The Suppressed
Madness
of Sane Men

The New Library of Psychoanalysis is published in association with the Institute of Psycho-Analysis. The New Library has been launched to facilitate a greater and more widespread appreciation of what psychoanalysis is really about and to provide a forum for increasing mutual understanding between psychoanalysts and those working in other disciplines like history, linguistics, literature, medicine, philosophy, psychology, and the social sciences. It is planned to publish a limited number of books each year in an accessible form and to select those contributions which deepen and develop psychoanalytic thinking and technique, contribute to psychoanalysis from outside, or contribute to other disciplines from a psychoanalytical perspective.

The Institute, together with the British Psycho-Analytical Society, runs a low-fee psychoanalytic clinic, organizes lectures and scientific events concerned with psychoanalysis, publishes the *International Journal of Psycho-Analysis* and the *International Review of Psycho-Analysis*, and runs the only training course in the UK in psychoanalysis leading to membership of the International Psychoanalytical Association – the body which preserves internationally agreed standards of training, of professional entry, and of professional ethics and practice for psychoanalysis as initiated and developed by Sigmund Freud. Distinguished members of the Institute have included Wilfred Bion, Anna Freud, Ernest Jones, Melanie Klein, John Rickman, and Donald Winnicott.

NEW LIBRARY OF PSYCHOANALYSIS
— 3 —
General editor: David Tuckett

The Suppressed Madness of Sane Men

FORTY-FOUR YEARS OF EXPLORING PSYCHOANALYSIS

MARION MILNER

TAVISTOCK PUBLICATIONS
LONDON AND NEW YORK

First published in 1987
by Tavistock Publications Ltd
11 New Fetter Lane, London EC4P 4EE

Published in the USA by
Tavistock Publications
in association with Methuen, Inc.
29 West 35th Street, New York NY 10001

©1987 Marion Milner

Printed in Great Britain by
Richard Clay (The Chaucer Press) Ltd
Bungay, Suffolk

British Library Cataloguing in Publication Data
Milner, Marion
The suppressed madness of sane men:
forty-four years of exploring psychoanalysis,
—(New library of psychoanalysis; 3).
1. Psychoanalysis
I. Title II. Series
150.19'5   BF173
ISBN 0–422–61020–8
ISBN 0–422–61690–7 Pbk

Librarary of Congress Cataloging in Publication Data
Milner, Marion Blackett.
The suppressed madness of sane men.
(New library of psychoanalysis; 3)
Includes index.
1. Psychoanalysis. I. Tuckett, David. II. Title.
III. Series.
RC509.M55 1987   616.89'17   87–9936
ISBN 0–422–61020–8
ISBN 0–422–61690–7 (pbk.)

To the British Psycho-Analytical Society
Warts and all – gratefully

Contents

Acknowledgements

I am very much indebted to Alexander and Miriam Newman of the Squiggle Foundation for their unfailing support to me in preparing this book and to the Foundation's Winnicott seminars. Also to Mary Pears, who read it all through, most helpfully, and to my colleague, David Tuckett, who edited it, especially for his patience over my slowness in getting on with it.

The author and publishers would like to thank the following for their kind permission to reproduce copyright material previously published elsewhere by the author: the *International Journal of Psycho-Analysis* (papers in Chapter 3, 4, 7, 9 and 10); Chatto and Windus: The Hogarth Press (lines from *The Hands of the Living God* quoted in Chapter 6); Heinemann Educational Books Ltd and the World Education Fellowship (paper in Chapter 13); and Jason Aronson Inc. (paper in Chapter 16). They would also like to thank the following for permission to reproduce personal letters: the Melanie Klein Trust for the letter from Melanie Klein (pages 109–11); the British Psycho-Analytical Society for the letter from Majorie Brierley (pages 269–71); Mrs Frances Bion for the letter from Wilfred Bion (page 271); Michael Eigen, Heather Glen, and Jean Kadmon for letters on pages 289–92; and J. D. Sutherland for the letter on pages 59–61.

The author and publisher have made every effort to obtain permission to reproduce copyright material throughout this book. If any proper acknowledgement has not been made, or permission not received, the copyright holder should contact the publishers.

Introduction

When asked by the British Psycho-Analytical Society to prepare a volume of my collected papers it was suggested that I should add some kind of thread that might link them together. I found great difficulty in doing this but eventually realized that there was something too constricting in this image of a thread and the preferable one was that of a tree of which I could recognize various branches. But if a tree, what about the roots? In short, where was I to begin? I decided that as the papers asked for are about the work of being a psycho-analyst I would begin with my earliest serious notions of what work I wanted to do in life. I therefore reminded myself that at the age of 11 I had decided that I wanted to be a naturalist. As I read that naturalists keep notes, I had started a nature diary, writing down anything interesting I saw, found, or heard, adding little drawings, and this went on for nine or ten years. In 1917 I left school after only one term in the sixth form because we had little money for the school fees and I had no thought of staying on to work for a university scholarship. Then, living in the country, in the spring of 1918, I was offered my first job, mornings only, to teach a small Canadian boy how to read. (It did not occur to me to ask why an intelligent boy of 7 had not yet learnt to read. What I did know was that his father was a Canadian officer fighting in the trenches in France.) I was paid seven shillings and sixpence (thirty-seven pence) a week. When the boy got the meaning of a word he was so delighted that he would say, 'Oh my, oh my!' After the lessons we would go out on to the heath to look for newts; strange how this so small job seemed to determine my future career. This was because when I told someone how much the boy and I had enjoyed

1

ourselves, she said, 'Have you read Montessori?' So I read her. It was a revelation. Here was somebody who actually believed that children could be trusted to know what they needed to learn and to do it by a concentrated kind of play, not just any play but using material especially provided so that the play really become work. Now I thought I could see more of the trunk of the tree whose branches were to spread through my life. In fact the question of what is the creative relation between work and play was to become an interest that finally landed me in the psychoanalytic consulting room or playroom, asking the analysand to say, or if a child, to do, whatever came to mind. In fact to play, whether with words or with toys. My task would be then to listen or watch and try to describe what I thought they might be really trying to say in the context of how they saw the meaning of their lives.

Having read the Montessori books I took steps to become a student at a Montessori nursery school training college. My only vivid memory from there is doing school practice in a slum nursery school, watching a small boy using the Montessori bricks to make a ring which he then tried to get into but found that he was too big. I was charmed by this and, knowing nothing of Freud, I did not think about ideas of getting back into the womb; I just thought he was trying to get an idea of his own size.

It was after one year at the college that an older far-seeing friend advised me to leave and take a university degree in psychology and physiology, at the same time arranging for me to get a grant to cover all my expenses, provided by an organization concerned with women's post-war training. At the university what was most exciting was learning the physiology, not the psychology, except for one course by J. C. Flugel on Freud's ideas about the unconscious as seen in relation to Sherrington's famous book, *The Integrative Action of the Nervous System.*[1]

The university degree led me on to work for the National Institute of Industrial Psychology and the interest in problems of concentration continued, now in the form of trying to improve my own by embarking on a postal course which claimed to do just that, but which demanded as a start that one decide one's aim in life. The attempt to answer this question led to more diary-keeping, this time studying the habits, not of the beasts and the birds, but my own ways of thinking. I can see now that the entries were far more to do with play than with work and often included ways of attending in trying to acquire physical skills in games. Eventually the result of the diary-keeping appeared in print in my first book, *A Life of One's Own* (1934).[2]

After a number of years in industrial psychology I happened on a pamphlet by a man I had never heard of, Elton Mayo, working at the Harvard Business School. It was about reverie in monotonous work. I immediately told my boss, C. S. Myers, that I would like to work with him, so Myers arranged a Rockefeller Travelling Scholarship (Laura Spelman) for me. Working with Elton Mayo meant attending seminars, which were intended to be training for the so-called Hawthorne experiment at the Western Electric Company of Chicago. We studied Pierre Janet on the neurosis, the early works of Freud, and Piaget's *Language and Thought of the Child*.[3] As far as I remember we never used Freud's words 'primary and secondary processes' but talked instead in terms of 'directed and undirected thinking'. The former, according to Mayo, aim at establishing truths, the latter at establishing relationships.

Back in England to a bit more industrial psychology and then my son was born. After that I had to go to work again, so began teaching psychology in evening classes for the Workers' Education Association in London's East End, including taking over a university tutorial class from Susan Isaacs who was by now a psychoanalyst. Next, in 1933, another branch of the tree sprouted for I was asked to undertake a research investigating the education system of the Girls Public Day School Trust. I decided to try and study the system via the girls who did not seem to be benefiting from it and eventually wrote an account of the work in a book, *The Human Problem in Schools* (1938)[4], edited by Susan Isaacs.

Subsequently I wrote a paper, published in *Occupational Psychology*, which gives a short description of this work in the schools.[5] Discussing the actual interviews with the girls, I wrote

'In the first years of the experiment the interviewing was almost entirely confined to an attempt to diagnose the factors entering into the girls' difficulties, without any direct help being attempted, each girl being seen only once. Later, however, as the nature of the problems became clearer, attempts were gradually made to deal with some of them directly.

The method used was to try to help the girl herself to see that her own behaviour had meaning and what the purpose of the behaviour that had been criticized as "mental laziness", "disobedience" and the like had really been. For instance, a girl who had good brains, as shown by the intelligence tests, but who continually evaded effort in her work and was inclined to be rude to the staff, began to talk about her mother and older sisters' mental gifts. Rather incoherently she tried to explain that she felt she was quite a different person from them, but that they were always trying to make her do the same sort of things as they had done. It was suggested to her that her rudeness and inability to accept the tasks set her by the staff were not necessarily due to some inherent mental laziness or incorrigibility, but might arise because, in the back of her mind, there was a confusion between the staff and those older than herself in her own family, so that she had, blindly and irrationally, felt that all adult demands were an attempt to force her into a mould of personality quite foreign to her nature.

Such blind defence of their own personality, leading often to an attitude of general negativism, was fairly frequently observed, and often found to be associated with a situation in the home where, on the part of the parents, there was excessive interference with the child's natural growth, through the imposing of quite inappropriate standards. In one such case, that of a girl of 13, the interferences took the form of a tacit assumption at home that the girl should always be at the top of her class, when in fact she had only average gifts. Finally this girl had found herself forced to stay away from school, because, although loving school life, she had an attack of sickness whenever she tried to come. Her doctor had reported that there was nothing wrong physically, but during the psychological interview it became clear that the girl had accepted her parents' exalted expectations, and was full of anxiety about the possible results of not living up to them; when these facts were pointed out to her she showed great sign of relief and was subsequently able to return to school.'

I have included this extract from my paper because it shows that I seem to have taken it for granted that my task was to look for the meaning of any girl's behaviour. In fact it was not until 1964 that I was to hear it clearly voiced, in J. A. Home's paper 'The Concept of Mind' for the British Psycho-Analytical Society, that what we as analysts are concerned with is the discovery of meanings, not of causes.[6]

It was after three years of trying to study the school system, using the required attitude of scientific objectivity, that another branch of my tree began to emerge. It began in the form of an increasing unease which finally led me to apply for a term's leave of absence, during which I wrote another book. This time it was not based on a daily diary but on memories from past holidays, images that had been increasingly intruding into my thoughts with a particular quality of still glow, a quality that was quite different from that of ordinary memories. So much so that I felt the need to try and find out what it might mean. The book that emerged was called *An Experiment in Leisure*, published in 1937 and blitzed out of print in the raids on London in 1940, but not before it had received some reviews which helped my own thinking.[7]

Amongst my papers I found, in 1985, one of these reviews. It was from the *New English Weekly*, written before the war and signed P.M. The writer quotes a bit of what I wrote because he liked it. I am reproducing it here because I was so astonished to see how what I wrote then so vividly prefigured the central problem I have ever since been struggling with, both in my patients and myself, the problem of how truly to trust 'the unconscious', trust the emptiness, the blankness, trust what seems to be not there.

> 'Expression, which I had felt to be the magical grip on the lion of desire, I now saw how it meant letting impulse and mood crystallise into outer form; not into purposive action determined by some outer goal, but expressive action determined by an inner vision – and this was the growing point without which the subjective temperament remains stagnant and enwrapped in its own egotism. And the inescapable condition of true expression was the plunge into the abyss, the willingness to recognize the moment of blankness and extinction was the moment of incipient fruitfulness, the moment without which the invisible forces within could not do their work. In other words the person who is by nature dominated by the subjective factor is committed to a life of faith whether he likes it or not, since all his important mental processes are unconscious. But if he does not continually seek expression for his faith, for his sense of the force by which he is lived, then it remains, unknown to himself, in the infantile stage of domination by ogres and ravening beasts, and the false opposition of gods of light and the underworld; and his dependence on the unseen within himself will be a continual torment.'

Yet another review, signed Kenneth Richmond, appeared in the *Observer* in 1938.[8] He wrote

> 'the drive towards self-subjection comes in for particularly interesting analysis and discussion, carrying explanation a good deal beyond the perverted pleasure principle, and the Freudian death instinct. Experiment shows that the deliberate suggestion "I am nothing", the deliberate letting go of all personal concern and fuss actually results in a great gain of personal (or should it be impersonal) stature. It seems a very possible view that the

progressive unconscious mind becomes sick to death of the ego and its attitudes and, thwarted and soured by subservience to this posturer, adopts punitive measures. One remembers how, in a different grouping of personality factors, the secondary personality, "Sally Beecham", tormented the prim and correct surface personality. Such an explanation in no way discounts the undoubted entanglement of pain seeking with erotic motivation.'

The virtual disappearance of the book and the necessary preoccupations with physical survival during the war years, together with the struggles over my apprenticeship for a new profession, meant that the implications of what I felt I had discovered in the experiment became somewhat blurred, indeed I almost forgot about the book. It was not until twenty years later that in 1957, having lent one of the few remaining copies to a friend, I was to receive from him a long critique of it entitled 'The Creative Surrender', a term which was to prove of great value in my struggles both with art and with patients.[9]

Soon after my return to work on the other side of my tree, that is to the objective study in schools, partly for my own sake and partly in order to understand some of the problems of the girls in the schools, I decided to have some Freudian psychoanaysis. It had to be rather intermittent because of times away in the provinces visiting the schools. Someone had suggested I should go to a Jungian but as far as I knew Jungians did not concern themselves then with work with children. It seemed to be by pure chance that I found myself neither in the analytic stream led by Anna Freud nor in that led by Melanie Klein, for I did not even know that there was a deep controversy both in theory and practice between these two pioneers of the psychoanalysis of children. I began part-time analysis with Sylvia Payne, someone I knew nothing about but who was in fact a founder member of the British Psycho-Analytical Society and later, through her chairmanship, able to prevent a split of that society into two as well as inaugurating what came to be called the Middle Group, 'Middle' because those in it belonged to neither of the opposing factions, but came later to be called the Independents. At the same time I not only came upon Melanie Klein's *Psycho-Analysis of Children* and read it excitedly but also happened to hear of somebody called D. W. Winnicott and began attending his Saturday morning clinics for mothers and babies at Paddington Green Children's Hospital.[10]

It was during the first years of Freudian analysis and before having had any ideas about applying for training that I found myself doing free association or doodle drawings; beginning with something that could only be called a scribble there had emerged pictures that had definite stories even though I had had no conscious awareness of what they were about while doing them.[11] I was so surprised at discovering this capacity that, in 1939, the very day that war was declared and I knew that my work in schools would be over because of the evacuation of the schools, I set about writing another book, making use of these drawings. I wanted to explore the nature of the capacity of one's mind that could produce such meaningful pictures without any conscious choice of meaning, in fact made in a mood of pure play with whatever medium I happened to have chosen. I wanted to consider this in the light of my work in the schools so I called the book *On Not Being Able to Paint*, because I thought that by exploring an activity in which I had failed to learn what I wanted to learn, I might find out something of what I felt was being left out of the school system.[12]

In the book I described how I had read that a good drawing should be a genuine expression of a mood, so I had tried the doodle method while concentrating on a particular feeling. For instance, once I did it when in a state of furious frustration and expected the drawing would be of total chaos, everything smashed up. Instead it had turned out to be a highly organized picture of a ludicrously hateful but also funny woman with the name Mrs Punch, which on reflection reminded me of the Duchess in *Alice's Adventures in Wonderland*. Next I had tried using the same doodle method of letting hand and eye do just what they wanted but keeping my mind fixed on something in the outer world that I wished to depict, such as a beautiful landscape. To my great surprise, at my first attempt, what emerged was the exact opposite of the peaceful scene I was contemplating, in fact an image of total destruction. In it the smooth lines of the Sussex Downs on a perfect summer morning had turned into a raging heath fire. In another a group of stately overarching beech trees had become two stunted thorn bushes in a snowy crag blasted by a raging blizzard.

In the book, instead of stopping to work out the meaning of this in psychoanalytic terms, I had gone on to review my early attempts to learn how to paint and come up against problems to do with visual perspective and outline. Hence the book contained some deliberate exploring of these aspects as well as further doodle pictures. Ideas about the use of the laws of perspective had then brought me to face ideas to do with separation and distance while outline brought in the whole question of boundaries. Having read what an artificial thing an outline is I had one day set about testing this statement and produced a drawing that was in fact going to turn up again and again

Figure 1   Two jugs

years later in my thinking about both art and psychoanalysis (see *Figure 1*). Perhaps it is worth quoting here my own account in the book of how this drawing came into existence.

'I noticed that the effort needed in order to see the edges of objects as they really look stirred a dim fear, a fear of what might happen if one let go one's mental hold on the outline which kept everything separate and in its place and it was similar to that fear of a wide focus of attention which I had noticed in earlier experiments.

After thinking about this I woke one morning and saw two jugs on the table. Without any mental struggle I saw the edges in relation to each other and how gaily they seemed almost to ripple now that they were freed from this grimly practical business of enclosing an object and keeping it in its place. This was surely what painters meant about the play of edges. Certainly they did play and I tried a five minutes sketch of the jugs. Now also it was easier to understand what painters meant by the phrase freedom of line because here surely was a reason for its opposite, that is the emotional need to imprison objects rigidly within themselves.

When trying to think about what might be the reason for this need to keep objects keeping themselves to themselves within a rigid boundary I remembered reading "the outline is the first and plainest statement of a tangible reality" (J. Gordon, *A Stepladder to Painting*, p. 19).

8

Thus the outline represented the world of fact, of separate touchable solid objects. To cling to it was therefore surely to protect oneself against the other world, the world of the imagination.'

In 1940 I was accepted for training with the British Psycho-Analytical Society. While attending the training seminars during the blitz and the blackout, there was a phrase lurking in the back of my mind, something to do with Samuel Butler having said that a misgiving is a warning from God to be attended to as a man values his soul. Indeed I tried to keep a diary of misgivings about the theory I was trying to learn and when I came to give seminars myself I sometimes advised my students to do the same.

Another branch of my tree sprouted when I was treating my first clinic patient. He was a young man of 17 who had been an infant prodigy on the violin but was now suffering from a total inability to practise while supposedly having lessons from a world-famous male violinist. While struggling with his problem I had one day wandered into the Marylebone Public Library and then happened on Blake's *Illustrations to the Book of Job*, which I had not known existed.[13] I found that the first picture showed Job and all his family sitting under a spreading tree surrounded by their flocks but on the tree are hanging musical instruments unused. However in the last picture, the twenty-first, they are all playing on them. After this I began to use Blake's series as a kind of handbook for trying to understand blocks in psychic creativity. Also I soon began to look for a connection between my own raging heath fire and blasting storm pictures and Blake's picture of Job's magnificent outburst when he curses the day he was born. However it was not until 1956 that I actually wrote about this use of Blake, both in thinking about education and art and psychoanalysis.

The first paper I wrote as a student was called 'The Child's Capacity for Doubt' (1942).[14] It was not written for psychoanalysts but as a lecture for the University of London Institute of Education. For me, doubt came to mean accepting emptiness, it meant a suspicion of what was supposed to fill the gap while at the same time being able to accept the gap, the not knowing, and even becoming able to relate oneself to it. I found another paper, also written in 1942 and also not written for psychoanalysts. It resulted from being asked to contribute an essay to an issue of the journal *Occupational Psychology* celebrating the twenty-first birthday of the National Institute of Industrial Psychology and in honour of its founder C. S. Myers. The subject chosen by me was 'The Toleration of

Conflict'.[15] I only realize now in 1986 when digging up these old papers that the choice of subject must have grown out of the struggles to find my bearings in the controversies then raging within the British Psycho-Analytical Society. Here is the conclusion of my paper.

> 'Conflict is essential to human life, whether between different aspects of oneself, between oneself and the environment, between different individuals or between different groups. It follows that the aim of healthy living is not the direct elimination of conflict which is possible only by forcible suppression of one or other of its antagonistic components, but the toleration of it – the capacity to bear the tensions of doubt and of unsatisfied need and the willingness to hold judgement in suspense until finer and finer solutions can be discovered which integrate more and more the claims of both sides. Thus it is the psychologist's job to make possible the acceptance of such an idea so that the richness of the varieties of experience whether within the unit of the single personality or in the wider unit of the group, can come to expression.'

I can see now that what I meant by unsatisfied need referred to the need for certainty; I was thinking of an inability to acquire what I even then thought of in terms of what Keats called negative capability. I have spoken about this paper here because many years later I once discovered that a qualified psychoanalyst who had come to me for further analysis expressed the belief that the aim of psychoanalysis was the elimination of conflict, thus ignoring the idea of the creative use of it. Also I myself needed the continual reminder that, as William Blake said, without contraries there is no progression.

Finally, since most of the papers in this book have been published before, and written for various audiences, there is bound to be a certain amount of repetition. I hope that this will be less a cause for irritation than a help in clarifying the main shape of the tree.

1986

References

1 Sherrington, C. (1906) *The Integrative Action of the Nervous System*. New York: Scribner's.
2 Milner, M. (1934) *A Life of One's Own*. London: Chatto & Windus.

3 Piaget, J. (1926) *The Language and Thought of the Child.* New York: Humanities Press.

4 Milner, M. (1938) (ed. S. Isaacs) *The Human Problem in Schools.* London: Methuen.

5 Milner, M. (1939) A Psychological Approach to Some Educational Problems. In *Occupational Psychology* **13**: 295–301.

6 Home, J. A. (1966) The Concept of Mind. *International Journal of Psycho-Analysis* **47**: 42–9.

7 Milner, M. (1937) *An Experiment in Leisure.* London: Chatto & Windus.

8 Richmond, K. (1938) Review in *Observer.*

9 Ehrenzweig, A. (1957) The Creative Surrender. *The American Imago* **14**: 3.

10 Klein, M. (1937) *Psycho-Analysis of Children.* London: Hogarth Press.

11 Only recently have I remembered that sometime in the late 1930s I had seen paintings by a psychoanalyst, Dr Grace Pailthorpe, and a young man, R. Mednikoff, using what I have called the doodle method and it was this that had stimulated me to try myself (*see On Not Being Able to Paint*).

12 Milner, M. (1950) *On Not Being Able to Paint.* London: Heinemann.

13 Blake, W. (1826) *Illustrations to the Book of Job.* London: Methuen (1904).

14 Milner, M. (1942) The Child's Capacity for Doubt. (Unpublished paper.)

15 Milner M. (1943) The Toleration of Conflict. *Occupational Psychology* **17** (1).

1

1942: The child's capacity
for doubt

This lecture was given to the Institute of Education, University of
London, 7 February 1942.

What sort of a citizen do we want to produce by our education? What
are the qualities that we think necessary in a citizen of a real
democracy? People usually try to answer this question with a list
such as courage, initiative, independence of judgement, and so on.
Recent research corroborates common sense by showing that in
general such 'good' qualities depend on a person's belief in
something good inside or outside him which will help him to 'make
good' in face of difficulties, trouble, pain, and loss instead of 'going
to pieces'. It seems that this belief in something good can come from
many sources, from the pride of belonging to a certain race or class
or family, from having been to a certain school, from having a
certain gift, or believing in a certain creed, or from the love of a
certain person, or even partly from having many possessions. But if
one tries to summarize people's ideas of what they seem to want in a
democratic citizen, he seems distinguished from other types of good
citizens by the kinds of good things he depends upon in order to be a
good person; he is a person who does not depend for the good things
he believes in exclusively on the physical and emotional levels of
experience. That is he does not depend entirely on material
possessions for his sense of his own value, nor upon physical
achievements and prowess, nor upon purely emotional relationships,
such as adoration of and subservience to a leader or his own capacity
to assert himself and dominate over others. Rather, he believes in

something that I can only call 'psychic process'; that is he believes in the value of independent judgement and thought and feeling, in fact, he believes in the value of individual experience, both in himself and others.

How does such a belief in experience come about? As far as we know at present it comes

1 through having good experiences, living out one's capacities for fullest mental, physical, spiritual enjoyment.
2 through coming to be aware of the nature of experience itself, that is the difference between inner reality and outer reality.

I think the first way is beginning to be fairly well understood in the primary phases of education, certainly in nursery schools, though less certainly for the older children.

The second way is not so well understood. I am calling it the way of doubt. Why? Because a child is not born knowing what is going on in his own mind and what he sees in the external world are separate and different kinds of reality. He has slowly and laboriously to discover by experience that thought is different from things. Just as he cannot know, till he has painfully experimented, that physical nature obeys special laws, that fire burns, that china breaks, that water spills, so he cannot know what the psychical nature can do. For instance, he assumes at first that it is sufficient to think or wish a thing to make it happen, by the omnipotent magic of his thought. In order to know the nature of his own experience, or that of others, he has to learn to doubt this original belief that his own ideas are omnipotent and all there is. Before he has achieved this doubt he always *thinks he knows*. His beliefs seem to him as solid and unchanging and certain as tables and chairs are.

Why is it so difficult to know the nature of this psychic reality?

1 Because of its form, it is essentially *process*. It is always changing, developing.
2 Because of its content. It contains things that are frightening to know, 'bad' things as well as 'good'.

These two aspects are connected, for the most disturbing change in the inner reality of feeling is from good moods to bad, loving can so quickly change to hating, knowing to not knowing, happiness to misery. Also many of our thoughts and wishes in childhood are too violent and terrifying to be known; some of them are too shocking to be known because they offend against the standards of the adults on whom we are dependent, but some of them are too powerful, or seem so, to be recognized, for if to think a thing is as good, or as bad

13

as to have done it, then better not know that you have even thought it. As a result of such fears some children retreat altogether from any attempt to know their own experience, give up all interest in 'insides', in favour of exclusive concern with external things.

How do we in fact ever come to know the psychic reality?

1 By the clash of our wishes and beliefs with those of others, which forces us to give our ideas some outer expression, if they are to be defended and forces us to realize our own ideas are not 'all there is'.
2 By the mind's apparently innate capacity for symbolizing experience.

It seems that the elusive inner realities of feeling are continually taking to themselves the form of outer realities. It seems that the discovery of the inner life is made in terms of the outer world, the same and yet also different, like the differences Alice found when she penetrated Wonderland and Through the Looking Glass. This symbolizing capacity of the mind, its inifinite capacity for using metaphor in expressing psychic realities, flows out in a tremendous stream which has many branches: the imaginative play of childhood, art, symbolic rituals, religion. Words become the central mode of expression for most people, after early childhood, and bridge the gulf between the inner and outer realities. But words also become caught up in the original confusion between the two realities and are too often given an absolute value, as when something is believed because it is seen 'in print'. Delight in verbal nonsense probably expresses relief at escape from this false dominance of words.

Confusion between the inner and outer realities leads us and the child either

1 to take the symbol for an external reality and so distort the outer reality into the shape of our own unacknowledged wishes and · fears, or
2 to deny the value of the symbol altogether and so impoverish the whole of the inner life.

Examples of these extremes are shown in attitudes to fairy tales and possible answers to the child's question 'is it true?' The answer 'It's true for inside you' can be accepted by a 5-year-old.

What are the implications for educational practice? Two questions arise here. First, how far does a general teaching method which gives marks for knowing and penalizes 'not knowing' objective facts, hinder the process of coming to know the psychic reality? How far does it help the child to realize the inner reality as process, if this realization does, in fact, require the ability to tolerate doubt and the willingness to wait in uncertainty?

Second, with regard to religious education in schools, how far does the fact that institutionalized religion emphasizes belief in dogma interfere with the process of coming to know the psychic reality? Is it not perhaps encouraging a clinging to certainty which in fact interferes with learning how to experience to the full? Does it tend to fix experience and so prevent growth? What attitude does the teacher of Scripture take towards those recently collected facts of our racial inheritance which are described in Frazer's *The Golden Bough*, such as the rituals connected with the theme of the Dying God, the sacrifice of the king's son for the good of the people, the human scapegoat taking upon himself the sins of the rest?[2] Is there a possibility of a dangerous split in consciousness if the Gospels are taught as a reality of unique historical external fact rather than as true for the inner life? Do teachers try to silence the child's doubts in this field or do they agree with Samuel Butler, who said 'a misgiving was a warning from God, which should be attended to as a man values his soul'?[3]

What are the results of the psychic reality knowing itself, not *about* itself, as something to discuss, but an act of perceiving in the living moment of 'now'? We are only beginning to know a little, but there seems to be a continual enlarging of the horizons of experience.

References

1 Frazer, J. G. (1890) *The Golden Bough*. Part Three: 'The Dying God'. London: Methuen (1923).
2 Butler, S. (1873) *The Fair Haven*. London: Watts & Co. (1938), p. 48.

2

1943: Notes on the analysis of a 2½-year-old boy

Amongst my papers I found a few typed sheets giving my notes on a few sessions of supervision with Melanie Klein, working on a 2½-year-old boy while we were waiting for the 3-year-old (Rachel) I needed for my training. The boy came because he was disturbed by his mother's second pregnancy. I think I must have typed out these sessions to remind myself how Melanie Klein dealt with what she felt to be the child's inner world at this time of crisis in his life. I was particularly interested in the way he tried to mend the toy man that had got broken.

Session 39

Marched in, turned and fetched M. Made me fetch bowl. Took broken man out happily, asked for seccotine. Waved to M as she went away.

Rocked the broken man (no feet) on his arms, pleased. 'You are glad to find that he can still move, still be alive inside although a bit broken.'

(Mrs K – 'Broken man stands for
1 internal father who guides him inside,
2 external father wherever he is, probably in bed with mother,
3 his own penis.')

Went to tap, much turning on and off and staring up at the hole, and putting stopper in and out. Said 'Daddy' when heard the water run away.

'You want to see if your wee wee and Daddy's still work all right, even if the things inside are a bit broken.'

16

(Mrs K – 'Tap play shows the doubt whether father inside is all right. Hence need for continual tests to see if it works even though a little injured.')

Fetched bowl, put it down, pushed all the toys off the table, picked up trucks and engine, put them on the table, spent a long time, with much perseverance, joining them together, they kept coming undone, studied the joints, staring at them, finally made me do one.

Turned the bowl upside down, tried to hang train across it, but it fell apart. Joined train and carried it held taut with arms outstretched.

(Mrs K – 'Note that way of dealing with destroyed M and F is to put the penis back into M, then everything is all right, F's potency is restored and M has all her babies.

Holding out the train is an internal situation, saying "Now they are all right inside".')

Asked for seccotine and touched joints of train with nozzle, trying to join them magically.

(Mrs K – 'Magical restoration with faeces. The young child can only restore by magic, if not magic, then never.')

Took seccotine pin to jab in the pillar, climbing on the sofa beside me, trying to make me do it (when he could not reach), by means of imperious but incomprehensible words of command.

'You feel you have got me, Daddy, inside you, and can make me do just what you want.'

(Mrs K – 'Speech used for control of inner chaos.')

Put seccotine pin to his mouth, teasingly sucked it, spat when he got the taste, and went to sink to spit it out. Laughed and spat again and blew towards me.

(Mrs K – 'Interaction with outside, when he takes the pin, it is one way of testing the internal. It is part of the inner control to eat the object. Doubts are stirred if reality says it tastes bad. May lead to feeling internal objects are not good.')

'Now you are putting the bad jobbies into M, me.' Went to the door, played with the key, put seccotine on it, took the seccotine to M, putting pin through hole of key. Left a bit early.

(Mrs K – 'What makes me bad is here the doubtful thing, he puts the jobbies into me – M – then has to go and see what the real M thinks of it.')

17

Session 47

Clinic reopens after January holiday.

M reports that he and she both had bronchitis, not well yet. He brought M in, at playroom door wanted to turn back, she picked him up, he cried a little.

'You feel, while you have not been coming to see me, that I have turned into a bad person.'

Sat on M's knee, whimpering, then pointed to her to go to the toys. I brought them out. He sat tight on her knee, picked out a broken arm, used a bid of wood as if it were seccotine tube; I produced seccotine, he used two armless men to put some on them, climbed down from M and played, standing, turned to the drawers and wanted the key put in the lock of top drawer (not his).

(Mrs K – 'I had gone wrong, bad, soiled, dead inside him.')

M reported here that for seven nights he had slept in his own cot, then refused to be put in at all, had to go in their bed, thinks it's the bars that worry him.

(Mrs K – 'Internal objects must have improved if he was able to lie in cot alone. Should have referred to M's remarks.')

I sent M away.

He found trucks in drawer, very delighted, took to table, put together, etc., etc.

Spent rest of hour seeming to be going over all the things he does in playroom, recapitulating, testing to see if I am the same, including banging on jutting out bit of wall and making me do it while he goes to the other side to listen (this is new).

Asked to be lifted to window sill, opened and shut window, and several times pointed to things in yard outside.

'You want to know just what is inside M, me, you, and about the baby inside M.'

(Mrs K – 'Noises, banging, is also the noise the baby is going to make.')

Session 48

M reports gave him medicine, no result yet.

In waiting-room was standing with back to me, lay down, and

began to scream (first time) when M told him to come in, stopped when she picked him up and carried him in, sat on her knee, with occasional [notes missing here].

Session 50

Rocked his foot, slightly kicking the wall and scratching with his finger.

'You want to scratch and kick and get inside and see what the baby is like, it may be a bad scratching screaming baby, you don't know what it is like, you may have made it bad with your jobbies and wee wee water that you want to put into M., like you do wee wee on my floor'. Stood absolutely still.

'You feel if you keep quite still and don't move at all then you won't hurt M, or me, and I won't hurt you back and you'll be quite safe.' Pressed his face hard against wall, nose all squashed against it, some mouth movements.

(Mrs K – 'Leaning against wall, wants to go into body, hide there, also see what he had done, wanting to find out, M and me dead when we are away, what is it he has done, fear and depression.

Can't move because things inside are dead, me, M can't move any longer. Screaming may be bringing them to life. Mouth movements because baby is going to suck?')

His eyes were shut, his head lolled sideways, I put an arm round to support him, suddenly he fell sideways into my arms, and woke himself up crying miserably.

(Mrs K – 'Falling asleep may be what he is doing in the evening, because of his terrors, wants to go into his body, to get away.')

I carried him to door, he walked to M, smiled while she brushed his coat, but he would not say goodbye.

Next day M reported he has been as 'good as gold' since this session, no crying.

Session 51

Cried when he saw me, turned to M, I picked him up and brought him, struggling. Screamed, put my hand on handle of shut door to make me open it. Interpretations given between screams.

'When you didn't come and see me you felt you'd lost D's wee

wee inside you. When we played, I did just what you wanted me to, like having me inside you. And now you can't make me open the door you feel you haven't got me to use for what you want. Or you have me inside but I am bad, not helping you do things for yourself?'

Whenever I said I was a bad person inside the screams became worse. When I finally opened door, he stopped screaming and went on serenely down passage, having waited while I slowly put his cap on. In waiting-room, sat on M's knee, and looked with unseeing stare at the wall.

(Mrs K feels he has me bad inside and cannot really put me right, so if I cannot be put right anymore, I have to go to hospital.

Tries to make me into bad injured M so he can keep his real M all right.

The stare is looking into his own inside, still trying find what they are like inside.)

1944: A suicidal symptom in a child of 3

This was written in 1943 as my membership paper of the British Pyscho-Analytical Society, the work was supervised by Melanie Klein, since in those days one was permitted do a membership paper on a supervised patient.[1] Also it was written only a year and a half after I qualified for associate membership, being pushed into doing it so soon because of the shortage of training analysts, so many being away doing war work. It was read in the basement of 116 Gloucester Place, the ceiling of the room being supported with wooden struts because of the bombing. In fact the attack on London by the V1 German bombs had begun that very day.

The analysis I am about to describe is of Rachel, aged 3, who came for treatment because of an acute inhibition of eating. I am going to try and give an account of what she seemed to be doing in her play and show some of the evidence leading up to my main hypothesis of what she was actually trying to do when refusing to eat. When I was actually working with the child it certainly seemed to me that the hypothesis I am about to put forward explained a large number of the facts of her behaviour; but when I came to consider how to present the material I did not feel certain that I might not have made certain theoretical assumptions that I could not substantiate from the evidence. It is true that the child got better, but I did not feel this was sufficient proof that what I had tried to tell her was necessarily the true explanation of what she was doing. In fact, I began to consider the whole question of the sense of conviction of the truth of one's interpretations which I suppose every analyst has, at least much of the time, when conducting a successful analysis. And I came to the conclusion that in fact I could not prove my hypothesis at all from the material, for though the material in the analysis may seem to provide convincing proof, for the analyst conducting it, of the truth of his theory, for anyone else I think it can only provide illustration of the theory. I think this must be so, since the material presented to anyone else must always be a selection from the great richness of varieties of behaviour (including gestures, manner, tones of voice) and must therefore always be selected on the basis of some theory; thus one can never prove that one's selection of the material is unbiased and that one has not omitted other facts which would prove some different theory. Thus I thought that the only way of evaluating the conclusions, as distinct from illustrating them, would be by trying to show their utility in explaining other facts, beyond the analysis, and in throwing light upon other psychological theories. With this in mind I had intended to test some of the theoretical ideas emerging from this analysis by considering their relation to quite different scientific theories, in fact, to certain formulations of general psychology. I had thought also that by trying to formulate the conclusions in terms which the general psychologist, with his more thorough training in scientific method, would consider valid, I might achieve something else: I might avoid the danger of slipping unawares into the uncritical use of concepts which may be common coin amongst psychoanalysts, but which I might not have sufficiently defined in my own thinking.

Clearly, however, such a task was impossible in a single paper. I have therefore limited this paper to the presentation of the material and hope to try and relate the findings to certain aspects of general psychological theory some time in the future.

The analysis, which the mother brought to an end after 118 sessions, began when Rachel was 2 years and 9 months old, and it was carried out with the help of weekly discussions with Mrs Klein. The disturbance in eating was so acute that just before coming for treatment the child had refused all food and drink for three days. She was a pretty, dainty, intelligent little girl and the mother reported no other symptoms, but under analysis it became clear that she had many deep-seated difficulties: her charming ways had a hint of artificiality which soon showed itself to be an expression of very deep mistrust of herself and others.

Here is a brief account of her history, as given by the mother. She was a first, and, so far, only child, born prematurely after eight months, weight 4 lbs. She was at the breast for two days, till the milk failed, and at 4 months she was only 6 lbs. in weight; she then had three weeks in a nursing home, then showed steady gain till 1 year, but had measles at 18 months. She was spoon-fed at 10 months and took the food well, but difficulties began when she started sitting up in a high chair: she would only eat when her mother interested her in something else. Difficulties increased till one day she ceased to eat or drink (she was just over 2), and signs of dehydration developed. A specialist suggested leaving bits of food about the house and this worked for a time. After this she insisted on sitting on her mother's lap, saying 'Mummy feed me', for a period of six months. Then she went to a nursery school and again began refusing all food, at school and at home, and screamed when her mother offered it, and again took nothing at all for three days. While she was waiting to begin the analysis her mother sent her to her grannie, where she ate enormously and was happy, but when her mother arrived she at once asked to sit on her lap and again refused to eat. She was brought home to begin the analysis and would eat a little for breakfast if her father gave it and her mother was not in the room. After the first day of analysis she would eat a little, provided that she could feed her mother with half of it from her own plate. Her mother reported that in character she was extremely independent, always refusing help at school, wanting to do what the older children did and wanting to use an adult knife and fork at meals; she played happily by herself, had many friends and slept very well. She slept in the parents' room till 18 months, but her mother insists that she always seemed fast asleep during parental intercourse.

I will now try and describe first certain main lines of the child's play during the analysis. Incidentally, there was a technical difficulty, in that the child, contrary to her behaviour at home, would not at first allow her mother out of her sight; so, at least until the ninth session, most of the analysis had to be carried out in the mother's presence. And even after the ninth session the mother was continually being fetched into the playroom for short periods.

Throughout the analysis her play continually showed that she wanted to destroy something, for she would cut up paper, day after day, and she continually tore up red flowers (fuschias) which she would bring in from the bush at my gate. She also gave many indications of why she wished to destroy something, for, time and again, she showed that she felt something was being withheld from her. For instance, she continually wanted to open another child's drawer and asked why she could not. And often, beginning in the second hour, she tried to scratch open the painted door of a little wooden house, and asked who was inside and why it would not open, sometimes, as in the fourth hour, shaking it and pretending she could hear something rattle and saying, 'There's a man inside.' She also continually showed that she felt something was being withheld from her in a tantalizing way, only she did not show this directly: she acted it out by tantalizing me, giving me the flowers she had picked to eat, and then snatching them away again and shouting, 'Don't!' Actually this stopping my eating them was also what she did to herself in her refusal to eat; for in the first hour she began by sitting on her mother's knee and looking at the toys, but not allowing herself to play with them; instead she made gnashing movements with her mouth. And when she did begin to play with them she often pulled off the feet and arms of a little man and also cut at the wooden house, again gnashing her teeth. But she also showed that she wished to repair what she had destroyed, for she told her mother to take the man home and mend him, and she often tried to stick on the man's feet herself with gum, though she always pulled them off again. In the sixth hour she actually tried to put the gum all over her mother's breasts. She also tried to show what it was that she wanted and felt was being withheld from her; for she indicated, I think, that it was all that her mother had that she wanted, by often making her mother or me sit in a certain spot in the room, and then herself taking her mother's place, or mine. In the fourteenth hour she showed how this feeling of what she wanted being withheld from her provoked a desire for bodily attack, for she suddenly said that she wanted to bite my finger.

Having shown that she felt she wanted something that she could not have and that what she wanted to do with it was to bite it and eat it, she also showed what she felt happened to things she ate and why eating had become so dangerous: not only because of wanting to eat things that must not be eaten, but also because of doubts about what happens to what one eats. For she showed that she was concerned with the fact, not only that eating means biting, but also that things you eat disappear and she did not know what they turn into. She showed this doubt partly by a continual interest in her urine and faeces, and, for instance, by once asking me: 'What do you think weewee really is?', and by testing water from the tap in various ways, sometimes taking it in her mouth and spitting it out and saying it was nasty, sometimes wanting to mix water and urine and wash the toys in the mixture, and so on. But she also showed that eating had become dangerous because she was so uncertain about what any external object, whether food or toys, really was. For once she had brought herself to play with the toys she continually expressed uncertainty about what they really were. She would take a dog kennel, for instance, and say it was teapot and use it for her play of pouring out tea, but then say, 'Is it really a teapot?' And often she would reverse phantasy and external reality, telling me to eat something 'really and truly' when she meant 'pretend to' and vice versa. Of course this may have been partly a difficulty of language, but I think it also expressed an inner doubt and inability to separate external and internal reality. For she seemed to be saying that she had no means of knowing whether the actual food which her hunger made her want to eat was not also at the same time the forbidden thing which she felt was being withheld from her. And I thnk we can connect this doubt and uncertainty about the difference between ideas, phantasies, in her mind, and external realities, with her doubts about her own feelings and wishes; for she wanted to play with the toys, but could not allow herself to, she wanted to feed me with the flowers, but snatched them away again. And I think, also, that it was because she wanted to eat up everything she liked, as symbolized by the toys, and because she felt she had actually done so, as shown by her feeling that there was a man inside the little house, that she could not distinguish between something that was only in her mind, inside her, and the external reality. For she went on to show how she felt that taking food inside her was as if she was taking in the actual people who were the objects of her longings and angers, but also showed a whole series of doubts and fears about what it was she really had inside and what happened to it. This sense of confusion was dramatically shown in the eighteenth hour, when she put two dolls and a pig and a car in the kennel saying, 'That's Daddy and Mummy' and added, 'That's bread and butter', and then tore fiercely at some paper, rattled the kennel, and tried to dig the toys out again with a pencil. Then she suddenly sat back, whimpering, put her hand over her eyes in a dazed way and said, 'Have I had my breakfast? Yes, I have.' And I think it was this doubt about what she had got inside, whether we see it as doubt about the nature of her own feelings or doubt about what she felt she had in phantasy taken inside, that linked with her inability to eat in her mother's presence. For if what she wanted, and felt that she could get by eating was all that her mother had, then she could not feel sure that her mother was not a dangerous person who was robbed from and eaten up. This mistrust of her mother emerged very clearly in later play about a 'nasty lady'. It also showed in some very interesting material in which she accused me of stealing her voice. Thus, after frequently telling me that I must not talk because I was a baby, she said one day in the forty-sixth hour that I must not have any toys, and when I

25

asked why, said it was because I had taken her voice. She then began to scribble and said she was drawing her voice. In the fiftieth hour she said, having just put two bricks in her own mouth, 'You're greedy, you want to bite my voice, take away my voice.' And in the fifty-second hour she showed, I think, the connection between voice and her father's penis by interrupting some interpretation of mine, in which I mentioned Daddy, by screaming, 'You mustn't, that's my song, you mustn't', and hitting me and adding, 'He's my Daddy, not yours, you haven't got one.' Later she again talked of my stealing her voice when I was trying to give an interpretation. In fact, it looks here as if my voice, by which I gave her the interpretations which she needed in order to get better, became the symbol of all goodness, of all she wanted from her father and felt her mother was withholding, and of the breast that her mother took away so soon – of all she wished to steal and which she felt would therefore be stolen from her. I think also that this doubt about her own feelings partly explains what was a marked feature of her behaviour in general, that is a subtle artificiality. She was a most gifted little actress, and once, when making me play the part of a crying baby, she was so disgusted with my poor performance that she gave me a demonstration of how I should do it, giving a most heart-rending portrayal of passionate sobbing and despair. It was as if everything she did was half pretence, as if she felt that to express her real feelings was far too dangerous, since they were so jealous and destructive. And it was only quite near the end of the analysis that she was able to burst into a fury of genuine indignation on discovering that I possessed a bicycle.

Now I should like to return for a moment to the material following the doubts about her breakfast; for in the next hour, the nineteenth, she pretended to cut my coat with scissors and wanted me to do the same to her, and also spent a long time undoing and doing up the zip fastener of her mother's trousers. And in the next hour she showed more than usual anxiety at being alone with me and had a hallucination that her mother was calling her; on her way to find her mother in the waiting-room, which was on the floor above the playroom, I interpreted her fear of retaliation from me for her wanting to cut and bite me, and as she went in to her mother she said to her, 'Someone bit my finger.' It will be remembered that in the fourteenth hour she had wanted to bite mine. It was after this hour that her mother reported a very marked improvement in her eating.

Having shown this projection of her desire to bite by the feeling that someone outside had bitten her, she gradually began to show, during weeks of analysis, how she felt that the thing she had injured was also inside her and attacking her from inside. In the seventy-sixth hour she struggled to deny this feeling, for she began by tearing the flowers she had brought and putting them in two piles, and then said, 'I can skip', and began to demonstrate it. She then found a leaf and said, 'Does it prick? Let's pretend it's pricked us both and put cream on!' Then she found a torn bus ticket, and put it in her mouth and said, 'My leg doesn't hurt.' And then she saw the loose leg of a stool which she had previously tried to pull off and now touched with her foot, saying, 'It pricks', and then threw the stool away. Here I think we can say that she wanted to show me that she could skip in order to try to feel that she was all right inside, full of life and skills; or, in the language of the unconscious, having a good uninjured penis inside. And she continued to try and uphold this belief by denying that her leg hurt; but what she was really feeling was that the pricking leaf and the leg of the stool which she had injured, which she had eaten, as she ate the flowers and the torn bus ticket, were now inside her and making her leg hurt so that she could not skip. In the end she tried to get rid of the persecuting injured stool, as if by defaecation.

In the next part of the analysis we shall see, I think, her gradual realization that it was her own angry and greedy impulses that were worrying her. She gradually came to realize more and more deeply that the thing that she felt was inside and attacking her, the pricking leaf, was also the biting cutting scissors with which she had tried to attack me – her own greedy, angry wishes, like a greedy mouth possessing her within.

I will now give an account of certain hours occurring a little later which led up to what seems to me a very clear indication of the feelings underlying her play in the first hour when she refused the toys. For she gradually showed how she felt herself to be such a danger to her mother and everything inside her mother that she felt that she herself ought to be got rid of, that she herself ought to be dead. In fact, it is material which seems to me to show that the refusal of food had in itself a suicidal intention, as well as being the attempt to protect herself against taking inside something which she felt was injured and would therefore attack her and destroy her from inside. Actually there was a new external factor influencing these later hours: her mother's second pregnancy. But I think the conscious knowledge of the new baby only reinforced phantasies that she had been struggling with all the time, of there being something inside her mother which she wanted to get for herself, something which she wanted both to destroy and to save.

The play which I now wish to describe occurred on her return from a month's summer holiday. Her mother reported that during the first week of the holiday she ate very little indeed, but that after that feeding was normal and it did not seem to matter whether her mother was present or not. The mother also told me of her own pregnancy but said she had not yet told Rachel. But she said that Rachel often took her own baby-clothes out of the drawer and that she (the mother) always told her that they were being kept for the next baby.

The play in the first hour of return was very confused. She talked a lot of gibberish, but also said, 'Are you as tall as Daddy? Have you a Daddy? I'm as tall as Daddy.' And finally, when sitting on her pot, she said, 'Kaki is awfully awfully.' In the next hour she spent a long time cutting paper and at intervals made such remarks as, 'I've been on holiday, you haven't', 'I've had my tea and dinner, you haven't', 'I've stroked Jenny, you haven't', 'These are *my* shoes, not yours', 'My finger's bigger than yours'. She had begun the hour by giving me a sweet and taking the wheelbarrow up to her mother, and I now interpreted that she had done this because she felt she had taken everything for herself and left me, representing her mother, quite empty, so that she now wanted to give something back. Her answer to this was, 'Let's walk closer together', and she then took some toys in her pinafore and gave me a few. The tone of her remarks, about what she had and I had not, had been triumphant and taunting, but now her mood changed, and she began a new game in which I was the baby and she the mother going to hospital. She had taken my ring off and now, with her back to me, folded it in paper, saying, 'No darling, you can't have it.' Then, turning to me, she said, 'It's soap, really and truly soap, really and truly put it in your mouth!' and put it in her own. Here I think it seems fairly clear that her triumphing over me, at the beginning of the hour, could not last because she was too afraid that her mother, from whom she felt she had taken everything, was ill, and therefore must be in hospital. This meant that now *she* had to become the mother who restrains the greedy baby, that is herself, and say, 'No darling, you can't have it.' *She* was now playing the part of the super-ego, but it was a kind and gentle one, in marked contrast to the cruel one that she dramatized in the next few hours.

In the following hour she continued to make me be the baby and showed me in various ways how a mother should treat the baby – partly satisfy it, partly restrain it. There is a little gate at the top of the stairs between the waiting-room and the playroom, and she shut this between herself and me, calling it a cage; she then went into the waiting-room saying she was going to get meat for me from the

28

butcher. The game continued with such remarks as, 'Go in your cage, baby', 'Go downstairs', 'Go to sleep', 'Here's your Teddy', 'Here's balls for Mummy and Daddy and a little one for you'. From the way she treated me, as the baby, wanting to keep me shut up in the cage and sending me away downstairs, I find it very difficult to believe that she did not already know about the new baby, in part of her mind, and also feel resentful that she had not been actually told. For in the next hour she began by talking gibberish and then said, 'You don't know what that is – I do', and spent a long time trying to smack my face and chest, and saying, 'Now cry'. Also she had three-halfpence which she rolled in her vest and then tucked into her knickers and made me try to get from her, shouting, 'You *can't* have it, try and get it, cry'; it was here that she showed me so dramatically just how I was to cry. I had to spend almost the whole hour crying, and once she shut me in the 'cage', saying 'I won't be long', but telling me to cry and say 'Yes, you will'. When I cried she banged the door on me in a frenzy of dramatic cruelty.

During the weekend her mother told her about the new baby and her comment was, 'How will you get it? Will you buy it?' And her mother had answered, 'No, we'll make it.' Then followed a sick attack and Rachel was not well enough to be brought to analysis on the Monday. When the child returned on the Tuesday she repeated much of the same play of shutting me out, as the baby, and making me cry, also feeding me and telling me to choke. There was much playing with her vest and showing me her tummy, and on the following day, she said, 'I'll hit your tummy, I'll bite you', but instead, pretended to feed me with orange juice and said, 'Are you ill, baby? – Say "yes".' She then became very gentle and loving, and asked, 'Baby, do you want to talk to Daddy?' and went off to her mother in the waiting-room upstairs, saying, 'Daddy, baby wants to see you'. Having brought her mother down, she picked a little man from the drawer and gave him to me saying, 'Baby, here's your chocolate, here's more, but you can't have it all to-day.' The next day she brought in four fuschias, did not tear them, but put them in a row and said, 'Which do you want, baby? – Say "that and that and that and that"', but added 'You can't have them'. She then repeated the game of leaving me and making me cry, but asked, 'Are you sick, baby?' and went to her mother, calling, 'Daddy, baby wants you'. In the next hour, when asked if I wanted some fuschias, I had to say in a very gruff voice, 'Yes, I do', and she answered, 'You can't, they're for Daddy, and I'm going to smack your face, your tummy'. She then told me to go and turn the tap on and let it run, but became frightened and made me turn it off again; she then played with two cups, putting the rims together and letting the water trickle out, and saying, 'Baby, do you want to do this? – Say "yes".'

Here I think we can say that all this material is very clearly a response to the external situation, first, of not seeing me in the holidays, and second, of being told about the new baby. We can say that she was trying to show how she, as the baby, wanted to have her father's penis, and how she felt she ought not to have it and ought to be stopped, and how she felt that the new baby would be as greedy as she was. Also, judging by the gruff way in which the baby had to talk, she felt the baby and her father identified. But she also felt that, in her anger and jealousy against her mother who would not let her have her father, she wanted to attack her mother with the tap, which seemed to stand for urination. And we can say that she then played the intercourse game with the two cups and told me how she wanted to do it too. We can also say, I think, that making the baby, who symbolized herself, talk in a gruff voice, meant that she felt she had actually realized her wish and got her father inside her. We can then predict that she would soon be showing how she felt that her mother was now, through being deprived, turned into an enemy. This was borne out in the next hour, when she played with a spoon, and said to me, as the baby, 'This is Mummy's best spoon, don't lose it – say "I *will* lose it", snatch Mummy's best spoon'; for she then washed my hands, saying, 'Darling, I won't hurt you' and told me to say, 'Yes, it *does* hurt' and snatch my hand away. For I think we can only conclude that it was because the water stood for poisonous urine that there was need to deny that it hurt, and that she was really feeling that her mother was going to do to her what she had wanted to do to her mother with the tap.

So much for what she felt about the external situation after the holiday and for material which I think was clearly the expression of infantile sexual wishes towards the actual external parents. But now she began to show also more of what she felt was happening inside. She began to express ideas which I find it difficult to explain without the hypothesis that she felt she had got the injured mother with the baby inside her. She introduced the material by showing how she felt she got her mother inside, that is through her bad and greedy mouth. For she brought in a fuschia flower which was fully open and said, 'This has a mouth, tear it up.' (Actually, some time after this, the mother reported that she said at home one day, 'Mummy I could eat if I didn't have to put it in my mouth.') After herself tearing the fuschia she said to me, 'Cry, and say "I'm the Mummy cooking the dinner".' In the light of her reference to the mouth I can only assume that she meant, in feeling that she was the mother, that she had taken her inside through her mouth. She then argued about this, trying, I think, to deny it but, at the same time, wanting it; for she said to me, 'You're not the Mummy, you're only three and a half. – Cry and say "I'm not three and a half".' She then gave me some stalks to eat, saying, 'Spit it out if you don't like it', introducing the idea, which she developed later, of getting rid of the mother she had taken inside. She said, 'I'm cutting your chalks, they're nasty. I'm going to cut your paper – Say "You're not going to".' When I said this she retorted, 'Yes, I am' and repeated it many times in a taunting, quarrelling voice. Here, by the way, it is interesting to compare a piece of earlier material in the fifty-fifth hour, when she had been washing the toys in a bowl of water, fiercely stirring them round, and had suddenly said, 'If you come inside me I'll make you cry', and had then added, 'What sort of a Mrs Milner are you?' as if trying to cling to the reality of me in the external world and get away from the idea of what she was doing inside. In this present hour, too, after insisting that she was going to cut my chalks and paper, she suddenly, I think, tried to escape from the anxieties about what she was doing to me inside by trying to cling to the external reality, for she suddenly said, 'I'm Rachel Sheridan, you're Mrs Milner – say that'; but when I repeated it she retorted at once, 'No, you're not'. And again it seems that she was trying to defend herself against taking me inside, for suddenly she said, 'Say "I won't open the door to you when you come" – Say "I'll hide when you come"', and she made me try and snatch the paper from her. And here I think the external situation was also shown, for the guilt about the wish to snatch and cut the baby was expressed in the idea that I, as mother, must hide to save the baby: it was *she* that should be shut out because she was such a danger to both her mother and the baby and also to her father's penis standing for the baby. For all this time she was cutting a newspaper and threatening to cut me and was saying, 'Look, I'm cutting Mummy and Daddy, *your* Daddy' (this was a photo of a man's face in the newspaper).

In the next hour she continually ordered me about saying, 'Stand here! No, here! here! go downstairs! no, come here! Go and play with the children! no, don't go in the road! there's traffic.' And I think we can say that on one level she was expressing her aggressiveness towards the baby – that it was a nuisance wherever it was – but that, on another, she was expressing her concern for the baby, as was shown in the reference to the dangers of traffic, and in her feeling that *she* was everywhere in the wrong place, a danger to everyone. Her mother reported that her eating had been very bad since the sick attack and that she was refusing meat (which she had liked before), always saying it was hard.

Now we come to a critical point in the internal situation, for the two hours following showed a sudden moment of insight into her own guilt and then the emergence of suicidal ideas. After the usual nagging quarrels of the 'I'm . . . You're not . . . ' type, she began smacking my face in a frenzy of real attack, then suddenly wanted to take the wheelbarrow to her mother, and on the way upstairs to her said to me, 'You're a darling, I'm not a darling.' When I said it was 'time' she began to scream, this time real screaming. This was interesting, because, three sessions before this one, she had started piercing dramatized screams for Mummy and had tried to make me do it too, and when I refused she had said, 'You'll go to the doctor and he'll make you able to scream, do something to your throat.' So it seemed that now I, as doctor, had made her able to scream. Her mother reported that her eating was a little better, but that she still refused the foods she particularly liked before.

She began the next hour, the ninety-ninth, with putting the fuschias on the floor and saying she was going to mess them up, then the usual repartee and quarreling, ending up with, 'Say "you're a naughty mummy not to let me have a . . . (nonsense word)".' She then absorbedly scribbled in chalk on the newspaper inside her toy drawer and finally tore the paper off saying, 'It's a nasty scribble, I'm going to cut out the nasty lady.' Now these two pieces of material coming together suggest, I think, that the nasty lady was the mother who would not allow her the penis or baby, and that this rival mother was not only an imago precipitated by the external experiences of frustration, but also the rival mother which she felt was inside herself (inside the drawer, in her play) and which she wished to cut out of herself because that was the actual way in which she experienced her own aggressive rivalry towards the external mother: it was her own badness which she wished to cut out of herself, an instinctual impulse within her – but she could not think of it as that, she could only try to deal with it in terms of the frustrating mother who stimulated it. This was confirmed by her saying, in the next hour, 'Cut *yourself*, your leg, pretend to, say "oooooh! help!".' Following this there was much ordering me about and when I obeyed her she continually said that I did it wrong. When I gave an interpretation beginning 'Whatever I do, you say it's wrong because . . . ', she interrupted with 'Whatever I do I cut myself' and then 'D'you know, Mrs Milner, my Mummy got a bleed with a pin.' I then interpreted that the hurt Mummy was inside, like the nasty lady, and she went on pretending to cut her own arms and fingers, then threw the scissors away and said, 'Let's pretend we're dead, we must take our shoes off.' She began cutting the brown fur trimming off her slippers and then suddenly hugged her tummy and went off to her mother saying, 'Mummy, I've got a pain in my tummy.' As she went I interpreted that the pain was the hurt mother and the baby inside without she brought a biscuit back from her mother ate it, and then returned to tell her mother that the pain was all right. Here she seemed to be saying that she felt she could not cut out the nasty lady inside feeling dead herself, also that she felt the nasty lady as equivalent to faeces, that is the brown fur on her slippers.

The next hour showed the extent to which she felt herself controlled and at the mercy of the nasty lady inside, how she felt she had a real bad agency within herself. For she began by not wanting to stay in the playroom but, when I interpreted that she felt the playroom was her mother's inside full of the cut-up babies, so that she was frightened of it, the anxiety disappeared and she no longer wanted to leave. Actually I think the interpretation here was only partly right and that the playroom stood more for her own inside, with me as the nasty lady. For she began to cut paper, while I held it, and then said, '*You* made me tear it, *you* made me drop the scissors, you're a horrid Mrs Milner and I won't open the door to you', and while saying this she put the paper over her mouth. By this last gesture with the paper she seemed also to throw direct light on her symptom, as if by refusing to eat she could avoid having the nasty lady inside. When I interpreted that she felt I was the nasty lady, the bad mother inside making her do bad things, she yelled and would not listen.

In the hour following she showed the first genuinely loving gesture to her mother that I had seen. She had begun the hour by refusing to come down to the playroom, and when I interpreted again that I was the nasty lady she had said, 'You aren't' and had come down at once. There she made us spend a long time dancing gaily round the table in a very free and happy way. She had often danced before, but it had always been in a highly sophisticated way, wriggling her body and swinging her arms and legs like a music-hall dancer. And once she had twirled round and round like a whirling dervish and said she was the doctor. But now she danced just like a little girl, and finally stopped, saying, 'It's nice, isn't it? I'm going to tell Mummy.' She brought her mother down and made us all three dance, then ran and gave her mother an affectionate hug. In this hour there was none of the rivalry and possessiveness and taunting that had been so frequent before, and it is particularly interesting that this capacity to show genuine affection followed directly after the interpretation of her aggressiveness in terms of the nasty lady inside, rather than after the many interpretations that I had made previously in the direct terms of her aggressive wishes as such, and not as internal bad objects. She ended the hour by saying to mother, 'Mrs Milner's nice'; but this did not last, for, unfortunately, the analysis now had to stop for a fortnight as I was ill. When she came back all the intense rivalry feelings had returned and her aggressiveness against me was very marked. For instance, while washing her hands she threw away the towel, saying, 'I've killed your towel, I'll throw away your head in the mirror.' Thus I think she was again trying to get rid of me inside herself, and in the following hour she showed how strongly she felt that I was inside her, for she burst into a fury of real tears, and gripped my arm in a frenzy of anxiety when I did not understand exactly what she wanted me to do although she had not told me. It seemed to me that this behaviour could only be explained by the assumption that she felt that I was inside her and therefore *ought* to know, and that everything I did not do was therefore felt by her as an act of obstruction and hostility. Probably also she felt me so hostile because she felt that she had made me ill and that now I was retaliating.

Her rivalry material now showed more aspects of penis envy. After saying one day, 'You haven't got toys in your room – I have', she added, 'We've got to hide from Daddy', as if to say that if she takes the penis her father then becomes the enemy. Actually her mother now reported that Rachel was very clinging with her and uneasy with her father, which reversed the earlier situation; also she now talked about the new baby, but called it 'he' and said it would be 3 and a half. And in the fifth hour after her return she brought her teddy and cut the hair on its tummy saying, 'He doesn't mind, . . . oh, yes, he does, he's crying.' She then happened to see my bicycle through the window, for the first time, and burst into a high-pitched tirade of fury and indignation, saying, 'Someone'll take it, it isn't yours, it's worsable, it's unkindable to have one, they're hard to get, it's too big . . . ' and so on, with much repetition.

In the next few hours anal material was uppermost. She brought a leaf in, tore it to bits, and put the bits in her mother's pocket. In the lavatory I heard her say to her mother, 'Mummy, why does kaki and weewee come out of there and not out of legs and eyes?' She had shut me out of the lavatory and when she came out I interpreted her not wanting to have me there as to do with feeling that she had bitten me up, like the torn leaves, and now wanted to get rid of me, and that the kaki would show what she had done. She indignantly interrupted with, 'I don't eat kaki and weewee; you said I do, I don't'. The connection between faeces and the nasty lady has already been seen, and here she was showing the fear that whatever she ate turned into faeces, that her mother, and what her mother gave, so easily became the nasty lady, felt as attacking faeces. That it was poisonous faeces and flatus which were the danger to the new baby was shown when later she tucked her doll, Belinda, into the wheelbarrow and said she was ill. In a dreamy voice she explained, 'She got in my pram and in the wind, catch the wind, she didn't like it and she ate some leaves, poison stalks.' Then she took some plasticine from the drawer and ran round with it, shouting, 'Let's pretend there's a real monkey', and shrieked when near the supposed monkey and called out in a different voice, 'I don't like you, Rachel Sheridan'; then in her own voice, 'Then I don't like you, monkey'. She made the pasticine into rolls and said she was making lovely things for Belinda, and cuddled her, but added, 'The monkeys say they don't like my yellow plasticine.' Here the monkeys seem to have stood for both the real mother outside and the super-ego mother inside, both telling her she must not poison the baby with her yellow faeces.

It was at this time, in November, that the analysis came to an end, as the mother could not continue to bring her; and also the mother did not feel it necessary to go on as the symptom had disappeared and she felt that Rachel was now an entirely normal child. I tried to explain to her that there was still much to be done.

The subsequent history is that the new baby (a girl) was born last April and that Rachel was sent away to a residential school in the country for six weeks at the time of the birth. Her mother reported that she came back quite changed, and though 'eating like a horse' was very silent and withdrawn; also that her face only lit up when she talked to the baby, but if the mother tried to cuddle her she 'went stiff'. This condition gradually improved and now the mother reports that Rachel is quite herself again.

Naturally there are many gaps in this study, both because the analysis itself was so short, and because so small a part even of a short analysis can be described in a single paper. But I will try to summarize here some of Rachel's main anxieties and the ways in which she was trying to escape from them. Her central anxiety seemed to be fear of what she might do, or felt she had done, in connection with her Oedipus wishes, and what might be done to her in retaliation and punishment; and she felt her Oedipus wishes largely in oral terms. Thus if she ate she felt she robbed her mother and her mother then became an enemy. But her father also became an enemy because he also was robbed of his penis. Thus if she ate she felt she would have no one good to turn to at all. Not to eat seemed to be the only way out, at home. But in the analysis she showed other ways also of trying to escape from this basic conflict between her wishes and what she felt would happen if she satisfied them. For instance, she tried to escape in the following ways.

First, by projection: she tried to feel that I was the person who wanted to bite, I was the bad and greedy child, not she.

Second, by denial: she tried to deny the actual fact of her own smallness and dependence, a denial that was shown for instance in her taunting rivalries. Here the mechanism seemed to be that, owing to her early frustration, her own smallness and dependence had become something acutely dangerous, in that it put her at the mercy of such destructive feelings towards her parents. But if she could deny this dependence on them, and make herself believe that she already had all she wanted, and that what she already had was the best, then she felt she would be saved from the angers at not having, which she felt were such a danger to all concerned.

Third, by control: for by controlling her own behaviour according to some imposed pattern, continually acting a part, instead of allowing herself to behave freely and spontaneously according to her own impulses, she felt she could be safe from those impulses. And by so often trying to control me and make me copy exactly what she did, she was, I think, showing me what she was doing inside herself, as well as trying to avoid the responsibility for her impulses by sharing it. For it seems to me that her method of defence by control here included the idea of getting all her external objects, including me, inside herself, and the failure of this defence was shown in her intense anxiety when I did not know what she wanted me to do without being told. It was as if her artificiality was a picture of her internal situation, in which she felt so dominated by the people she had taken inside that she could not be herself at all.

By the vehemence and persistence of her denials we can see, I think, the poignancy of this child's dilemma, and most of all by the fact that her chief defence, the refusal to eat, was a threat to life itself. For if we ask how the instinctive self-preserving need to take food and drink can be so inhibited, if we ask what can be stronger than the instinct to preserve physical life, I think we can only answer that the need to preserve something good to believe in can be stronger. For this little girl felt that if she ate she robbed her mother and her mother then became an enemy and therefore could no longer be believed in. And if she ate she also then had the enemy mother inside her and so there was nothing good to believe in, either inside or out, and life would not be worth having. Thus what she was really doing in not eating was trying to save something good to believe in from the destructiveness of her own greedy and envious impulses.

In a second paper I shall hope to test this idea of a need that is stronger than the need to preserve physical life, against certain general psychological theories about the basic springs of action. I shall hope also to consider certain implications of the material about the nasty lady inside in relation to general psychological theories about how we do in fact come to perceive ourselves and what is inside us. I want to consider certain problems to do with the question of the terms in which a child can, in the years before speech, come to perceive its own impulses; in what terms the child's consciousness, as the organ of inner perception, apprehends the experiences which this little girl expressed as the nasty lady inside; and exactly why my putting this experience into words for her had such a marked effect in relieving her anxieties and making her able to show genuine love for her mother.

In conclusion I should like to express my gratitude to Mrs Klein for all the help she has given me in conducting this analysis.

Seven months after reading this paper I was asked to undertake the analysis of a girl of 23 (I called her Susan) whose analysis, centring around her drawings, I eventually tried to describe in the book *The Hands of the Living God*.[2] During the analysis she told me how she had, a few week before, left hospital, where she had been persuaded to have ECT (electroconvulsive therapy) and what she felt it had done to her. She said that since having it she had no boundary to the back of her head and that the world was no longer outside her. This meant that she felt terrified of the bombing, since there were no boundaries; it meant that she was everything so the bombs were bound to fall on her. She also told me that, before going into hospital, at the age of 19 and when working on a farm, she had 'broken down into reality' and discovered for the first time that if you walk away from things they get further away from you. Since I had just been writing about questions to do with boundaries and visual perspective in my book about painting I was all alert to see what she could teach me about such problems, especially after Rachel's concern with doubts about 'what is really real' and what is 'pretend real'. In fact, my next paper was an attempt to get some idea about what kinds of reality we were struggling with, so I tried to relate some of these clinical findings to the general psychology I had learnt about in the university. Particularly also this next paper was deeply stimulated by this 3-year-old's question, 'What sort of a Mrs Milner are you?' In fact this was a question which pointed forward to a number of adult patients I was to struggle with, mostly those who came to be called 'borderline' (between neurosis and psychosis) people who had great difficulty in accepting the fact that, in their feelings and ideas about me I was both Mrs Milner and some figure from the past – or even part of themselves.

References

1 This paper was read before the British Psycho-Analytical Society, 21 June, 1944, and published later that year in the *International Journal of Psycho-Analysis* 25: 53–61.
2 Milner, M. (1969) *The Hands of the Living God*. London: Hogarth.

4

1945: Some aspects of phantasy in relation to general psychology[1]

In a previous paper (see Chapter 3) I tried to give an account of a partial analysis of a little girl of 3, called Rachel, who came for treatment because of an acute inhibition of eating.[2] I stated my intention of trying to consider the relation of some of the theoretical ideas emerging from this analysis to certain aspects of general psychology; I wanted to do this in order to define these ideas more clearly in my own mind, through trying to find out how far they were based on common ground of agreed theory in the two sciences. I know it is sometimes said by analysts that no such common ground is possible; it is sometimes said that general psychologists, if not analysed themselves, have too great a resistance against accepting those facts about the unconscious mind which are disclosed by the special psycho-analytical method of research. Though there may be some truth in this view I feel it is a dangerous one for analysts, because it tends to make us assume, when faced with criticism from scientific workers, that it is only the content of our findings which they cannot accept. But it may also at times be the form in which we present our findings which causes the general psychologist to have misgivings.

With this plan in mind I chose a modern textbook of general psychology written by a lecturer in a university. The particular textbook I have chosen is Sprott's *General Psychology* published in 1937.[3] I selected this because of its recent date and because, in his foreword of acknowledgment to Professor F. C. Bartlett and Dr C. S. Myers, the author puts himself in the direct tradition of English academic psychology. Having selected this book, I then found that the writer makes many references to Freudian theory; for instance, he gives it eight out of fourteen pages in the chapter headed 'Development' and twelve out of twenty-eight in the chapter headed 'Conflict'. In Chapter 1, headed 'The Springs of Action', Sprott gives a modified form of MacDougall's famous list of the fundamental drives and then says

> 'Another and shorter list has been suggested by the Freudian school of psycho-analysts. For them there are two fundamental drives – love and destruction. . . . Such a simplification is attractive because it satisfies the demands of the principle of scientific economy. The question which we shall have to face later is: on what evidence are so many diverse purposive activities linked up with, and considered manifestations of, the love instinct?'
>
> (p. 17)

In the chapter on 'Development', after briefly describing the theory of the phases of the libido, he says, 'Whether the theory will stand the test of future investigations, we cannot say, but (1) it helps us to explain much that is left out of other psychological theories, (2) if it is true it is of very great importance' (p. 138).

Further, in describing various views on the meaning of play, Sprott refers to Melanie Klein's work and says 'In the play, impulses which are responsible for psychological disturbances betray themselves, sometimes with startling clarity' (p. 114).

Finally, with regard to general Freudian theory, he says

> 'The value of this complicated interpretive framework lies, of course, in its utility. If it helps us to understand behaviour it has value for that fact alone; if it helps us to influence behaviour it gains thereby increased probability, and the fruits of psycho-analytic practice certainly warrant our taking the theory seriously, however unexpected it may be in detail.'
>
> (p. 170)

I have quoted these extracts from Sprott in order to give some idea of the position of general psychology in regard to Freudian theory, and to see what common ground I can take for granted in trying to relate some of the findings from Rachel's analysis with general psychological theory.

The idea arising from this analysis which I am particularly interested in and wish to clarify in my own mind is that connected with the child's play of the 'nasty lady' and my interpretation of it

40

both in terms of myself in the transference, and also in terms of the 'enemy mother inside'. At the end of my first paper I said

> 'For this little girl felt that if she ate she robbed her mother and her mother then became an enemy and therefore could no longer be believed in. And if she ate she also then had the enemy mother inside her and so there was nothing good to believe in, either inside or out, and life would not be worth having. Thus what she was really doing in not eating was trying to save something good to believe in from the destructiveness of her own greedy and envious impulses.'

But the question I have to ask myself is, what exactly do I mean by the statement that the child feels she has an enemy mother inside? And, if my observations and inference from her play are accurate, how can I justify in their own terms, to general psychologists, an idea which is so remote from common-sense experience, however familiar it may be to imaginative experience in poetry, literature, and religion?

In order to answer this question I looked for an account of any similar phenomena in general psychology and I found a passage to do with the structure of the personality which seemed to me to be relevant. Thus Sprott says, in the chapter on 'Development':

> 'The development of character consists in building up a well-organized structure, such that there is a certain relation of coherence between what we do at one time and what we do at another. We develop certain skills, such as reading, writing, typing and walking, and these are at the disposal of our desires to use for their satisfaction. But the desires themselves grow into a system.'

> (p. 142)

And again, when referring to Shand's work on character:

> 'The point here is, not so much that the impulses and tendencies get integrated into a personality system, as that our interests and therefore the liability to emotion, get centred round relatively permanent objectives. . . . We live our lives in a world of persisting entities, towards which we have attitudes or, as Shand calls them "sentiments", and these sentiments, while not facts of experience, are hypothetical structural features of ourselves in virtue of which we have certain emotional experiences, and certain liabilities to behave in certain ways, under suitable circumstances.'

> (p. 144)

41

Certainly this little girl had a persisting attitude towards the persisting entity of her mother as a food-giving person. In Shand's terms, I suppose we could say that she had developed a primitive sentiment towards her external mother as food-giver, though a negative rather than a positive one, and perhaps we might say that this had become part of the structure of her personality – the way in which her most fundamental desires had become organized. But such a statement offers no clear idea about the way in which this attitude had become part of the structure of her personality. My task then seemed to be to try and find out whether such material as that of the enemy mother inside could possibly be used to throw light on the exact nature of these hypothetical structures of ourselves, and to decide whether, when the general psychologist talks of sentiments and the psychoanalyst of internal objects, we may not in fact be talking about the primitive form of the same thing.

In order to do this I thought it best to begin by trying to clarify in my own mind the concept of phantasy. It seemed to me that there are certain distinctions in the meaning of the word phantasy which are implicit in parts of current psychoanalytical theory, but which I should have to try and make explicit before attempting the comparison with general psychology. And in so doing I also hoped to be able to define the meaning I had myself been giving to certain aspects of Melanie Klein's theories and to find out how far it is the meaning given by other analysts or not.

Incidentally, the word 'phantasy' does not appear in the index of Sprott's book, though it does in the text. But the word 'imagery' does appear in the index, and here I want to use the word image for whatever is precipitated from already lived experiences and becomes the basis for interpreting the present and expecting the future – with the note, that the image may be built from memory traces of all kinds of sensory experiences, kinaesthetic and visceral as well as visual and auditory.

When I tried to summarize psychoanalytic theory on the functions of the image I began with the basic distinction between its function in the service of the pleasure principle and its function in the service of the reality principle. That is (1) its function of providing the means by which past experiences can be compared with and brought into relation to present ones; in fact, its function as the vehicle of memory, recognition, judgement, knowing; and (2) its function as a substitute for the action in the external world which the child is too weak to perform or is prevented from performing; that is its use for conjuring up wish-fulfilments in a hallucinatory way which carry with them the feeling that the child has actually performed the action she wished to; in fact, its function as a primitive form of acting rather than of knowing, of conation rather than of cognition.

But if we say that the function of the image very early branches out into two, the primitive form of knowing or interpreting experience and the primitive substitute for action, then the first function surely also branches out into two, owing to the ever-present fact of the difference between the subjective and objective realities. One branch must consist of images which do actually belong to the real nature of external experiences. They are as it were tied to it; and, though they are derived from the child's own past emotional experience with the object and subjective interpretation of its nature, they do refer, even if in a distorted way, to something that is really there. For they are the images which are evoked to fill out the meaning of any perceptual experience, they are the records of past experiences evoked in fresh relationships to explain what is not immediately given in the present; as, for example, the images from past experiences with people that are evoked to fill out the meaning and intentions that lie behind a particular facial expression or gesture. But they are memory images based on actual external perceptions and so can be continually tested against further external perceptions, and so become progressively 'true' of the outside world. The second branch must then consist of images which are the expression and content of the child's own psychic reality of wishes and feelings and moods. And these, although also originally derived from actual experiences with the external object, do seem to remain in the mind, not only as memories of past external experiences and hopes for future ones, but also as a means of knowing present internal ones. Thus they are, I think psychoanalytical theory is suggesting, the only means by which the child can represent to herself the psychic processes going on inside; and they can therefore be said to be 'true for inside her'.

If these distinctions are correct, there are then three functions for the image: first, the primitive action substitute or conjuring-up function; second, the primitive knowing or giving meaning to external happenings; third, the primitive knowing or giving meaning to internal happenings.

It is I think the extreme form of the first of these functions of the image which, in popular presentations of Freudian theory, is often given especial if not exclusive emphasis. And it is this bias that is expressed in the often wholesale application of the word 'escapism' to much of the imaginative creations of the mind. But I think it is only by considering the second and third functions, in their relation to the first function, that it is possible to find any logical justification for the inferences I have drawn from the material of the 'nasty lady inside'. Also, the first function cannot be separated from the others by a hard and fast line, for when not in its extreme form it does in fact lead on to knowing. When the urgency of the need for immediate magical satisfaction of the wish is not too great, the conjured-up wish-fulfilment does seem to function as a kind of experimental rather than magical action. It enables the holding of action in suspension and imagining the probable results of it, and thus becomes the essential basis for experimental thinking and deliberate choice of means to ends.

That such a three-fold distinction is implied in psychoanalytical theory, although ignored in popular presentations of it, is shown, I think, in Freud's essay on 'Negation'.[4] Clearly, the first function of the image is only possible when the contrast between subjective and objective is not being taken into account, when the thought or image of an action and the action itself are felt to be identical. And Freud says of this contrast that it is not there from the beginning but only arises from two conditions: first, from the mind's capacity for reviving a thing which has been perceived by reproducing it as an image; and second, from the fact that a real external object has been lost which once afforded real satisfaction. Then surely the second function of the image arises with the attempt, as Freud describes it, to re-discover externally the real object which has been preserved internally in the form of an image – in fact with the attempt to convince oneself that it is still there. Thus the image which has been preserved internally is then put out again into the outside world in response to the inner demands of instinct, and when the sensory experience of the moment is sufficiently like the original experience to raise the hope of finding the lost object once more. So the projection of the image leads to action towards it in the real world and reality-testing begins. This is the sense in which I meant that images used in the way of the second function can become progressively 'true' of the outside world. But Freud adds: 'What is not real, what is merely imagined or subjective, is only *internal*; while on the other hand what is real is also present *externally*.' And what is present internally is not only images or memories of past perceptions of the external world; there are also the present psychic realities of feelings and wishes and moods, which are real internal experiences, as are also the memories of past ones. Thus it is my problem here to try and consider psychoanalytical theory on the way in which these psychic realities are experienced by the self that owns or disowns them, and how the idea of the enemy mother inside illustrates this.

These three aspects of the image are implied by Joan Riviere:[5]

'The phantasy-life of the individual is thus the form in which his real internal and external sensations and perceptions are interpreted and represented to himself in his mind. . . . I would draw your attention to the conclusion that phantasy-life is never "pure phantasy". It consists of true perceptions and of false interpretations; all phantasies are thus *mixtures* of external and internal reality.'

[Paragraph deleted.][6]

Such a hypothesis certainly seems to explain the child's behaviour in the ninety-ninth hour of the analysis, when she had accused me of being a 'naughty mummy' for withholding something from her and had scribbled on the paper inside her toy drawer and then torn out the scribble saying it was 'nasty' and that she was cutting out the nasty lady. In my first paper I put forward the hypothesis that the nasty lady was the mother who would not allow her the penis or the baby, and that this rival mother was not only an imago, or external memory image, of what her mother seemed like to her during frustration, but also the rival mother felt to be both inside herself and part of herself, part of the structure of her personality, which she wished to cut out of herself. It was felt to be part of herself because she could not separate the bad wish from the bad object of it; thus it was the whole experience which she wished to cut out of herself. And I went on to suggest that this idea was confirmed in the next hour by her game of pretending to cut herself.

Such a use of phantasy is also, I think, definitely implied by Freud, when, in *The Ego and the Id*, he introduces the problem of how internal reality is perceived, and says:[7]

'Whereas the relation between external perceptions and the ego is quite perspicuous, that between internal perceptions and the ego requires special investigation. . . . Internal perceptions yield sensations of processes arising in the most diverse and certainly also in the deepest strata of the mental apparatus.'

(p. 24)

For he goes on to say, when taking the particular example of the perception of pleasure-pain:

'Suppose we describe what becomes conscious in the shape of pleasure and "pain" as an undetermined quantitative and qualitative element in the mind; the question then is whether that element can become conscious where it actually is, or whether it must first be transmitted into the system Pcpt. Clinical experience decides for the latter.'

He also refers to the part played by words in internal perception: 'The part played by verbal images now becomes perfectly clear. By their interposition internal thought-processes are made into perceptions. It is like a demonstration of the theorem that all knowledge has its origin in external perception' (p. 26). He does not, however, actually discuss what external perceptions could fulfil the same function as words before the child learns to talk. But he does, in another connection, point out how visual images of things (which must surely mean people, parts of people, or inanimate objects which are symbols of these) can be used as the vehicles of thought, though not specifically indicating thought about the internal world. Thus he writes:

'We must not be led away, in the interests of simplification perhaps, into forgetting the importance of optical memory-residues – those of *things* (as opposed to *words*) – or to deny that it is possible for thought-processes to become conscious through a reversion to visual residues, and that in many people this seems a favourite method.'

(p. 23)

Incidentally I feel it necessary here, for the sake of clarity, to assume that this 'becoming conscious' includes both simple knowing one's own experience, as well as knowing that one knows. For I think clinical material forces us to assume that the patient does in fact know all his own experience even though he does not know that he knows. And it is the question of the form which this first knowing takes, before experience is verbalized, which is my problem in this paper.

If it is true to say of the child's dramatic internal upheavals of love and hate, that they have to be translated into the system Pcpt. and so are felt as people inside doing things, because the original incorporation phantasy provides her with such a convenient way of representing them, what about all the other psychic processes, cognitive as well as conative and affective, to which we give the abstract psychological names of judgement, recognition, intuition, habit, and so on? Obviously in this child of 3 such processes are in full swing, she is judging, wondering, learning by practice, and so on, all the time, in connection with what is going on around her and inside her. But how do such activities *feel* to her? Even the basic

46

mental capacity of perception must lead to confusion, before we have slowly come to realize that there is a fundamental difference between thoughts and things. This point has been dealt with in detail by Susan Isaacs, who asks how it is that we come to know that perception is a mental process of taking in, not a physical one.[8] Thus she says: 'How do we come – you and I, psychologists and ordinary people alike – to know this distinction, to realize that what we have "taken inside" is an image and not a bodily concrete object?' And she goes on to show that it is only after a long and complex process of development that 'it is realized that the objects are outside the mind, but their *images* are "in the mind".' And, if simple perception is felt in concrete terms, what, for instance, does the psychic state of conflict between impulses feel like? Surely it must feel like its counterpart in the external world, like two people in conflict. And harmony between impulses must surely feel like a loving accord between people. Also I have often wondered what does that surprising thing, habit, getting used to something, learning by practice, feel like, when one has no words, such as 'learning' or 'practising' to describe it? At all ages one can suddenly and mysteriously find difficult tasks getting easier. Does that feel to the child like a good helping person appearing inside? It seems to me we get nearest, apart from the material given in an analysis, to a picture of how psychic processes must feel to a child from the mythical cosmologies, such as those of the Greeks, for instance. Here we find the loves and quarrels of the gods of Olympus, in an endless complicated pattern, continually controlling, both helping and hindering, the hero's endeavours.

I should like to find a name for this way of looking at the phantasy of the internal object, by borrowing from Silberer and calling it the functional interpretation. What I do not feel certain about is whether *all* internal objects carry a functional meaning, or only some.

The above is, briefly, an attempt to define what the idea of the enemy mother inside meant to me in this analysis. I have in fact tried to define it in terms of a special aspect of the funciton such an imaginative creation may serve in the child's total dynamic situation, and have in so doing been led to emphasize the distinction between the three functions of phantasy. I will now try to compare this distinction with Sprott's formulations. The first function of phantasy, the primitive action substitute or wish fulfilment is fully described by Sprott, though under the heading of Piaget's concept of 'ego-centricity' rather than under the concept of phantasy. Thus he says, in the chapter on 'Development':

'Another symptom of "ego-centricity" is the "omnipotence of

47

thought". If the outside world does not have to be taken into account because its independence is not yet fully appreciated, the all-important distinction between reality and desire is not likely to be made. This means that the wish will be tantamount to the act. . . . This is why there are unconscious feelings of guilt in the breast of the blameless, and this accounts for the development of symbolic representation. What matters to the unconscious is that aggressive desires are harboured, and since there is no essential difference between the desire and its gratification, guilt and fear are aroused by the presence of the desire alone.'

(p. 147)

Again later, in the chapter on 'Imagery and Imagination':

'The theory is that our behavioural world is more a matter of our own creation than we are used to think, and that at an early stage the real has not been distinguished from the imaginary, so that it is almost as satisfying for an impulse to manifest itself in the form of imaginary satisfaction as for it to clothe itself in "real" performance. This rather startling view has great explanatory value.'

(p. 329)

In the chapter on 'Conflict' he actually uses the word 'fantasy' though only in a passage describing Freudian theory, not as an essential concept in general psychological theory: 'If socially respectable satisfaction is impossible, we can relieve the tension somewhat by indulgence in fantasy. Dreams, day-dreams and myths are safety valves for unconscious desires' (p. 166).

What I have called the second function of phantasy, that of filling out the meaning of our perceptual experiences is referred to by Sprott in the chapter on 'Imagination' under the heading of 'make believe'. He says, 'although it is important to distinguish the image from the perception as an experience, there is nevertheless a strong imaginal factor playing a part in all our percepts, which is the more dominant the less developed we are' (p. 332). He refers specifically to primitive people and children, and writes, 'It appears that very primitive peoples invest any strange phenomena with "power", they see it as the abode of supernatural force, impersonal, dangerous and contagious. From this projection of their emotions has developed personal deities' (pp. 331–32). And: 'We cannot have any idea of what the world looks like to the child, but its behaviour gives us the impression that . . . it ensouls all that helps or hinders it in the satisfaction of its desires' (p. 189).

In another place Sprott enlarges on the imaginal element which plays a part in all our perceptions and shows how it enters into scientific discovery:

'In the fields of invention and scientific discovery imagination is used to elaborate the behavioural world and the hypotheses we construct as to its "real" nature, and under such circumstances the imagination is tied by external factors; the framework of a hypothesis is tied to the facts it has to explain, and the invention is a dream until it works.'

(p. 328)

But, with regard to the task of scientific discovery that is involved in finding out about the real nature of other people, he says:

'If they [that is, other people] cross our paths we are apt to regard them as hostile throughout; if they help us they are seen as kindly throughout. . . . The object we apprehend is apprehended as having qualities which go beyond the evidence. So vulnerable are most of us that the characteristic of hostility is planted in others with much greater ease than is the characteristic of friendliness. . . . It is not only our conscious experiences which determine . . . our apprehension of what other people are like: our unconscious desires and aspirations often clothe other people . . . with qualities we should like them to possess, or ascribe to them sinfulness which really lurks in ourselves. . . . And when two people are linked up by the sentiment of love, the qualities ascribed to the mind of the lovee are indefinitely variable and frequently remote from the truth.'

(p. 190–91)

In terms of Rachel's analysis, here is the description, in Sprott's words, of how the real experience of her mother crossing her path, in the course of all the inevitable frustrations of childhood, had produced in her mind the picture of the hostile enemy mother. But to this observation that we ascribe to others the sinfulness that really lurks in ourselves psychoanalysis adds that we do it because we are moved by a very strong urge to escape the guilt of our bad feelings, and also because we expect to have done to us what we unconsciously wish to do to others. So the hostility that Rachel felt at the frustrations she suffered had led her to implant the hostility in her mother, to ensoul her with it, so that her mother finally became such a dangerous figure that it seemed unsafe even to eat in her presence. Rachel had in fact used her imagination to elaborate the behavioural world, represented here by her mother, and attempted to construct a hypothesis as to her real nature. But the process had become

49

distorted by her inability to recognize certain aspects of her own real nature, that is her hostility. But the next problem is how this hostile mother came to be felt to be inside herself, and this brings us to the whole phenomena of introjection.

Although Sprott does not put forward the concept of introjection as an accepted part of general psychology, he does refer to it, as a part of Freudian theory. For instance, in the chapter on 'Conflict', he says:

> 'The hostility of the outside world is proportional to the child's own feelings rather than to the "real" facts of the case. The organism is therefore in a predicament. If desires arise which cannot be satisfied (a) unbearable tension is set up, and (b) danger threatens because of projected hostility. Something has to be done, and the organism is believed to take into itself ("introject" – oral technique) a parental control which operates nearer the source of the trouble and stems the impulses which are responsible for its difficulties. This is the basis for the "super-ego".'
>
> (pp. 164–65)

Also, when giving a list of the various ways, such as displacement, projection, reaction-formation, and so on, by which, according to Freud, men seek relief from what Sprott calls the internal dynamic situation, he includes introjection and says: 'The organism may take an external objective into itself. We have seen that this is the mechanism involved in the setting up of the super-ego. It is also thought that a lost love-object can be introjected' (p. 169). He does not actually suggest that the phantasy of the introjected object is used, amongst other things, in the service of endopsychic memory and endopsychic perception; possibly however an indirect reference to this line of thought may be found in the fact that he does, in connection with the experimental rather than the analytic approach to the study of dream imagery, refer to Silberer's experiments, as described by Freud on how abstract ideas clothe themselves in visual imagery.[9]

I should now like to return to the problem of the relation between the concepts of sentiments and internal objects; and to take, in order to limit the field to a more nearly manageable size, the particular problem of the self-regarding sentiments. And I should like to ask in this connection, how in fact do we come to regard ourselves and what is it that we regard? Here Sprott, in his chapter on 'Other People', quotes Stout: 'Stout points out that the mentality of others is brought to the fore in all situations in which the perceived organism facilitates, or hinders, or completes the satisfaction of our desires.'

He then adds, 'It is suggested that our awareness of ourselves as ourselves and our awareness of other people come about at the same time, and, for all we know, this may be the case' (p. 189). But here psychoanalysis can surely add a whole field of observations of how our awareness of ourselves and belief in ourselves does seem to depend directly upon what we have wanted to do to other people, both when they hindered our activities and also when we wanted to hinder theirs. In fact, it has much evidence to show that our feelings about ourselves, our own gifts and qualities and our ability to use them depends directly upon the use we have made of other people in our own minds. It shows, for instance, how we often destroy in our anger the perception or memory of what hinders our desires and rouses our rage and envy; and, in so denying and destroying the knowledge of part of our external reality, we also deny or destroy part of our own inner reality, that is the wish that is stirred by the denied external reality. And the result may be obsessive doubts about external reality which are linked to doubts about ourselves. As Freud has said, he who doubts his love, doubts everything.[10] So the many doubts which Rachel showed about the exact nature of the toys can be related to the fact that she cannot trust herself to be loving towards her mother, and later, towards the actual baby inside her mother; because she cannot trust the bad and frustrating mother, who is both outside, as the real mother who frustrated her, and also inside, as the internal perception of her own bad feelings when frustrated. Further, her feelings about her mother hindering her activities and desires link with her own desire to hinder her mother and father's activity of making the new baby. Thus what we regard when we regard ourselves would seem to be a mixture. It consists partly of our consciously recognized attitudes, capacities, experiences. But underneath this, at a deeper level of organization, there would seem to be a whole inner world of hurt or preserved introjected figures. For instance, clinical material seems to show that the particular state of self-regard, or lack of it, known popularly as 'an inferiority complex', rests upon a feeling of doubt or despair about the nature and condition of the introjected objects. Thus such a state can be said, if we are describing it intellectually, to be the endopsychic perception of our own guilty wishes; but it is felt as if we were continually harbouring, carrying about inside us, not the guilty impulses, but the magically achieved results of them, the hurt and robbed people themselves.

Sprott defines sentiments as liability to emotion centring round relatively permanent objectives. This does not specify whether the objectives are internal or external, but it raises the question of what happens to this organization of our emotions when the external objective is not immediately present to us. Sprott says, again in the chapter on 'Other People': 'When a person goes out of the room, even though there is no sense-data of them, they are, for a longer or a shorter time, continuing in the present behavioural world in some sense' (p. 190). But psychoanalysis can surely add that a whole world of struggle and hope and misery lies behind this single reference to what happens to a person, in our minds, when he is not there; for the interaction of the three functions of phantasy surely means that the hostile wish to destroy what frustrates us can destroy the memory image or imagined perception of the loved person. When they are absent, they can be destroyed in our minds by the hate we felt at their going; and the destroyed image can be felt as an inherent part of ourselves because it is the psychic representative of our own power to love them. In this way the common description of a person as 'going to pieces' under emotional frustration and strain, can be linked with the idea of the temporary disintegration of the structural features of the personality, and this again linked with the amount of hostility directed towards the outside world of loved and hated people.

Although I have tried to make use of this three-fold distinction in the function of phantasy, I personally often find it difficult in actual analysis to decide at what moment a particular phantasy or dream should be interpreted in terms of the external or internal world. This raises the question of whether there is any special type of symbolism associated with phantasies of the internal world. In Rachel's analysis, she did not of course actually say that the nasty lady that she wished to cut out was inside her, she only tried to cut out the picture of the nasty lady which she herself had drawn on the paper inside her toy drawer. I should like to ask, if this distinction holds good, then when is it legitimate to take the symbol of people inside something, such as houses or trains or cars, as an indication that the phantasy needs to be interpreted in terms of the inside world, that is in terms of the inner structure of the personality, as well as in terms of objective experience? Perhaps, however, this difficulty only arises from a mistaken way of stating the problem. By hypothesis, the inner experiences of wish and feeling that are felt imaginatively as the activities of people inside are in fact originally based on actual experiences with people outside. Thus in one aspect the internal object phantasies are the imaginative interpretation of real feelings and bodily experiences with certain actual external characters as they seemed to the child to be in reality. Then the decision for the analyst is not so much whether the phantasy or dream figure represents an outer or inner reality; it is rather a question of the nature of the interplay between the two realities, and of what stage or level in the assimilation of an experience the patient is concerned with at the moment. And if the analyst does interpret the phantasy figure as felt to be inside and part of the patient's inner reality, part of his repressed ego, then it is with the mental reservation that this internal figure will eventually, as analysis progresses, be traced back to an actual figure from the external world, and bearing the particular qualities which the child really judged him to possess at the moment of introjection. But I think it is important to emphasize that such a reservation does not detract from the importance of these internal figures and does not mean that such a mechanism for representing internal reality can ever be dispensed with in the psychic organization of even the most extensively analysed person.

In the first place, if we think how long it takes to put into words all our feelings about someone we are intimately concerned with, how immensely subtle and complicated human relationships necessarily are and how continually we have to make decisions and take immediate action on the basis of such subtle and rich mixtures of feeling, and if we consider the marvellous economy of thought so often shown in the condensation of a dream image or symbol, by which we can represent to ourselves a whole range of past and present feelings in a single symbolic figure – then it seems likely that to imagine we could analyse away the internal objects would be to think that we could rob the mind of one of its most valuable instruments. In fact I think it would be comparable to the attempt, in matters of external perception, to try to make the patient use solely rational judgements on the ground that intuition is more easily affected by emotional distortion than is rational judgement. I think such an analogy is valid because the imaginative symbol formation represented by the internal object does seem to provide the basis for intuitive endopsychic perception, just as the direct expression of feeling in words provides the basis for rational endopsychic perception. Thus the analyst's task is surely to enable the patient to bring this instrument of intuitive self-knowledge up to date and appropriate to present needs, rather than attempt the impossible task of eliminating it on the grounds of its archaic form.

And secondly, through providing such a basis for knowing our own deepest feeling experiences, internal object phantasies do provide also a means by which we can continue assimilating, reflecting upon, developing our past experiences. They do seem to provide the vehicle by which the psyche can carry on its relation to its first loves, developing and enriching this throughout life and long after these loved people no longer exist in the external world; and this continuous development itself enlarges and enriches the boundaries of the ego, through widening the range of endopsychic perception and therefore also of endopsychic relationship. As Freud said, in *The Ego and the Id*, of the process of introjecting the loved object: 'this transformation of an erotic object-choice into a modification of the ego is also a method by which the ego can obtain control over the id and deepen its relations with it' (p. 37). And this process not only deepens the relation with the id, for Freud goes on to say:

> 'The transformation of object-libido into narcissistic libido which thus takes place obviously implies an abandonment of sexual aims, a process of desexualization; it is consequently a kind of sublimation. Indeed, the question arises, and deserves careful consideration, whether this is not always the path taken in sublimation, whether all sublimation does not take place through the agency of the ego, which begins by changing sexual object-libido into narcissistic libido and then, perhaps, goes on to give it another aim.'
>
> (pp. 37 f.)

This would seem to imply that we do go on throughout life, in so far as we are psychically well, serving and taking care of and fighting and contending with our good and bad internal objects, by projecting them continually into the external world in the form of our permanent interests, and so continuing the never-ending process of discovering more of ourselves and more of the world.

I will now give an example, from an adult patient, of a dream in which the symbolism seems to me to include marked references to the internal situation as well as to infantile external experience and present physiological changes. The patient is an unmarried woman, nearing 50, and had shown great anxiety over the approach of the menopause, together with disturbance of the self-regarding sentiments, an acute sense of unworthiness being convered by marked aggressiveness and criticism of others. Here is the dream:

> 'There was a hansom cab, a relic of past days and anomalous, out of date and unnecessary, and it was being driven by a woman. Her husband had driven this antiquated vehicle, but had died, and she carried on with the work. . . . She was dressed in black. I think a dark man . . . was a passenger in the cab. . . . There were definitely two horses. If horses they can be called. They were poor little frail things, not much bigger than dogs or pigs. In fact they were like this because they had been worked out or played out, they had

54

something of the primitive precursor of the horse that we know: the prehistoric forerunner of the horse with the somewhat pointed snouted nose. The poor little things were piebald, and they were so frail or old that they were not even black or white, but a sort of pallid brown and white. Though so old they had also the suggestion of being very young. I realized that they were nearly at their end and they *could* not pull the vehicle any longer.'

The above is in the patient's own words, but I will summarize the rest of the dream. The little horses faltered at crossroads and stopped; one curled up with its feet in the air; the dreamer thought it was dead. She knew that the day before they had been cruelly over-driven. The woman driver got out to make them go on, but did nothing to force them to; the man, who was now driver, got out and she was afraid he would beat them. Instead he pushed the cab and they went on a little, though she was filled with pity as they were not fit. Their stables lay in a turning to the right and they were to go there to die. The patient was glad of this so that they would not be worked so cruelly any more.

I would say here that the responsibility and guilt about the external parents (and the analyst) were clearly shown, the prehistoric horses being the original external parents, shown as little because they were, in fact, so big. But the little horses also stood for incorporated objects. They stood both for her own unborn babies and the recreated internal loved parents; that is in terms of instincts, for her own creative and constructive urges. And their dying showed, in functional terms, the psychic situation of these impulses being overwhelmed by her sadistic domineering greedy wishes, represented here by the cruel driving mother: just as, in wish-fulfilment terms, their dying represented the wish to make powerless the terrifying dangerous parents. The patient herself was in fact very depressed by the dream, which occurred during the holidays and was sent to me by post.

Clearly there is a great deal more to be said about this dream which I cannot enter into here. But there is one further point I should like to make, in connection with a passage of Sprott's given after he has been explaining the mechanism of the Freudian super-ego:

'The principle is that we increase our stock of inhibitions in order to gain security from real or imaginary dangers; they are the price we pay for love and social approval. At the same time we put a terrific strain upon ourselves. . . . When we come to the positive dictates of conscience, the position is not quite so clear. Granted we avoid doing this or that because we hope to secure love by inhibiting ourselves, do we set up our ideals in accordance with the same principles? The ideals which cause the bother are our anti–individualistic ideals, and the odd thing is that though they frequently do not pay, and frequently cause us a good deal of trouble and pain, we persist in pursuing them. . . . It is interesting to reflect that the psychology of "badness" is complicated and full, but goodness makes us feel a little shy.'

(pp. 140–41)

This touches on the point, in Rachel's analysis, of how the instinct to preserve physical life by taking food can be inhibited by something stronger, the need to preserve something good to believe in, both inside and outside. But it also bears on the contrast in this dream between the little horses overwhelmed by their task and the drivers who demand such tasks; for surely here the drivers stand partly for the repressive super-ego form of control, the repressive aspect of the parents, while the little horses stand for control through love rather than through force and fear. I mean they represent the patient's concern for her good objects, ultimately the breasts, but a concern which she feels were better dead because of the intolerable burden of the guilt that it carries with it. So her relief that the horses were going to die aptly expresses the internal state in which she is continually denying her love because of the pain it brings with it. Actually her best friend had died of cancer during the period of her analysis and she was continually worried that she had not been able to experience any grief over the loss. Thus I cannot help thinking that the symbolism of the little horses as prehistoric forerunners of the modern horse does perhaps refer to the forerunners of the super-ego. There is the idea that behind the domineering driving introjected parent figure there is a more primitive and more directly instinctive factor making for the control of aggression, the love and concern for the object; and that this is in fact actually expressed in direct emotion in the patient's tenderness towards the little horses. But the dream-thought includes the idea that this factor making for control brings so much pain, through guilt, that the cruel driver figure has to be introjected to deal with the situation, at a later stage of development and drawing its character partly from the external parents, who did in fact treat her cruelly, partly from the destructive id-impulses themselves which were aroused by such cruelty.

The symptoms for which this patient came to analysis included extreme lack of self-confidence and inability to make use of her own marked intellectual, practical, and artistic gifts, also an inability to maintain satisfactory social contacts, and, from time to time, an inhibition of eating. The main point I wish to make, in quoting this dream, is to suggest that the symbols in it are used partly in a functional way, to describe what the patient feels to be her own internal dynamic situation; and that this dynamic situation is felt by her to be an interplay between hurt and hurting people. In fact, her difficulties, which, in terms of general psychology, are disturbances of her self-regarding sentiments, are here seen as based on disturbances of her original other-regarding sentiments, her actual relationships to the loved and desired and hated father and mother who have been taken inside and form the basis of the structure of her personality. Thus the phantasy of the little horses dying, which she herself consciously felt as a symbol of her own state of mind, the state in which she felt dead inside, is a phantasy referring to her present inside world and the present structure of her personality. But its basis is the complex of feelings in actual past experiences of her childhood when she wished her parents dead, because she felt that they used her so cruelly, but when she had also been filled with sorrow and guilt about the pain she wished to inflict, and then again denied or killed this aspect of her love because of the pain it cause her. Thus under analysis the phantasies of the present inner world gradually become recognized as actual wishes and experiences in relation to the past outer world.

Although Sprott does not explicitly describe the functional aspect of phantasy he does, I think, refer to it in an attempt to compare Freud and Jung:

'For the Freudian the symptom and the myth are rather unpleasant necessities, while for the Jungian they are expressions of valuable non-rational aspirations. Both admit non-rational forces as the basis of existence, but for the Freudian it would be possible theoretically so to organize education, social life and therapeutics that we could live frictionless and reasonable lives, allowing due satisfaction to our desires and preventing the accumulation of repressed material. The Jungian, on the other hand, pays greater respect to irrationality. According to him we shall always require mythology, religion, poetry, not because we are too stupid to arrange our lives without such ridiculous safety-valves, but because they express a part of our natures that cannot be satisfied in any other way.'

(pp. 176–77)

Sprott does not here enlarge on the exact nature of this more than safety-valve and wish-fulfilling function of phantasy, and I think it is clear that a comparison in such terms does in fact omit certain very important aspects of Freudian theory. Granted that Freud's views on the subject sometimes seem contradictory and that the revealing statements are often scattered and hard to piece together, or else so concentrated that the reader easily misses their full import, I think it will be agreed that Sprott's summary cannot be regarded as an adequate account. For instance, in the passage in the essay on 'Negation' which I have already referred to, Freud points out how the concern of what he calls the 'reality-ego' is whether a thing which is present as an image within the ego can also be re-discovered in perception. But he also says that this actual presence of the image within the ego, which makes reality judgements and reality testing possible, is felt to be the result of the phantasy of introjection; he writes, for instance, that 'Judging has been systematically developed out of what was in the first instance the introduction into the ego or the expulsion from the ego carried out according to the pleasure-principle.' Surely he is here saying that the image, in all its functions, is the essential basis of our psychic existence, since he is saying that it is this which makes reality testing possible, and therefore makes possible the whole development of the ego.

It seems to me that it is in connection with the mental phenomena included under the term phantasy that the general psychologist and the psychoanalyst can most fruitfully meet. Thus if the psycho-analyst, with his special instrument for the study of phantasy, and the general psychologist, with his greater knowledge of techniques for studying overt behaviour outside the consulting room, could combine their findings, then surely the understanding of human behaviour would be greatly enriched. And if general psychology has become sufficiently convinced of the importance of Freudian theory to include it in general psychology rather than relegate it to psychopathology, now is surely the moment for further attempts to integrate the findings from the two different approaches. Moreover, if Freudian hypotheses are in the main true, then many of the problems of general psychology can be seen in a different light.

It took Freud's genius to grasp fully and begin to work out the immense implications of the idea that the organism is a whole and that the psychic life is always a total situation; but the detailed integration between the resulting theories of the instinctive life and the cognitive life has still to be done. I can imagine general psychology textbooks of the future which, although not necessarily written by psychoanalysts, will discuss all psychic capacities in terms of what the whole person is doing, that is, in terms of his deepest loves and hates; and I think that the co-operation between psychologist and analyst needed for the writing of it will bring a further elucidation of psychoanalytic theory.

After reading this paper through (in 1986), what has stayed in my mind over the years is feeling grateful that Freud did allow that people like me, who think mostly in images, do exist. But I did wonder why he mentioned only optical memories; why not also auditory, kinaesthetic, or even olfactory ones, all of which must play an essential part in mental activity before the advent of speech.

I then began to wonder what changes in the views of general psychologists might have taken place in the intervening years. I therefore sent a copy of this paper to J. D. Sutherland, as I knew him to be someone who always kept in close touch with developments outside psychoanalysis. He wrote back at length and, although calling his letter 'only ramblings', he has given me permission to quote from it.

'22 September, 1985

Dear Marion,

I have been very interested to read your paper on Phantasy as I believe it has become highly relevant to the rising flood of interest in the self.

Your questions about the functions of images and their place in the structuring of the person seem basic to the issues that challenge the status of psychoanalysis as a science and as a professional discipline. I find it rather good that your own aspirations from so many years ago in wishing to have general psychology and psychoanalysis more closely related have proved so prophetic.

I have always believed, ever since Fairbairn put forward his ideas, that Freud's libido theory was a handicap to the theoretical development of analysis. Our theories with their underlying asumptions of fundamental forces having to be conceptualised in what was assumed to be "really real!", i.e. based on physiological speculations about "energies", prevented analysts from getting enough confidence to base their views on what is our actual reality, namely, psychological data. H. Guntrip was to me on very solid ground when he criticised Melanie Klein's energic basis for her views about the revolutionary psychological data from young children's phantasies that she brought forward.[11] Her findings were surely all requiring study of the questions you raise.

The enormous development of infant–mother studies has become increasingly drawn to the processes governing the early structuring of the person. There is still a very wide gap between the mind and the necessarily behavioural standpoint adopted in most of these, yet the general psychologists who are being most creative in this field are alive in many places to the need to bridge this gap between what they infer and what we feel driven retrospectively to imagine as going on in the baby's mind.

A major step, I believe, is getting away from our traditional way of looking at the baby as much more "separate" psychologically from its mother than it really is. The great rise of interest in Winnicott is concerned with this theme and Bowlby's work has given us an indispensable start in the way the ethologists are conceptualising the equipment of the neonate. The danger with his work – not of his making – is that it can be used to support a rather mechanistic view of development from the innate systems. It is seized upon by so many psychiatrists and psychologists as "respectable science" because it appears to leave aside the critical subjective forces affecting mother and infant interaction. (I like a recent trend arising in some of Kohut's associates that defines our field of study as that of "inter-subjectivities".) And just as you found, when trying to make sense of Rachel's mind, that you had to get some understanding of "images", so are many of the developmental studies concerned with them. What they are up against, however, is that to postulate relationships with inner objects with the content that Klein's work suggests, is almost impossible to square with the findings on cognitive development. Thus, to imagine Rachel feeling great guilt at an early stage implies a differentation of a self-structure that can appreciate what it is doing to a differentiated object. This is conceivable for most researchers as the second year goes on but not in the first when Klein's oral sadistic phantasies are so powerful in their implications.

I do not have any doubt about analytic work with adults and young children forcing us to assume a highly structured phantasy activity being active in the first year – indeed, in the first half of the first year if we accept the reality of the phenomena subsumed by "the depressive position". You make your own view such that this can be possible if we allow for imagery well in advance of verbal levels. The growing evidence from the observational studies is all in favour of the early mental relationships being "perceptual – affective – action" systems viewed as a whole which motivate the child to seek from the mother what it needs. This is a highly active process from the baby's side with a great deal of "learning" in its fitting in with mother (who also adapts actively). Imagery from the action must be very pronounced from the way in which learning takes place; but it need not give rise to an imagined object separated from the self until there has been much more cognitive development.

The capacity to create the inner object must, I think, come from frustration as you suggest and simultaneously must be accompanied by a growing feeling about a "self" as the other end of the experience. The implications, however, of the clearer conceptions of the relationship as action systems – not a separate thing called the self relating to objects – do help towards the basis for the image being inside the conative processes. This action system certainly seems to characterise the first relationships and, of course, in them the self has not yet been separated. Perhaps at this stage, say the first six months, we could see how Melanie Klein's referring to the "concrete object" being felt as right inside would represent how things felt.

Once the self has begun to be "self-conscious" there must be a different relation of "me" and "not me" to the images, though here I am really thinking of not so much "me" and "not me" as "me" and this image of the other.

I had broken off these ramblings and then your phone call came. I repeat again your paper is so much at the centre of this fundamental area that it will fit well into your later work as well as being so relevant.

Although I mentioned Lichtenberg's *Psychoanalysis and Infant Research* as a useful presentation of what is being done to bridge the behavioural and the analytic viewpoints, it does expose the gap between them.[12] How we shall get it closed I don't know; we do need some clues from infant studies of the fantasy activities that start from play and the more imaginative area. It is striking for instance, there is no mention of "transitional objects" – perhaps because this has to be a more "naturalistic" type of observation than the kind the "scientists" find congenial.

It was delightful to speak.

Yours affectionately,
Jock'

References

1 This paper was read before the British Psycho-Analytical Society, 24 January, 1945, and published (1945) in the *International Journal of Psycho-Analysis* 26: 144–52.

2 Milner, M. (1944) A Suicidal Symptom in a Child of Three. *International Journal of Psycho-Analysis* 25: 53–61.
3 Sprott, W. J. H. (1937) *General Psychology*. London and New York: Longman.
4 Freud, S. (1925) Negation. *International Journal of Psycho-Analysis* 6: 367.
5 Riviere, J. (1936) On the Genesis of Psychical Conflict in Earliest Infancy. *International Journal of Psycho-Analysis* 17: 399.
6 I have omitted this paragraph, because I do not now understand just what I meant by it.
7 Freud, S. (1923) *The Ego and the Id*. London: Hogarth.
8 S. Isaacs contributed to a Special Discussion held by the British Psycho-Analytical Society, 20 October, 1943.
9 Freud, S. (1932) *New Introductory Lectures on Psycho-Analysis*. London: Hogarth.
10 Freud, S. (1909) Notes upon a Case of Obsessional Neurosis. *Collected Papers*, III: 376.
11 Guntrip, H. (1961) *Personality Structure and Human Interaction*. London: Hogarth. Chapters 10 and 11.
12 Lichtenberg, J. D. (1983) *Psychoanalysis and Infant Research*. New York: Analytic Press.

5

1947–48: Some signposts – blackness, joy, mind

During the next four years there were various signposts that were to become crucial issues for me, although I did not always recognize them at the time. For instance, in 1947 I was asked to contribute to a symposium on 'black' at the Tavistock Clinic. I spoke about a child patient who, when painting the roof of a house black, had said, 'There's lovely shiny black and there's horrid black.' He also once said to me, 'I wish you and I were the same person.'

About this time too there was another theme emerging in my preoccupations: a wondering whether psychoanalysis could concern itself with joy as not entirely the same as what the English translations of Freud spoke of as pleasure. This preoccupation first found a voice one day when Clifford Scott was giving a paper to what was then called The Progressive League, a group of all the progressive societies in England. He had to leave early and I was asked to introduce the discussion. What he had been talking about was pleasure and unpleasure, but I felt the mood of the meeting was a bit anxious and bothered, so I said that perhaps they would find it easier if we talked more in terms of joy and woe as William Blake does – I even quoted Blake:

> Man was made for Joy and Woe;
> And when this we rightly know,
> Thro' the World we safely go
>
> (*Auguries of Innocence*)

Amongst the clutter of my mostly unclassified old notes I found a contribution I had intended to make to Clifford Scott's paper on the Body Scheme presented to the Society in 1948.[1] The part of the

63

paper which I particularly wanted to discuss was the bit about mind as illusion, and Scott's asking whether the difference between external and internal stimulation is more than a spatial difference. It was here that I looked up James Ward's *Psychological Principles*[2] and quoted his talking about the relation between subject and object and their inseparability, and how it was Kant who first recognized this; also that subject is a better word for the self than 'ego' because subject implies an object, whereas an ego can be thought of as a thing in itself. I told how Ward defined psychology as the science of experience, and points out that this avoids some of the difficulties we get into if we define it as the science of the mind. He defines experience as a unity which is differentiated, but though differentiated, not disintegrated.

I found I had written that this is what I assumed Dr Ernest Jones and Dr Scott meant at the discussion in the society when they said that the idea of mind was an illusion. I assumed they meant that the idea of mind as a thing in itself is an illusion, but that mind as the word for one term in the relationship that we call experience is not an illusion. I had gone on to write that this seemed to me to be the main position of modern biological philosophy so far as I had been able to dip into it. Its position seemed to be that thought is a reality, the subject of experience is a reality, with unique and special characteristics that are different from those of non-thought. It's not just physics and chemistry and can't be reduced to the laws of those. It is something new which happens when physical and chemical processes are organized into living bodies and nerves and brains. Thus it seemed that the main trend of modern biological philosophy was not mechanistic materialism, but is the result of acceptance of reality as process. Here I added that a detailed formulation of this position is given by M. Follett in her book *Creative Experience*,[3] written in 1930 and based on scientific study of industrial conflict. Thus Follett says

'The full acceptance of process gets us further and further away from the old controversies. The thought I have been trying to indicate is neither conventional idealism nor realism. It is neither mechanism nor vitalism. We see mechanism as true within its own barriers. We see "elan vitale" still a thing in itself, as a somewhat crude foreshadowing of a profound truth.'

And again she says

'Any analysis of society which seems not to take into account the responses to a relating gives us the determinism of the last century. Biology has made large contributions on this point, for biologists have for some time shown us the interactive influence of organism and environment as a whole activity.'

Also

'Of course, the subject is no mere reflex arc than it is an evangelical soul, nor are subject and object products of a vital force. For a century roughly speaking objective idealism had given us existence as a unitary experience which upon analysis resolved itself into the two great generic differences which had been called subject and object. Now physiologists and psychologists in their response are approaching this view.'

Or, as Ward puts it, 'There is duality but not dualism'.

I found that I had also written that such accounts of change in the current philosophical climate had a direct bearing on Scott's paper. For example, Follett says that the full acceptance of reality as process gets us away from the old philosophic controversies, but such a getting away must also change aspects of our thinking in other ways. It must bring changes that are bound to affect psychoanalysis, though of course psychoanalysis itself has also contributed to the change. Thus there is, I said, no doubt that there is an intellectual revolution going on around us and whether we like it or not it is influencing our own and our patients' thinking. I said that Dr Scott in his paper seemed to be saying the same thing, that we had better try and know what is happening and how it is affecting us.

It seems that I wrote this small contribution but did not have the courage to read it to the meeting, partly because of being unclear about what the clinical implications of such a standpoint must be, and never liking to get too far from clinical experience.

References

1 Scott, W. C. M. (1948) Some embryological, neurological, psychiatric and psycho-analytic implications of the body scheme. *International Journal of Psycho-Analysis* 29.
2 Ward, J. (1933) *Psychological Principles*. Cambridge: Cambridge University Press.
3 Follett, M. P. (1930) *Creative Experience*. London: Longman.

6

1948: An adult patient uses toys

I now want to describe a certain experience in my clinical work during 1948 that I can now see contained the seeds of later developments far more than I realized at the time. It was an experience in the very long analysis of the patient I later called Susan (see Chapter 3), whose analysis had begun in 1943, after she had been given ECT. All this time I had been trying to use the techniques I had learnt in my training for the analysis of the neuroses. However, owing to the extreme slowness of our progress, I gradually decided that it might be possible to use a somewhat different approach. As I was to describe this change in the book which I eventually wrote about Susan's analysis in the 1960s, I think I can best indicate what happened by quoting a bit of what I wrote there.[1]

'I will now try and describe certain changes in technique that I found myself developing in response to what seemed to be her particular needs and difficulties, but first I must explain something more of her early attitude to me. Over the years of analysis she gradually came to remember more about what she was like before the ECT. As she did so she became more and more critical of me and arrogant, because she said she had got somewhere, before the ECT, and knew things other people did not know, and how could I help her because I did not know them. It was not until she happened to come across and read my first book that this attitude changed. Her comment on the book was that it was so like her that she felt I must have thought that she had been reading it before. After this she felt I did perhaps know a bit about what she was talking of, and her open arrogance subsided. Increasingly she became preoccupied with the question of what had really happened to her in hospital before the ECT, and how she was to evaluate it. On the one hand she felt it as an intensely valuable experience, so that if at moments she did begin to come slightly more alive, the feelings of this were constantly disparaged and even rejected because she said it was nothing like the intensity that she had felt before. But on the other hand there was this idea that she must have been crazy.

One day, I think it was before reading my book, she had come in and said she had just discovered the word "mystic" and thought that she must be one in the light of what had happened to her. Here I remembered that she had told me how, during her four years of working in the fields of the farm, she had discovered how to become aware of every muscle in her body. She had just discovered it, nobody had told her; and I also remembered that one of the recognized methods for beginning the training for mystical experience is to learn to become aware of the inside of parts of one's own body. So I began to speculate whether she had not perhaps stumbled into experiencing certain phases of mystical consciousness as a result of this work on herself, but on a very precarious basis because of not yet having firmly established that ordinary consciousness which is bounded by the awareness of separateness.

I was also to write in the book about another difficulty she had in the analysis.

'But here we came up against the block of her continued inability to grasp the idea of unconscious mental activity, expressed in her incredulous question, "But in what part of my mind do I think these things?" So I had the recurrent doubts about the value, certainly at this stage, of trying to talk to her about unconscious phantasies, or even unconscious wishes. In fact I gradually found myself experimenting with a change in technique. Instead of trying to put into words for her what I considered to be the unconscious phantasy causing the anxiety of the moment, I began trying to keep her to the point of herself seeking to find an exact word for what she was feeling. Thus, when she said, as she often did, "Oh, it's useless, it's impossible to describe", I would try to show her how she seemed to be putting a rigid barrier between the describable and the indescribable. When she tried to get away from the issue by talking of something else, I would point out the evasion, and very often she would in the end find a word or words or image for what had been indescribable. This was an empirical procedure on my part. It was a long time before I was able to become clearer about the theory by which I could justify the change in procedure. Eventually, however, I came to realize that part of what we were faced with was a defect in her thinking, one connected with the relation between the articulate and the inarticulate forms and phases of it. My first awareness of any kind of defect in her thinking had been when I noticed the great difficulty she had in taking in any interpretation that depended upon finding a hidden symbolic meaning for something she had told me. She would say crossly, "A thing is what it is and can't be anything else." In fact she seemed to cling fiercely to Aristotelian logic, rules which of course she had never heard of, and I slowly came to see the problem in terms of this deep-seated split between the articulate and inarticulate level of her thinking. I began to try to understand more about the relation of this to symbol formation. Here I remembered what she had told me about her difficulties at school to do with symbolical or metaphorical expressions, for instance, how she had said in connection with geography, "What on earth did they mean by talking about the head or mouth of a river", implying that if a thing is what it is and nothing else, then how could a river have a head or a mouth. It certainly seemed that her difficulty in recognizing separateness had also resulted in a block in that recognition of duality which makes it possible to accept that a symbol is both itself and the thing it stands for, yet without being identical with it.'

I now have to go back to the time before I had worked out this change of technique, for something quite surprising had happened. I was to sit by throughout one session and watch this woman who complained that she could not understand symbols create a cluster of startlingly vivid ones. It was one day when both of us were feeling very stuck, and Susan, knowing that I had child patients who used toys, asked if she could have some too. Accordingly I had brought her a trayful from the playroom; little animals, houses, people, also plasticine. Without a moment's hesitation she knew exactly what she wanted to do with it. She made a large ring out of green plasticine, calling it a farmyard. Amongst the toys was a set of those tiny Chinese boxes that fit into each other; she set about filling them all with the red plasticine, and then took some little pigs and buried their heads in the clay, their tails sticking up in the air. She also stuck a similarly filled box on to the muzzle of a little horse. In addition there was a tiny teapot that she also filled with red plasticine, and then stuck a tiny man's feet in it, while putting his head into the clay of another of the little boxes – a very stuck situation indeed I thought.

There were also three tiny zebras, and for them she made halos out of the red clay, but for one of them she made the halo so big that the zebra fell over on to its nose. But she also used the clay, not to blot out the faces and imprison the feet, nor as a too heavy halo, but as a ground and support. Thus she once used it to symbolize water, making a flat base on which a little swan is swimming. In another construction she used it as part of a complex symbol in which a goat is passing under an arch-shaped brick, both goat and arch being supported on a four-square lump of red clay, which itself rests on an up-turned red wooden brick. (In fact, the brick had tall windows marked on it, so that it must have once been part of a tiny church.) Here I came to think that she might be trying to communicate to me her memory of the sense of her own weight four-squarely on the ground – something that she said she had discovered for the first time at the farm, including the awareness of the distancing of objects when she walked away from them, the sense that she felt she had lost after the ECT. As for the goat halfway through the archway I thought it could be depicting an idea of the baby half in the world and half still inside the mother, as well as possibly showing the attempt to achieve the idea of some kind of creative intercourse going on both inside her and in the relationship between us.

On the tray there was also a tiny green steam engine. On the roof of this she put two of the little figures in a sort of nest of green clay. She said she thought they stood for the couple, Dr X and his wife, who had been giving her a home all these years.

This play with the toys made such a vivid impact on me that in the evening I made coloured copies of most of what she had done (see *Figure 2*). As for interpreting, I doubt if I said very much. In fact during the days after there was a catastrophic intrusion from the environment in that Susan became aware of real trouble in the marriage of the two people depicted on the top of the steam engine. This trouble was to lead to the break-up of their home and to Susan going into such a regressed state that she could not get to me by herself, having to be brought every day in a taxi by the friend of the X's who was by now looking after her. All this is described in the book I subsequently wrote about her analysis, but in it for some reason I did not describe the session with the toys or publish my copies of them. I suspect that I felt that I did not then understand

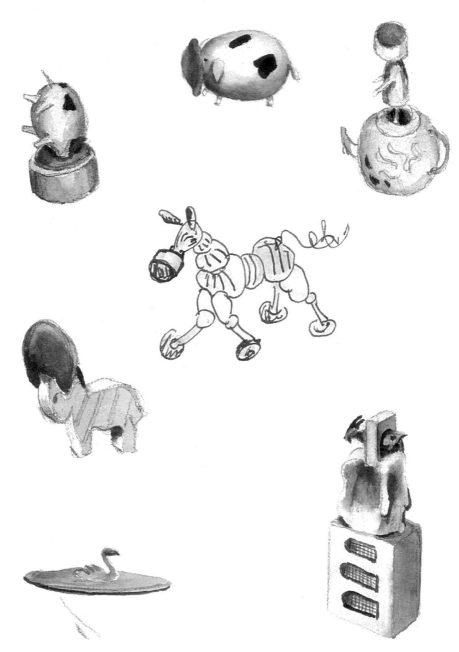

Figure 2   Susan's toys

them enough, but I am including them now because I do feel they vividly illustrate a theme that became clearer later on. However, I did even at the time have something to say to Susan about the zebras with the clay made into halos and the intensely innocent look it gave them. I asked, could this be her way of telling how she had set herself the task of struggling with her mother's depression, not only by a compulsive gaiety, always trying to make her mother laugh, but also by setting up within herself an ideal of perfection. She had to be perfect in order to help her mother believe in herself. Certainly it did seem that her mother had tried to battle with the feeling of her own deadness within by believing that she had at least produced a wonderful live daughter (Susan had reported her elder sister as saying that it was always assumed in the family that Susan would be something wonderful).

When I looked at the too good to be true little zebras, including the one that fell forward on to its nose, I began to wonder if it could be said that, while she knows intuitively that it is the so exalted self-image that is both the very devil and the prison from which she cannot escape, yet to give it up is surely felt to be risking the death of her mother, and so come to feel she is her mother's murderer; I remembered how once in the first weeks of analysis Susan had said to me with marked anxiety, 'What would happen if she wanted to kill me?' She had added then that she was very strong, having worked on the farm. I think I said she wanted to know if I was as depressed as she was or would I defend myself because I did not want to die. Here I remembered too that Susan had told me of how her mother would often say she was going to die – she would say it when Susan was sitting on her knee, and would sing the most unhappy songs. So I came to ask myself, could the repeated symbol of the face buried in the round object full of dead clay be Susan's way of telling me of her feelings about her mother's inside as containing only dead people.

Some time later too I came to see what other levels of meaning there could be in the little figures and animals having their heads or faces buried in the clay. I asked myself is this also a symbol of unconsciousness, could it not be her way of expressing the idea of the blanking out of consciousness as actually experienced by her in the fits she had been given in the ECT?

It was soon after the environmental crisis leading her to the regressed state and having to be brought in a taxi (January 1950), that Susan had again felt the need for visual as well as verbal expression in her analysis, for one day she asked for pencils and paper and began to draw. She said she wanted to show me what she felt had happened to her since the ECT, how she felt she was now existing only in a very small area at the top of her head. But after this she went on to make doodle drawings, sometimes in the session and sometimes between sessions, once bringing me ninety of them all in the one day. Eventually she produced several thousand, a selection of these being shown in the book I came to write about her. Incidentally I was intrigued to note that while her drawings began in 1950 my book about my own free association drawings was not published until Easter, so I do not think she can possibly have known about it before it was published.

As the years went on I was to find myself making increasing use of her drawings in my own thinking on the psychoanalytic process. In the meantime there was the whole problem of symbolization that increasingly interested me, as well as the effects of different kinds of concentration.

Reference

1 Milner, M. (1969) *The Hands of the Living God*. London: Hogarth.

7

1949: The ending of two analyses[1]

Although there is perhaps no such thing as a completed analysis, most patients do, sooner or later, stop coming to analysis. Perhaps we, as analysts, are handicapped in knowing all about what ending feels like, for by the mere fact of becoming analysts we have succeeded in bypassing an experience which our patients have to go through. We have chosen to identify ourselves with our analyst's profession and to act out that identification – a thing which our patients on the whole are not able to do. But we have to manage as best we can; and here is an attempt to describe what no longer coming to analysis meant to one particular patient.

This ending was not something which happened as a logical result of the patient's being considered cured; in fact, the ending preceded the cure by many months, for it was not until the analysis had actually stopped that the symptom began to move at all.

The patient, an unmarried woman of 33, had had a headache since the age of 13. When she was sent to me, the diagnosis had been hysteria with a hypochondriacal under-layer. Her own description of the headache was that it was like a black cloud or fog that separated her from everything and penetrated into her brain, making her utterly incapable.

She had had three years' analysis with another member of the Society, and was approaching the end of her second year with me when the question of termination was raised. She maintained persistently that the headache was no better, that she was utterly bored in her work, and could never hope for a better job as she was untrained; also that the money available for her analysis had almost run out. All this was true, with the further difficulty that I had too

73

many low-fee patients at that time to be able to carry on at a merely nominal charge. Moreover, I did not feel justified in encouraging her to continue, in view of the results so far obtained after five years' work. We therefore mutually agreed that the analysis could be looked upon only as a failure, so far as the symptom was concerned, and had better stop.

One characteristic of the analysis during the two years with me had been the patient's complete detachment. Although she had brought plenty of significant material and described extreme emotional states, she always kept me entirely out of the picture and her conscious attitude remained oblivious of all transference interpretations. During the two months or so after the decision to stop but before actually stopping she told me: (1) that she had never let analysis influence her; (2) that she had had no belief in it anyway; (3) that she would not know what she thought of me until I chucked her out. Then we stopped. I knew, of course, that it was a risk, but I felt it was a risk that had to be taken. I told her also that I was not going to fill up all her hours at once. Two of them, which had been in the late evening, I intended to keep free, so that she could telephone if she ever wanted to come.

She came five times in the following six months. Eight weeks after the last of these visits I had a letter saying she was getting married. She added that analysis alone had made this possible and that she was deeply grateful. A year later I heard through a friend that she had never been so happy in her life, and was successfully adjusting to all the conditions of married life, which, in her case, included step-children and frequently a house full of guests. Two years later she herself wrote to me to say how happy she was. There was no mention of the headache.

The first of the five visits occurred two months after the official ending of the analysis. Among other things, she said:

> She has been feeling utterly ghastly, a burning sort of pain weighing her down, down the whole of her front, a terrific weight on her chest. . . .
> Dream, can't get it out of her mind.
> In some sort of colossal prison hall full of people.
> Next to her was an old grey woman with wispy hair.
> She and the woman were tied down by guards with sort of tent ropes reaching to the floor.
> A young man is brought in, and defies the guards.
> She decides to try too, though with no belief that she *can* free herself; but she finds the pegs give way and she goes off with the ropes clattering round her neck.

She runs down frightful passages . . . and suddenly begins to feel she is racing down and down into the black depths of her own soul.

She reports utter rage and fury against me for not finding her a decent job or curing her headache.

The old woman was directly associated with her mother.

The second visit, again after a two months' gap, contained definitely admitted hope. The third, after a six weeks' gap, brought an admission that the headache did vary in virulence. The fourth, a week later, brought a dream-phantasy that left the headache 'different'.

In phantasy she saw herself as a little child, lying in glorious sunshine, utterly relaxed, like a cat by the fire.

Then mother had appeared, like a thundercloud, and fiercely punished her.

She'd called out, 'Why! Why! Why!' and her cry had echoed through the mountains.

Afterwards she had felt utterly in disgrace, everyone against her.

But for several days since, the headache has been less overwhelming – just a headache.

At the fifth and last visit, another week later, she reported for the first time enjoying lovely spring sun, and also admitted, indirectly and for the first time, to having sexual wishes.

Obviously many things can be said about this material and the conditions under which it appeared. The point I want to make at the moment is the effect of the stopping on the relation to the mother, as lived out in the transference. Her first analyst's comment to me had been that he felt the mother 'had really been a bitch'. But in analysis, all my attempts to help the patient to see how fiercely she was denying this fact had been quite fruitless. She seemed to be forced to feel herself completely on her mother's side in every way, just as she had tried to keep herself completely on mine. And this had led to great conflicts, because the mother had certainly been pegged down all round on the subject of sexuality. So apparently (though this of course is a great over-simplification of what happened) the break with me, felt by her as a 'chucking out', did enable her to risk having a separate existence and therefore separate standards and a morality of her own. Thus the dream-phantasy of intense sensual enjoyment, with its passionate cry of 'Why! Why!' to the mother's prohibitions, did represent her first taking responsibility for her own sexuality, as shown also in the next session when she admitted it to me.

Certainly such material as this is commonplace in psychoanalytic experience. But what is of interest is that it all happened after the official ending; also that before the ending there was nothing classical about the analysis, in the sense that what looked like appropriate interpretations did not seem to have any effect. It was almost as if the analysis had been done while the patient herself was not there – and the headache had remained immovable. But her first reported dream after stopping contains the image of racing down into a black pit and away from the pegged-down mother. Certainly it is possible to look on this image as borrowing some of its significance, if not from actual memories of the physical experience of being born, at least from the symbolic idea of birth. Also the utter sense of helplessness that the headache produced, combined with choking and strangling sensations fitted in with this idea. Apparently the analysis could not begin to 'take' until after she had lived through this psychic experience of being born; also she felt that she could not be 'born' except by leaving analysis. It looks, too, as if, when she did get herself born, the work done in analysis, which apparently had had no effect, began to take effect retrospectively.

Obviously this was not an ideal way to end an analysis. On looking back I can see that it might have been possible to avoid such an ending if I had understood more clearly why the interpretations, although based on evidence in the material, were not causing changes in the symptom. If I had understood more about how far this patient had not yet taken the risk of feeling herself a separate person in a world of separate people, and how the capacity to take this risk develops, the course of the analysis might have been different and the ending perhaps different also.

As it was, the ending and its sequel were, I think, determined by the fact that the patient's mother, although according to family tradition adored by all, was often really bad, in the sense that she stultified the child's development. So it was not until the patient had felt that I had been really bad to her, by 'chucking her out', and at the same time I had taken the responsibility for it, that she had become able to recognize her hate of her mother, and so become free enough to begin life as a separate person with standards of her own. The question why it is so necessary for some patients to find that their analysts really are what the patients, in the transference situation, believe them to be, is beyond the scope of this paper.

Reading this paper again after so long naturally made me wonder what part my confession of total failure to change her symptom (the headache) and also my offering 'on demand' analysis had had in such a dramatic sequel.

In the original form of this paper there was an account of the ending of the analysis of another woman patient, also in her thirties, who felt she had never had any period in her infancy when there was any one person devoted to trying to understand her and her needs. She said that this was something she had been looking for all her life. In fact she was so determined to find it that she steadily created in me the analyst she needed, even endowing my interpretations with an aptness and insight that was sometimes beyond what I would have seen in them myself.

She certainly thrived on this relation to a partially self-created reality, in contrast with her babyhood when, so she said, she had grizzled and pined and nearly died. Obviously for her the ending of the analysis had to be a slow process of de-illusioning. But it had a rather special aspect connected with her Oedipal problems and this raised another question to do with the ending of an analysis.

Her history was that she was born too soon and should have been a boy. The whole of her childhood, she felt, was spent in trying, unsuccessfully, to make her mother love her, and in being terrified of her father who adored her. During the first three years of her analysis she felt she had achieved great things (as shown in much freeing of ego capacities). The last and fourth year was almost entirely taken up with the ending problem. Acute crises came when she began to dare to miss a day (for the sake of some necessity of her work), and also when, by mutual agreement, we cut down the number of days per week. The awful thing about this was, for her, not so much the actual missing the hour, but the having to admit to herself that she could want something other than to come to me; for this meant, to her, admitting that she could want father.

When she did finally admit it, by staying away, I turned into such an acutely avenging persecutor that she had to come dashing up in a taxi for the last few minutes of the hour, just to see that I was not wanting to kill her.

The point I wish to raise here is to do with the fact that, although I had tried to analyse much Oedipal phantasy, it had never struck home, in a manageable way, until we had actually begun ending by cutting down hours. I say 'in a manageable way' because there had been several acute crises earlier, when she had been offered another job which would have meant working both with a man and in a place that would have made carrying on analysis impossible. The anxiety raised then by the need to choose was of great intensity, and it seemed that her external life had precipitated an emotional situation which she was not yet at all ready to manage. But now in the ending situation, it was something we were able to deal with, at her own speed, with the gradual cutting down of sessions according to internal and external needs.

Reference

1 The first part of this paper was read at a symposium on the termination of psychoanalytical treatment at the Tavistock Clinic, at a meeting of the British Psychoanalytical Society, 2 March, 1949, and published in 1950 in the *International Journal of Psycho-Analysis* 31: 191–93.

8

1952: The framed gap

During the year 1952 I was asked to give two lectures on any subject I liked. Neither was published, and I am including parts of the second one as I see it as leading up to the next long paper, about symbolization, written in honour of Melanie Klein (see Chapter 9). The first one was given to the medical staff and nurses of the Cassell Hospital. I chose the subject 'The Uses of Absentmindness', thus again thinking about aspects of concentration. During the discussion everybody started telling me about the settings in which they were able to enjoy undirected thinking, reverie, or absentmindness. For one it was when she was using a vacuum cleaner; it made a sort of cocoon of sound. For one of the men it was when he was driving his car at a particular speed on a nice road, and of course for some of the men it was fishing.

Next, also 1952, I was asked to go to Leeds University to a hand-picked audience of staff, including Marjorie Hourd who was working there on a fellowship and writing *The Education of the Poetic Spirit*.[1] Again I was asked to talk about whatever I liked. What I said was never published, and my notes are by now somewhat dismembered. However, I have assembled some of them to quote here, because although they are not ostensibly about psychoanalysis, clinical experience was at the back of them. The title seems to have been 'Aspects of Absentmindness in Relation to Creative Process'. I said I was going to present certain beads of experiences of my own and hoping with the help of the audience to spin a thread for some of them. I began by talking about different ways of trying to draw, using experience that I had already tried to describe in the book about not being able to paint.[2] I told how I had discovered two ways of drawing from nature; first with the object in front of one, carefully, painstakingly, one's eyes hopping to and fro from object to pencil so as to be sure to get it right, with the model and one's drawing as two quite separate things, and probably a growing despair about the wideness of the gap between them. But the second way was keeping one's eyes on the subject, while drawing quickly, excitedly, only looking down at the pencil and the drawing when you have finished one line and have to start again somewhere else, but still having your mind totally concentrated on the excitement about the object, not split into two. I also talked about ways of drawing from imagination, for instance, not thinking to oneself, 'now I am going to draw a donkey, how does a donkey go, oh like this, oh that isn't right', and so on, but drawing lines quickly, at random at first, not knowing what will come, letting the lines themselves suggest ideas of what one is drawing, but of the quick give and take between the line and the thought. I added that there comes a moment, when painting some object from the outer world, when the excitement about whatever it was made you want to paint it and the immensely complicated practical problems of how to represent that feeling in colour, shape, texture, and so on, all disappear as conscious problems. One becomes lost in a moment of intense activity in which awareness of self and awareness of the object are somehow fused, and one emerges to separateness again to find that there is some new entity on the paper.

Having told how startling to me the results often were, showing a rhythm and pattern and integrated wholeness far beyond anything I had ever achieved by a deliberate plan, I now told how I had tried to make a list of what factors seemed to have been playing a part; (1) muscular action with a medium, a little bit of the outside world that was malleable, chalk, paint, etc., (2) within a limited space, a frame, the edge of the paper, even a wall, (3) a sacrifice of deliberative action or working to a plan, instead allowing the hand and the eye to play with the medium. I told how under these conditions of spontaneous action in a limited field with a malleable bit of the outside world it seemed that an inner organizing pattern-making force other than willed planning seemed to be freed, an inner urge to pattern and wholeness which had then become externally embodied in the product there for all to see. It was then that I talked more about the frame and how there had to be to start with a blank space, a framed gap.

I told how I saw the frame as something that marked off what's inside it from what's outside it, and to think of other human activities where the frame is essential, a frame in time as well as in space; for instance the acted play, ceremonies, rituals, processions, even poems framed in silence when spoken and the space of the paper when written. Also the psychoanalytic session framed in both space and time. I said I thought that all these frames show that what is inside has to be perceived, interpreted in a different way from what is outside; they mark off an area within which what we perceive has to be taken as symbol, as metaphor, not literally.

Then I came back to the role of the will, how in painting it seems to come in through restricting one's attention to the blank space to be filled together with the model, still life, landscape or whatever, and one's own feelings about this. The will making a kind of frame for what I have come to call contemplative action, contemplative to distinguish it from expedient action, action to distinguish it from pure contemplation, through bringing in the movement of the hand. Later I would have to add attention to one's own whole body awareness while moving with one's hand (see Chapter 14).[3]

The theme of the framed gap, emptiness, seemed to have led me on to talk about gaps in one's own self-awareness, for instance, the kind of concentration that we call 'losing oneself in an activity', something that can be greatly longed for, delighted in, but which does require a safe setting, a setting that will still be there when one emerges again into ordinary self-awareness. I remembered that my patient Susan had said she could never lose herself in a book when at home, when with her mother, but that she could when staying away. I even quoted Cezanne on the capacity to achieve unmindfulness.

I also talked about some more of the things I myself had learnt when writing the Joanna Field books, for instance,[4] about having observed that there were two kinds of attention, both necessary, a wide unfocused stare, and a narrow focused penetrating kind, and that the wide kind brought remarkable changes in perception and enrichment of feeling.

At one point I even found myself quoting the Bible and wondering whether the injunction 'Take no thought for the morrow' did not have something to do with this state of mind. In addition I had quoted from John MacMurray who said, 'The artist does not act by impulse, still less by the compulsion of rules, but by the nature of the reality which he apprehends'.[5] So it seemed that what the will did was to hold the attention, to embrace the reality: of what? Of the developing relation between oneself and what one was looking at. But then I thought that MacMurray was partly wrong, one did act by impulse under these special conditions of attention. One held the willed attention in passionate contemplation and then could let the hand do exactly as it liked, feel the form passionately, said the painter Bernard Maninsky to me when I was once a student in his life class. And didn't St Augustine say, 'Love and do what thou wilt', and Shakespeare in *Hamlet*, 'Readiness is all'.

And then I asked – can we summarize what the will has to do? It seemed that it certainly has to wait in very active present mindedness and be content with being a frame, holding the empty space if something new is to emerge, something that has never been before. I asked – can we say that it has to recognize its limited function, give up any hoped for omnipotence and bow before the more powerful function, the imagination? 'Oh human imagination, oh divine body I have thee cruxified', wrote William Blake. 'As dying yet behold we live', says St Paul. I told too how often experiencing the pattern-making aspect of the imagination begins to feel like an answering presence, even a 'you'. I told how I had even come to look on many of the sayings in the Gospels as providing a handbook for the process of creative activity.

It was years later that I happened to open at random my battered copy of *Selected Poems of William Blake* at a page which said 'The religions of all nations are derived from each nation's different perception of the poetic genius which is everywhere called the spirit of prophecy.'[6]

References

1 Hourd, M. (1949) *The Education of the Poetic Spirit*. London: Heinemann Educational.
2 Milner, M. (1950) *On Not Being Able to Paint*. London: Heinemann.
3 Milner, M. (1960) Painting and Internal Body Awareness. Published in the IV International Congress on Aesthetics, Athens.
4 Milner, M. (1934) *A Life of One's Own*; (1937) *An Experiment in Leisure*. London: Chatto & Windus. (1950) *On Not Being Able to Paint*. London: Heinemann. These three books were originally published under the pseudonym 'Joanna Field'.
5 MacMurray, J. (1932) *Freedom in the Modern World*. London: Faber.
6 Blake, W. (1904) *The Selected Poems of William Blake*. Oxford: Oxford University Press, p. 427.

9

1952: The role of illusion in symbol formation

In 1952 I was asked to write a paper in honour of Melanie Klein's seventieth birthday. It is about a boy patient whose analysis was, during the first part, actually supervised by Melanie Klein, as part of my training in child analysis.

The first version of this paper was entitled 'Aspects of Symbolism in Comprehension of the Not-self', and published in 1952 in an issue of the *International Journal of Psycho-Analysis* devoted to papers written in honour of Melanie Klein.[1] When these papers were reprinted in book form I used the title given above and shortened the paper.[2] However I have now restored the omitted portion as it seemed to express an important aspect of what had been going on between this boy and me. (In later papers I referred to him as Simon.)

Much has been written by psychoanalysts on the process by which the infant's interest is transferred from an original primary object to a secondary one. The process is described as depending upon the identification of the primary object with another that is in reality different from it but emotionally is felt to be the same. Ernest Jones and Melanie Klein in particular, following up Freud's formulations, write about this transference of interest as being due to conflict with forces forbidding the interest in the original object, as well as the actual loss of the original object. Jones, in his paper 'The Theory of Symbolism' emphasizes the aspects of this prohibition which are to do with the forces that keep society together as a whole.[3] Melanie Klein, in various papers, describes also the aspect of it which keeps

83

the individual together as a whole; she maintains that it is the fear of our own aggression towards our original objects which makes us so dread their retaliation that we transfer our interest to less attacked and so less frightening substitutes.[4] Jones also describes how the transfer of interest is due, not only to social prohibition and frustration and the wish to escape from the immanent frustrated mouth, penis, vagina, and their retaliating counterparts, but also to the need to endow the external world with something of the self and so make it familiar and understandable.

The identification of one object with another is described as the forerunner of symbolism, and Melanie Klein, both in her paper 'Infant Analysis' (1923) and in the 'The Importance of Symbol Formation in the Development of the Ego' (1930), says that symbolism is the basis of all talents. Jones describes this identification as a process of symbolic equivalence through which progress to sublimation is achieved, but adds that symbolism itself, in the sense in which he uses the word, is a bar to progress. Leaving aside for a moment this difference over the use of the word symbol, there is one point about wording which, I feel, requires comment. Jones describes the process of identification that underlies symbol formation as being not only the result of the forbidding forces, but also a result of the need to establish a relation to reality. He says that this process arises from the desire to deal with reality in the easiest possible way, from 'the desire for ease and pleasure struggling with the demand of necessity'. It seems to me that this way of putting it is liable to lead to misunderstanding. The phrase 'desire for ease and pleasure' set against the 'demand of necessity' gives the impression that this desire is something that we could, if we were sufficiently strong-minded, do without. The phrase reflects perhaps a certain puritanism which is liable to appear in psychoanalytic writing. Do we really mean that it is only the desire for ease and pleasure, and not necessity, that drives us to identify one thing with another which is in fact not the same? Are we not rather driven by the internal necessity for inner organization, pattern, coherence, the basic need to discover identity in difference without which experience becomes chaos? Actually I think Jones himself implies such an idea when he says that this confounding of one thing with another, this not discriminating, is also the basis of generalization; and he indicates the positive aspect of this failure to discriminate, in relation to discovery of the real world, when he says:

> 'there opens up the possibility . . . of a theory of scientific discovery, inventions, etc., for psychologically this consists in an

overcoming of the resistances that normally prevent regression towards the infantile unconscious tendency to note identity in differences.'

This was written in 1916. In 1951 Herbert Read writes:[5]

'The first perceptions of what is novel in any science tend to assume the form of metaphors – the first stages of science are poetic.'

Jones quotes Rank and Sachs when they make a distinction between the primary process of identification which underlies symbolism and symbolism itself. He quotes their description of how the original function (demonstrable in the history of civilization) of the identification underlying symbolism was a means of adaptation to reality, but that it 'becomes superfluous and sinks to the mere significance of a symbol as soon as this task of adaptation has been accomplished'. He quotes their description of a symbol as the 'unconscious precipitate of primitive means of adaptation to reality that have become superfluous and useless, a sort of lumber room of civilization to which the adult readily flees in states of reduced or deficient capacity for adaption to reality, in order to regain his old long-forgotten playthings of childhood'. But they add the significant remark that what later generations know and regard only as a symbol had in earlier stages of mental life full and real meaning and value.

Jones goes on to quote Rank's and Sach's statement that symbol formation is a regressive phenomenon, and that it is most plainly seen in civilized man, in conditions where conscious adaptation to reality is either restricted, as in religious or artistic ecstasy, or completely abrogated, as in dreams and mental disorders. Here it seems to me that a valuable link has been made between symbolism and ecstasy, but the context in which these two ideas have been brought together leaves out, in respect of the arts, what Jones has described in respect of scientific invention: that is that it may be a regression in order to take a step forward. Thus Rank's and Sachs' statement does not draw attention to the possibility that some form of artistic ecstasy may be an essential phase in adaptation to reality, since it may mark the creative moment in which new and vital identifications are established. In fact Rank and Sachs do not here allow for the possibility that truth underlies the much quoted aphorism that Art creates Nature; and so also they miss the chance of indicating an underlying relation between art and science. (Rank, in his later work, does in fact take a much wider view of the function of art.)

I think some of the difficulty arises here from lack of a sufficiently clear distinction between the two uses of the process which has been given the name of symbolization. Fenichel has made this distinction more clear.[6] He says:

> 'In adults a conscious idea may be used as a symbol for the purpose of hiding an objectionable unconscious idea; the idea of a penis may be represented by a snake, an ape, a hat, an airplane, if the idea of penis is objectionable. The distinct idea of a penis had been grasped but rejected.'

But he then goes on to say that symbolic thinking is also a part of the primal prelogical thinking and adds:

> 'archaic symbolism as a part of prelogical thinking and distortion by means of representing a repressed idea through a conscious symbol are not the same. Whereas in distortion the idea of penis is avoided through disguising it by the idea of snake, in prelogical thinking penis and snake are *one and the same*; that is, they are perceived by a common conception: the sight of the snake provokes penis emotions; and this fact is later utilized when the conscious idea of snake replaces the unconscious one of penis.' (The italics are mine.)

A distinction between two uses of the word symbol has also been described by a non-analyst. Herbert Read says:[7]

> 'But there is a very general distinction to be made between those uses of the word which on the one hand retain the sense of a throwing together of tangible, visible objects, with each other or with some immaterial or abstract notion, and those uses which on the other hand imply no such initial separation, but rather treat the symbol as an integral or original form of expression. A word itself may be a symbol in this sense, and language a system of symbols.'

The similarity between this second use of the word symbol and Fenichel's second use of it, is clear; although Read says earlier that he feels that it is a pity that he and analysts have to use the same word to describe different things.

Illusion and fusion

It is the use of symbolism as part of what Fenichel calls prelogical thinking that I wish to discuss here. In particular I wish to consider what are the conditions under which the primary and the secondary object are fused and felt as one and the same. I want to study both the emotional state of the person experiencing this fusion and what conditions in the environment might facilitate or interfere with it; in fact, to study something of the internal and external conditions that make it possible to find the familiar in the unfamiliar – which, incidentally, Wordsworth said is the whole of the poet's business.[8]

When considering what concepts are available as tools for thinking about this process of fusion or identification, the concept of phantasy is obviously essential, since it is only in phantasy that two dissimilar objects are fused into one. But this concept is not quite specific enough to cover the phenomenon; the word illusion is also needed because this word does imply that there is a relation to an external object of feeling, even though a phantastic one, since the person producing the fusion believes that the secondary object *is* the primary one. In order to come to understand more about the meaning of the word illusion I found it was useful to consider its role in a work of art. I had already, when trying to study some of the psychological factors which facilitate or impede the painting of pictures, become interested in the part played by the frame. The frame marks off the different kind of reality that is within it from that which is outside it; but a temporal spatial frame also marks off the special kind of reality of a psychoanalytic session. And in psychoanalysis it is the existence of this frame that makes possible the full development of that creative illusion that analysts call the transference. Also the central idea underlying psychoanalytic technique is that it is by means of this illusion that a better adaptation to the world outside is ultimately developed. It seemed to me that the full implications of this idea for analytic theory had still to be worked out, especially in connection with the role of symbolism in the analytic relationship.

In considering the dynamics of the process the concept of anxiety is clearly needed. Melanie Klein has laid great stress on the fact that it is dread of the original object itself, as well as the loss of it, that leads to the search for a substitute. But there is also a word needed for the emotional experience of finding the substitute, and it is here that the word ecstasy may be useful.

There is also another ordinary English word, not often used in psychoanalytic literature, except to talk about perversion, or lack of it, in neurotic states, and that is the word concentration. I wish to bring it in here because, in analysing children, I have found myself continually noticing the varying moods or quality of concentration shown by the children, and have tried to understand the relation of these variations to the kind of material produced. These observations have not been confined to the analytic situation; I have often noticed, when in contact with children playing, that there occurs now and then a particular type of absorption in what they are doing, which gives the impression that something of great importance is going on. Before becoming an analyst I used to wonder what a child, if he had sufficient power of expression, would say about these moods, how he would describe them from inside. When I became an analyst I began to guess that the children were in fact trying to tell me, in their own way, what it does feel like. And I thought I recognized the nature of these communications the more easily because I had already tried for myself, introspectively, to find ways of describing such states, most particularly in connection with the kinds of concentration that produce a good or a bad drawing.

Before going on to present and discuss some clinical material, there is one other concept which I think needs clarifying; and that is the meaning of the term 'primary object'. Earlier psychoanalytic discussions of symbol formation most often emphasized the child's attempts to find substitutes for those original objects of interest that are the parents' organs. But some also emphasized the aspect of the child's attempts to find his own organs and their functioning in every object. In more recent work these two views tend to be combined and the idea develops that the primary 'object' that the infant seeks to find again is a fusion of self and object, it is mouth and breast felt as fused into one. Thus the concept of fusion is present, both in the primary situation, between self and object, and in the secondary one, between the new situation and the old one.

Case material: A game of war between two villages

Moments when the original 'poet' in each of us created the outside world for us, by finding the familiar in the unfamiliar, are perhaps forgotten by most people; or else they are guarded in some secret place of memory because they were too much like visitations of the gods to be mixed with everyday thinking. But in autobiographies some do dare to tell, and often in poetry. Perhaps, in ordinary life, it is good teachers who are most aware of these moments, from outside, since it is their job to provide the conditions under which they can occur, so to stage-manage the situation that imagination catches fire and a whole subject or skill lights up with significance. But it is in the analytic situation that this process can be studied from inside and outside at the same time. So now I will present some material from child analysis which seems to me to be offering data about the nature of the process.

The patient is a boy of 11 who was suffering from a loss of talent for school work. During his first school years, from 4 to 6, he had been remarkably interested and successful and always top of his form; but he had gradually come to find himself very near the bottom, and at times had been totally unable to get himself to school at all.

The particular play that I wish to discuss had been preceded by a long period in which all the toys had been set out in the form of a village, full of people and animals; the boy would then bomb the village by dropping balls of burning paper upon it, my role being to play the part of the villagers, and try to save all the toys from actual destruction. The rules of the game were such that this was often very difficult, so that gradually more and more of the toys were burnt, and from time to time I had replaced them by new ones. (This boy had, in fact, lived through part of the blitz on London, and had started this play some time after my own house had been damaged by blast; and he had shown delayed interest in the extent of the damage when he came to my house for his analysis.)

In the session which I have chosen to describe, he begins by saying that we are to have two villages and a war between them, but that the war is not to begin at once. My village is to be made up of all the people and animals and houses; his of toy trucks, cars, etc., and 'lots of junk and oddments to exchange', though I am to have some oddments as well. He begins by sending along a truck from his village with half a gun in it, and takes various things in exchange. He then brings a test-tube and exchanges it for a number of objects, including a little bowl, bits of metal, a ladder, etc. When I comment on the amount taken in exchange he says, 'Yes, the test-tube is equal to a lot', but on the return journey to his own village he adds: 'I think those people were a bit odd, I don't think I like those people much, I think I will give them just a little time-bomb.' So he takes back his test-tube, sticks some matches in it, and drops it over my village. He then drops a whole box of matches on my village and says the villagers have to find it and put it out before it explodes. But then I have to come and bomb his village, and when I drop a flare, instead of putting it out he adds fuel to it. Then he says, 'You have got to bring all your people over to my village, the war is over.' I have to bring the animals and people over in trucks, but at once he says they must go back because they all have to watch the burning of the whole stack of match boxes (which he has bought with his own money). He makes me stand back from the blaze, and shows great pleasure.

He now decides that his 'people' (empty trucks) are to call on mine; his are explorers and mine are to think his are gods. The trucks arrive, my people have to be frightened. He tells me to make them say something; so I make the the policeman ask what they want; but he replies, 'You've forgotten, they think it's gods.' He now borrows the 'Mrs Noah' figure from my village and stands her in one of his trucks. Then, in a god-like voice, he commands that the villagers go into their houses and prepare food.[9] It is now the end of the session and while I am beginning to tidy up he plays with some melting wax, humming to himself the hymn-tune 'Praise, my soul, the King of Heaven'. He smears some wax on both my thumbs and says he is double-jointed, and asks if I am too.

At first I saw this material in terms of the bisexual conflict and I tried to interpret it in that way. I told him that I thought the war between the two villages was expressing his feeling that I, as the mother, the woman, have all the human values, while he has only the mechanical ones. This interpretation linked with earlier material in which he had spent weeks making Meccano models with sets that he brought to the session, and had continually shown me the models illustrated in the handbook, assuring me that 'You can make *anything* with Meccano'; but this play had stopped suddenly after he had tried to make a mechanical man, as specified in the book, and it had failed to work, that is move. And I had told him then how disappointed he was that he could not make a live baby out of his Meccano. So, in this village play, I pointed out how he had now attempted some rearrangement and exchange in which I was to be given some of the maleness (gun and test-tube), and he was to have something of the femaleness (ending up with getting the 'Mrs Noah' figure). I explained also how this compromise had not entirely worked, since jealousy had broken through, as was shown in his attempt to justify his impending envious attacks by saying 'I don't like these people'; that is to say 'I am not guilty because they are bad anyway, so it doesn't matter hurting them.' Also I told him that by burning his own village he was not only punishing himself, but at the same time expressing (externalizing) the state of anxiety in which he felt full of explosive faeces which might at any moment blow up his own body; and added that he had returned to the attempt to avoid the cause of jealousy by trying to mitigate the absoluteness of his split between 'mechanized' male and 'human' female. I suggested that he was trying to tell me how he could not stand the empty, depersonalized gods (trucks), so effected a compromise by borrowing the good mother figure to fill the empty truck. I pointed out how, after this, he could tell me that he was double-jointed; that is he combined both positions, and he hoped I could too.

In the next session immediately following this one, he spent the whole hour mending his satchel, a job that he said ordinarily his mother would do for him. Here I interpreted that the two villages were also mother and father, and that he felt he had succeeded in bringing them together inside him.

Certainly he did seem to be working out his conflicts about the relation between father and mother, both internally and externally, and trying to find ways of dealing with his jealousy and envy of his mother in what Melanie Klein (1928) has called the 'femininity phase'. Considered in this light, his mechanized village then also stood for his feeling about his school. For at this time he was constantly complaining how utterly uninteresting and boring his school work was, and he frequently brought material to do with waste lands and desert places: this being in marked contrast with the early school years during which he had been interested and successful. Thus one way of trying to describe the situation was in terms of the idea that the school, the place in which he must seek knowledge, had become too much identified with the destroyed mother's body, so that it had indeed become a desert; for the game of attacking and burning the village had been played throughout the period of his most acute school difficulties. But at the same time it was also too much identified with the desired mother's body, for such material certainly also pointed to intense conflict in the direct Oedipus situation, as well as in the 'femininity phase'; and for a long time it had seemed to me that the school difficulty was being presented largely in these terms. Thus the entry into the world of knowledge and school work seemed to be identified with the entry into the mother's body, an undertaking at once demanded by the schoolmaster–father figure but forbidden under threat of castration by the sexual rival father. In fact one could describe the situation here in terms of the use of symbolism as a defence, and say that because the school had become the symbol of the forbidden mother's body this was then a bar to progress.

The defence against the anxiety aroused by this symbolic identification took the form of a reversal of roles in his play with me; he himself became the sadistic punishing schoolmaster and I had to be the bad pupil. For days, and sometimes weeks, I had to play the role of the persecuted schoolboy: I was set long monotonous tasks, my efforts were treated with scorn, I was forbidden to talk and made to write out 'lines' if I did; and if I did not comply with these demands, then he wanted to cane me. (When asked if he were really treated as badly as this at school he always said 'no'; he certainly was never caned, and the school, though of the conventional pattern, did try most generously to adapt to his difficulties.) Clearly then there was a great amount of resentment and fear to be worked through in the Oedipus situation, but I did not feel this was the only reason for the persistence of this type of play. It was other aspects of the material which finally led me to see the problem as also something to do with difficulties in establishing the relation to external reality as such.

One of these was the fact that he frequently adopted a particularly bullying tone when talking to me, even when he was not playing the schoolmaster game, but he always dropped this tone as soon as he began imaginative play with the toys. This observation suggested that perhaps this boy could drop the hectoring tone, during this kind of play, because it was a situation in which he could have a different kind of relation to external reality, by means of the toys; he could do what he liked with them, and yet they were outside him. He nearly always began the session with the bullying tone and insistence that I was not ready for him at the right time, whatever the actual time of starting; but as soon as he had settled down to using the toys as a pliable medium, external to himself, but not insisting on their own separate objective existence, then apparently he could treat me with friendliness and consideration, and even accept real frustration from me.

The receptive role of the toys

This observation set me wondering about the exact function of this relation to the toys, and in what terms it could be discussed. I noticed how, on days when he did play with the toys, there seemed to develop a relationship between him and them which reminded me of the process I had myself tried to observe introspectively when doing 'free' drawings.[10] I thought that there was perhaps something useful to be said about the actual process of playing with the toys as compared with, on the one hand, pure day-dreaming, and on the other, direct expedient muscular activity directed towards a living object. In the play with the toys there was something half-way between day-dreaming and purposeful instinctive or expedient action. As soon as he moved a toy in response to some wish or phantasy then the play-village was different, and the new sight set off a new set of possibilities; just as in free imaginative drawing, the sight of a mark made on the paper provokes new associations, the line as it were answers back and functions as a very primitive type of external object.

About two months after the war-of-the-villages play something occurred which seemed to offer a further clue as to what was happening when he played with the toys; for the bullying tone suddenly vanished for four days, beginning with a day when he told me about something that had happened at school which clearly gave him great pleasure. For many weeks before he had been intensely preoccupied with a photography club that he and his particular friends had organized in their out-of-school hours; now he reported that their form master had given him permission to hold their meetings in school, during a time set aside for special activities, and had even given them a little room in which to work.

This sudden disappearance of his dictatorship attitude gave me the idea that the fact of his spontaneously created activity being incorporated in the framework of the school routine was a fulfilling, in external life, of the solution foreshadowed in the war between the villages play. What he had felt to be the mechanized, soulless world of school had now seemed to him to have become humanized, by the taking into its empty trucks of a bit of himself, something that he had created. But what was particularly interesting was the fact that he had only been able to respond to the school's gesture at this particular moment; for there had been many efforts on their part to help him before this, such as special coaching after his continual absences. One could of course say that it was because of the strength of his own aggression and his anxiety about it, that he had not been able to make more use of the help offered; but it seemed to me that these earlier efforts on the part of the school had not had more apparent effect also because they had not taken the particular form of the incorporation of, acceptance of, a bit of his own spontaneous creation. Now the school, by being receptive, by being in-giving as well as out-giving, had shown itself capable of good mothering; it was a male world which had become more like his mother, who had in fact been a very good mother. Much earlier he had foreshadowed this same need by one of his rare dreams, in which his mother had been present at school in his Latin class, Latin being the bugbear of his school subjects.

This view of the meaning of the villages play as partly to do with problems of this boy's whole relation to what was, for him, the unmitigated not-me-ness of his school life, threw light on one of the elements in the original situation when his difficulties first became apparent. Not only had his father been called away to the war just at the time when his baby brother had been born and when London was being bombed, but he had also lost his most valued toy, a woolly rabbit. As the analysis advanced I had come to realize how significant this loss had been, for it became more clear that one of my main roles in the transference was to be the lost rabbit. He so often treated me as totally his own to do what he liked with, as though I were dirt, his dirt, or as a tool, an extension of his own hand. (He had never been a thumb sucker.) If I was not free the moment he arrived, even though he was often thirty minutes early, I was reprimanded or threatened with punishment for being late. In fact it certainly did seem that for a very long time he did need to have the illusion that I was part of himself.

Play and the boundary between inner and outer

Here I tried to review the various psychoanalytic concepts of mechanisms that can be forerunners of or defences against object relations, and see which might be useful to explain what was happening. Certainly he split himself and put the bad bit of himself into me when he punished me as the pupil. Certainly he used threatening words which were intended to enter into me and cow me into doing what he wanted and being his slave. Certainly he tried to make me play the role of the all-gratifying idealized phantasy object; he once told me that he did feel himself quite special and that the frustrating things that happened to other people would not happen to him. I thought that this did mean that he felt at times that he had this marvellous object inside him which would protect and gratify him. And this linked with the fact that he would sometimes hum hymn tunes, such as 'Praise, my soul, the King of Heaven', although he explicitly expressed great scorn for religion. Certainly also he found it very difficult to maintain the idea of my separate identity; in his demands he continually denied the existence of my other patients or any family ties. The way he behaved could also be described by saying that he kept me inside him, since he continually used to insist that I knew what he had been doing or was going to do, when I had in fact no possible means of knowing. Yet I did not feel that these ways of talking about what happened were entirely adequate; for all of them take for granted the idea of a clear boundary, if I am felt to be inside him then he has a boundary, and the same if a bit of him is felt to be projected into me.

But there was much material in this analysis to do with burning, boiling down, and melting, which seemed to me to express the idea of the obliteration of boundaries. And I had a growing amount of evidence, both from clinical material and introspective study of problems in painting, that the variations in the feeling of the existence or non-existence of the body boundary are themselves very

94

important. In this connection Scott[11] restates Winnicott's view[12] about how a good mother allows the child to fuse its predisposition to hallucinate a good situation with the earliest sensations of a good situation. Scott then describes this as an 'oscillation between the illusion of union and the fact of contact, which is another way of describing the discovery of an interface, a boundary, or a place of contact, and perhaps at the same time is another way of describing the discovery of "the me" and "the you" '. He goes on to say 'But I think only a partial picture of union and contact is given by discussing the good situation. Equally important is the evil union and the evil contact and the discovery of the evil me and the evil you'.[13] He also talks of the extremes of the states in which all discriminations and interfaces are destroyed as in what he calls 'cosmic bliss' and 'catastrophic chaos'. And these extremes relate, I think, to behaviourist observations that can be made, both in and out of analysis, of the variations of facial expression between extreme beauty and extreme ugliness. I had, for instance, a child patient of 6 who would at times show an extremely seraphic face, and it occurred in connection with great concentration on the use or lack of use of outline in painting. I also observed a schizophrenic patient (adult) who would at times have moments of startling physical beauty counterbalanced by moments of something startlingly repellent.

One could certainly think of this phenomenon in terms of complete union with a marvellous or atrocious inner object, with the obliteration of inner boundaries between the ego and the incorporated object. But there was also the question of where the actual body boundary was felt to be. Did it mean that the skin was felt to include the whole world and therefore in a sense was denied altogether? Certainly the introspective quality of what have been called oceanic states seems to include this feeling, as does also the catastrophic chaos that Scott refers to. For the schizophrenic patient described above constantly complained that she could not get the world outside her and that this, rather than being a source of bliss, was agony to her. Certainly there is very much here that I do not understand. Also the whole question of beauty appearing in analysis, perceived by the analyst either as a varying physical quality of the patient or as the quality of the material, has not been much discussed in the literature, though Sharpe does mention dreams that the patient describes as beautiful.[14] When perceived by the analyst it can clearly be described in terms of the counter-transference, and used, just as any other aspect of the counter-transference can be used (Paula Heimann)[15] as part of the analytic data. Thus in trying to understand all that this boy was trying to show me I had to take into account the fact that at times there was a quality in his play which I can only describe as beautiful – occasions when it was he who did the stage managing and it was my imagination which caught fire. It was in fact play with light and fire. He would close the shutters of the room and insist that it be lit only by candle light, sometimes a dozen candles arranged in patterns, or all grouped together in a solid block. And then he would make what he called furnaces, with a very careful choice of what ingredients should make the fire, including dried leaves from special plants in my garden; and sometimes all the ingredients had to be put in a metal cup on the electric fire and stirred continuously, all this carried out in the half darkness of candle light. And often there had to be a sacrifice, a lead soldier had to be added to the fire, and this figure was spoken of either as the victim or the sacrifice. In fact, all this type of play had a dramatic ritual quality comparable to the fertility rites described by Frazer in primitive societies. And this effect was the more striking because this boy's conscious interests were entirely conventional for his age; he was absorbed in Meccano and model railways.

Aesthetic experience and the merging of the boundary

The fact that in this type of material the boy's play nearly became 'a play', in that there was a sense of pattern and dramatic form in what he produced, leads to many questions about the relation of a work of art to analytic work, which are not relevant here. But the particular point I wish to select for further consideration is that he seemed to me to be trying to express the idea of integration, in a variety of different ways. Thus the fire seemed to be here not only a destructive fire but also the fire of Eros; and not only the figurative expression of his own passionate body feelings, not only the phantasy representative of the wish for passionate union with the external object, but also a way of representing the inner fire of concentration. The process in which interest is withdrawn temporarily from the external world so that the inner work of integration can be carried out was, I think, shown by the boiling or melting down of the various ingredients in what he called 'the fire cup', to make a new whole. And the sacrifice of the toy soldier by melting it down both expressed the wish to get rid of a bad internal object, particularly the cramping and cruel aspect of his super-ego, and also his sense of the need to absorb his inner objects into his ego and so modify them. But in addition to this I think it represented his feeling of the need to be able, at times, to transcend the common-sense ego; for common sense was very

96

strong in him, his conscious attitude was one of feet firmly planted on the ground. For instance, when he did tell a dream, which was rarely, he usually apologized if it was at all nonsensical. And formerly also this boy had told me that he was 'no good at art' and he was extremely tentative in any attempts at drawing. But later this changed. For he told me one day, with pride, that he was good at both science and art, which he felt was not very usual amongst his schoolfellows; though he was still inclined to be apologetic about his aesthetic experiences. When he told me of the delight he took in the colours of the various crystals he had studied in his chemistry he added, 'It's childish to like them so much.'

Although an important factor in this development of his capacity to feel himself 'good at art' was his growing belief in his power to restore his injured objects, this is not the aspect of the material that I wish to discuss here; for I am concentrating on the earlier problem of establishing object relationships at all, rather than on the restoration of the injured object once it is established. Granted that these two are mutually interdependent and that anxiety in the one phase can cause regression to the earlier one, there is still much to be said about the earlier phase as such. Thus a central idea began to emerge about what this boy was trying to tell me; it was the idea that the basic identifications which make it possible to find new objects, to find the familiar in the unfamiliar, require an ability to tolerate a temporary loss of sense of self, a temporary giving up of the discriminating ego which stands apart and tries to see things objectively and rationally and without emotional colouring. It perhaps requires a state of mind which has been described by Berenson as 'the aesthetic moment.'[16]

> 'In visual art the aesthetic moment is that fleeting instant, so brief as to be almost timeless, when the spectator is at one with the work of art he is looking at, or with actuality of any kind that the spectator himself sees in terms of art, as form and colour. He ceases to be his ordinary self, and the picture or building, statue, landscape, or aesthetic actuality is no longer outside himself. The two become one entity; time and space are abolished and the spectator is possessed by one awareness. When he recovers workaday consciousness it is as if he had been initiated into illuminating, formative mysteries.'

Now I think it is possible to add something to my attempts to describe what happened in this boy during the play when his whole behaviour to me changed, and to link this with what an artist or a poet does. For observations in analysis suggest that experiences of the kind described by Berenson are not confined to the contemplation of works of art, but that art provides a method, in adult life, for reproducing states that are part of everyday experience in healthy infancy. Sometimes poets have explicitly related such states to their early experience: for instance, Traherne, and also Wordsworth, in his note on 'Intimations of Immortality from Recollections of Early Childhood'. Thus Wordsworth says that as a child he was unable to think of external things as having external existence, he communed with all he saw as something not apart from but inherent in his own immaterial nature; when going to school he would often grasp at a wall to recall himself from the abyss of idealism. I suggest that it is useful, in child analysis, to look out for the ways in which the child may be trying to express such experiences, when he has not yet sufficient command of words to tell what he feels, directly, but can only use words or whatever other media the playroom offers him, figuratively: for instance, as this child used candle light and fire and the activities of melting and burning, as well as the actual toys. And I think it may be useful also to bear in mind that if, when talking about this state, one uses only those concepts, such as introjection and projection, which presuppose the existence of the organism within its boundaries in a world of other organisms within boundaries, one may perhaps distort one's perception of the phenomenon. Thus it is important not to forget the obvious fact that we know the boundaries exist but the child does not; in the primal state, it is only gradually and intermittently that he discovers them; and on the way to this he uses play. Later, he keeps his perception of the world from becoming fixed, and no longer capable of growth, by using art, either as artist or as audience; and he may also use psychoanalysis. For, as Rank says, art and play both link the world of 'subjective unreality' and 'objective reality', harmoniously fusing the edges but not confusing them.[17] So the developing human being becomes able deliberately to allow illusions about what he is seeing to occur; he allows himself to experience, within the enclosed space-time of the drama or the picture or the story or the analytic hour, a transcending of that common-sense perception which would see a picture as only an attempt at photography, or the analyst as only a present-day person.

The need for a medium between the self-created and external realities

What I want to suggest here is that these states are a necessary phase in the development of object relationships and that the understanding of their function gives a meaning to the phrase 'Art creates Nature'. In this connection a later phase in the transference phenomena shown by this boy is relevant. It was after he had become deeply interested in chemistry that there occurred in analysis, for several weeks, a repeated catechism. He would say, 'What is your name?' and I would have to say, 'What is my name?' Then he would answer with the name of some chemical, and I would say, 'What is there about that?' And he would answer, 'it's lovely stuff, I've made it!'; and sometimes he would give me the name of the chemical which is used as a water-softener.

Here then is the link with the artist's use of his medium, what the *Concise Oxford Dictionary* defines as an 'intervening substance through which impressions are conveyed to the senses'; and this pliable stuff that can be made to take the shape of one's phantasies, can include the 'stuff' of sound and breath which becomes our speech. (This boy would sometimes tell me that I was a gas, or that he was going to dissolve me down or evaporate me till I became one.) So it seemed that he had become able to use both me and the playroom equipment as this intervening pliable substance; he had become able to do with these what Caudwell says the poet does with words, when he uses them to give the organism an appetitive interest in external reality, when he makes the earth become charged with affective colouring and glow with a strange emotional fire.[18]

As regards the use of the medium of speech,[19] there was a stage, after the war of the village's play, when it was very difficult to get this boy to talk. He would play, but silently, and when he did talk, it was always to try and teach me something; sometimes it was the language of chemistry, which he knew and I did not. And this I think expressed the need of the artist in him (and also the scientist, for he soon became determined to make science his career) to have a bit of his own experience incorporated in the social world, just as he had been able to have his own club incorporated in the world of school. For, as Caudwell points out, the artist is acutely aware of the discrepancy between, on the one hand, all the ways of expressing feeling that are provided by the current development of speech and art, in our particular culture and epoch; and, on the other hand, our changing experiences that are continually outstripping the available means of expression. Thus the artist wishes to cast his private experiences in such form that they will be incorporated in the social world of art and so lessen the discrepancy. Caudwell points out that it is not only the artist who feels this discrepancy and not only the discrepancy between feeling and current forms of expression of it; it is also the scientist, in respect not of feeling, but of perception and currently accepted ways of formulating it, currently accepted views of 'reality', who wishes to contribute something of his own to the changing symbols of science. Perhaps even he must do this if the already discovered symbols are to become fully significant for him.

Effects of premature loss of belief in the self-created reality

The phenomenon of treating the world as one's own creation is mentioned by Fenichel. He says:

> 'There always remain certain traces of the original objectless condition, or at least a longing for it ("oceanic feeling"). Introjection is an attempt to make parts of the external world flow into the ego. Projection, by putting unpleasant sensations into the external world, also attempts to reverse the separation of ego from non-ego.'

And he goes on to refer to the child who 'when playing hide-and-seek closes his eyes and believes he now cannot be seen'. Fenichel then says, 'The archaic animistic conception of the world which is based on a confusion of ego and non-ego is thus illustrated.'

Although there are differences of opinion about what he calls here 'the original objectless condition', about whether or not there is some primitive object relation from the very beginning, which alternates with the 'objectless' or fused condition, I think Fenichel's description is valuable. The example of the child playing hide-and-seek vividly shows the belief in a self-created reality; just as analytical material shows related phenomena such as the child's belief that when he opens his eyes and sees the world, he thereby creates it, he feels it is the lovely (or horrible) stuff that he has made.

The idea that these states of illusion of oneness are perhaps a recurrently necessary phase in the continued growth of the sense of twoness leads to a further question: What happens when they are prevented from occurring with sufficient frequency or at the right moments?

This boy had had in general a very good home and been much loved. But he had suffered very early environmental thwartings in the feeding situation. In the early weeks of his life his mother had had too little milk and the nurse had been in the habit of not getting the supplementary feed ready in time, so that he had had to wait to finish his meal and had shown great distress: an experience that was re-lived in the transference, when whatever time I was ready for him, he always said I was too late.

100

Although it is obvious that a child must suffer frustration, there is still something to be said about the way in which it should occur and the timing of it. I suggest that, if, through the pressure of unsatisfied need, the child has to become aware of his separate identity too soon or too continually, then either the illusion of union can be what Scott calls catastrophic chaos rather than cosmic bliss, or the illusion is given up and premature ego-development may occur; then separateness and the demands of necessity may be apparently accepted, but necessity becomes a cage rather than something to be co-operated with for the freeing of further powers. With this boy it was clear how the imposed necessities, regulations, non-self-chosen tasks, of a conventional school, had provided a setting for a repetition of his first difficulties in relation to the environment. In fact he often told me what his ideal school would be like, and it amounted to being taught by a method very like what modern educationists call the project method.

If one asks the question, what factors play an essential part in the process of coming to recognize a world that is outside oneself, not one's own creation, there is one that I think has not been much stressed in the literature. Thus, in addition to the physical facts of the repeated bodily experiences of being separated from the loved object, and being together with it, and the repeated physical experiences of interchange with the not-self world, breathing, feeding, eliminating: in addition to the gradually growing capacity to tolerate the difference between the feeling of oneness, of being united with everything, and the feeling of twoness, of self and object, there is the factor of a capacity in the environment. It is the capcity of the environment to foster this growth, by providing conditions in which a recurrent partial return to the feeling of being one is possible; and I suggest that the environment does this by the recurrent providing of a framed space and time and a pliable medium, so that, on occasions, it will not be necessary for self-preservation's sake to distinguish clearly between inner and outer, self and not-self. I wish to suggest that it was his need for this capacity in the environment that my patient was telling me about in his village play, when he said there was to be a war, 'but not yet'. It was as if he were saying that the true battle with the environment, the creative struggle of interacting opposites, could not begin, or be effectively continued, until there had also been established his right to a recurrent merging of the opposites. And until this was established necessity was indeed a mechanized god, whose service was not freedom but a colourless slavery.

Looked at in this way the boy's remark, 'I don't like those people', was not only due to a denial of an uprush of feared uncontrollable jealousy and envy, it represented also the re-enactment of a memory or memories of a near breakdown of relationship to the outside world. It was the memory, I suggest, of actual experience of a too sudden breaking in on the illusion of oneness, an intrusion which had had the effect of preventing the emergence from primary narcissism occurring gradually in the child's own time. But it represented also a later situation; for the premature ego-development, referred to by Melanie Klein as inhibiting the development of symbolization (or, in Jones's terms, of symbolic equivalents) was also brought about by the impingement of the war. For the sake of self-preservation, it had been necessary for him continually and clearly to distinguish between external and internal reality, to attend to the real qualities of the symbol too soon. Thus it was reported to me that this boy had shown remarkable fortitude when, with his father away in the Navy, he and his baby brother and mother had lived through the blitz on London. And also, later on, his reports indicated that he was very self-controlled in school, in that situation where self-preservation demands a fairly continual hold upon objectivity, since day-dreaming and treating the external world as part of one's dream are not easily tolerated by schoolmasters. But the fact that this amount of objectivity was only achieved at a fairly high cost in anxiety was shown in his analysis, for at one time he was continually punishing me for imagined lapses into forgetfulness, inattention, unpunctuality. It was only later that he was able to tell me about what he now called his absentmindedness, in a tolerant way and without anxiety.

Implications for technique

The considerations I have tried to formulate here are not only matters for theory, they have direct bearings upon technique. With this boy there was always the question of whether to emphasize, in interpreting, the projection mechanisms and persecutory defences and to interpret the aggression as such; but when I did this the aggression did not seem to lessen and I was sometimes in despair at its quite implacable quality. At times he treated me as if I were like the man in the Bible from whom a devil was driven out, but into whom seven more came, so that he went on attacking me with almost the fervour of a holy war. But when I began to think along the lines described above, even though I knew that I was not succeeding in putting these ideas clearly into words in my interpretations, the aggression did begin to lessen and the continual battle over the time of the beginning of each session disappeared. Of course I may be mistaken in thinking that the change in the boy's behaviour which accompanied the change in my idea of the problem was a matter of cause and effect, since the issue is very complicated and brings in many debatable questions of theory. But I think that it was significant that, near the end of his analysis, this boy told me that when he was grown up and earning his own living he would give me a papier-mâché chemical clock, which would keep perfect time and would be his own invention. He said it would be of papier-mâché because I had an ornament, a little Indian dog, made of this, and also I remembered how he himself had tried, during his play with me, to make papier-mâché bowls, but unsuccessfully. Granted that the idea of the giving of the clock stood for many things, including returning to me the restored breast and restored penis, and also represented his gratitude for the recovery of his own potency, I thought he was telling me something else as well. I thought that the malleability of the papier-mâché provided him with a way of expressing how he felt about part of the curative factor in his analysis. It was his way of saying how, in the setting of the analytic playroom, he had been able to find a bit of the external world that was malleable; he had found that it was safe to treat it as a bit of himself, and so had let it serve as a bridge between inner and outer. And it was through this, I suggest, as well as through the interpretations I had given about the content of his wishes towards outer and inner objects, that he had become able to accept the real qualities of externality, objective time standing as the chief representative of these. And in those phases when he could not make this bridge, because the fact that I had to work to a timetable forced on him an objective reality that he was not yet ready for, then I became merely the gap into which he projected all his 'bad' wishes, or internal objects representing these. When he could not feel that he had 'made' me, that I was his lovely stuff, then I was the opposite, not only bad but also alien, and bad because alien; so I became the receptacle for all that he felt was alien to his ego in himself, all the 'devil' parts of himself that he was frightened of and so had to repudiate. It seemed as if it was only by being able, again and again, to experience the illusion that I was part of himself, fused with the goodness that he could conceive of internally, that he became able to tolerate a goodness that was not his own creation and to allow me goodness independently. Exactly how an infant does come to tolerate a goodness that is recognized to exist independently of himself seems to me to have not yet beeen entirely satisfactorily explained; though the factor of the relief obtained from giving up the illusion of omnipotence is mentioned in the literature and was clearly apparent in this boy. The repeated discovery that I went on being friendly, and remained unhurt by him, in spite of the continual attacks on me, certainly played a very important part. For instance, there was another ritual catechism which would begin with 'Why are you a fool?' and I had to say, 'Why am I a fool?' Then he would answer, 'Because I say so.' Clearly if he had to feel that all the foolishness of adults was his doing, as well as their goodness, then he was going to bear a heavy burden. But I think he could not proceed to the stage of experiencing the relief of disillusion until he had also had sufficient time both to experience and to become conscious of the previous stage; he had to become aware that he was experiencing the stage of fusion before he could reach the relief of de-fusion. And it was only when he could become conscious of the relief of de-fusion that we were then able to reach his depression about injuries that he had felt he was responsible for, both internally and externally, in his family situation and in relation to me.

On looking back it seems to me that the greatest progress in his analysis came when I, on the basis of the above considerations, was able to deal with the negative counter-transference. At first, without really being aware of it, I had taken for granted the view of infantile omnipotence which is described by Fenichel:

> 'Yet even after speech, logic, and the reality principle have been established we find that pre-logical thinking is still in operation and even beyond the role it plays in states of ego regression or as a form of purposeful distortion. It no longer fulfils, it is true, the function of preparing for future actions but becomes, rather, a *substitute* for unpleasant reality.'

I had accepted this view but grown rather tired of being continually treated by this boy as his gas, his breath, his faeces, and had wondered how long the working through of this phase would take. But when I began to suspect that Fenichel was wrong here, and that this pre-logical fusion of subject and object does continue to have a function of preparing for future action, when I began to see and to interpret, as far as I could, that this use of me might be not only a defensive regression, but an essential recurrent phase in the development of a creative relation to the world, then the whole character of the analysis changed; the boy then gradually became able to allow the external object, represented by me, to exist in its own right.

Caudwell says that the artist and the scientist

> 'are men who acquire a special experience of life – affective with the artist, perceptual with the scientist – which negates the

104

common ego or the common social world, and therefore requires refashioning of these worlds to include the new experience.'

This boy had, I think, indicated the nature of this process by his reaction to the school's refashioning of a tiny bit of itself and its routines. For this had happened in response to the vividness of his belief in the validity of his own experience; a vividness which also had contributed to a refashioning in me of some of my analytic ideas.

Conclusion

On the basis of the study of such material as I have described here, and also from my own experiments in painting, I came to see the pertinence of Melanie Klein's statement that symbolization is the basis of all talents; that is that it is the basis of those skills by which we relate ourselves to the world around us. To try to restrict the meaning of the word symbolization, as some writers tend to do, to the use of the symbol for purposes of distortion, may have the advantage of simplification, but it has other disadvantages. One of these is that it causes unnecessary confusion when one tries to communicate with workers in related disciplines, such as epistemology, aesthetics, and the philosophy of science; it interferes with what might be a valuable collaboration in the work of clarifying some of the obscure issues about the nature of thought. This isolation of psychoanalysis, by its terminology, from related fields, may not have been a disadvantage in the early days of the struggle to establish analytic concepts in their own right, but now such isolation, can, I think, lead to an impoverishment of our own thinking.

Another advantage of not limiting the meaning of the word symbol to a defensive function would be a clarification of theory by bringing it more in line with our practice. The analytic rule that the patient shall try to put all that he is aware of into words does seem to me to imply a belief in the importance of symbolization for maturity as well as for infancy; it implies the recognition that words are in fact symbols by means of which the world is comprehended. Thus in the daily battle with our patients over the transference we are asking them to accept a symbolic relation to the analyst instead of a literal one, to accept the symbolism of speech and talking about their wants rather than taking action to satisfy them directly. And, as all analytic experience shows, it is when the patient becomes able to talk about all that he is aware of, when he *can* follow the analytic rule, then in fact he becomes able to relate himself more adequately to the world outside. As he becomes able to tolerate more fully the difference between the symbolic reality of the analytic relationship and the literal reality of libidinal satisfaction outside the frame of the session, then he becomes better.

Postscript

After completing this paper I began the analysis of another child (I called her Ruth), also aged 11 who presented a somewhat similar problem of persistence in what looked like aggressive attacks. This child fervently and defiantly scribbled over every surface she could find. Although it looked as if it were done in anger, interpretation in terms of aggression only led to increase in the defiance. In fact, the apparent defiance did not change until I began to guess that the trouble was less to do with faeces given in anger and meant to express anger, than with faeces given in love and meant to express love. In this sense it was a battle over how she was to communicate her love, a battle over what kind of medium she was going to use for the language of love. So intense were her feelings about this that, after the first two days of analysis, she did not speak to me again, except when outside the playroom, for six months, although she would often write down what she wanted to say. Gradually I had come to look at the scribbling in the following way: by refusing to discriminate and claiming the right to scribble over everything, she was trying to deny the discrepancy between the feeling and the expression of it; by denying completely my right to protect any of my property from defacement she was even trying to win me over to her original belief that when she gave her messes lovingly they were literally as lovely as the feelings she had in the giving of them. In terms of the theory of symbolism, she was struggling with the problem of the identity of the symbol and the thing symbolized, in the particular case of bodily excretions as symbols for psychic and psychosomatic experiences. She was also struggling with the very early problem of coming to discriminate not only between the lovely feelings in giving the mess and the mess itself, but also between the product and the organ which made it.

When I began to consider what she was doing in these terms I also became able to see the boy's battle of the villages in a wider perspective. Both the children were struggling with the problem of how to communicate the ecstasies of loving, as well as the agonies; and the boy's 'lovely stuff' was certainly both the lovely stuff of his lovely dreams *and* his lovely sensations which, at one level, he could only think of in terms of 'lovely' faeces. The phrase 'denial by idealization' is familiar, but the denial here is, I suggest, in the nature of the mess, not in the nature of the psychic experience of which it is the symbol. For this is the maximum experience of joy, ecstasy, which is a psychic fact, a capacity for heavenly or god-like experience possessed by everyone. The psychic agony came, and the anger, when this boy had to face the fact that there was discrepancy between the objective qualities of his messes, that is how they looked to other people, and his subjective evaluation of them as actually being the same as the god-like experiences. Thus both children were struggling with the agony of disillusion in given up their belief that everyone must see in their dirt what they see in it: 'my people' are to see his empty trucks and 'think it's gods'. In fact, he is saying what the poet Yeats said: 'Tread softly, because you tread on my dreams.'

But was this struggle to make me see as they saw in essence any different from the artist's struggle to communicate his private vision? I have suggested that both the artist and the scientist are more acutely aware than the 'average' man of the inadequacies of what Caudwell calls 'the common ego', the commonly accepted body of knowledge and ways of thinking about and expressing experience, more sensitive to the gap between what can be talked about and the actuality of experience. If this is true, then it is also true to say that what is in the beginning only a subjective private vision can become to future generations, objectivity. Thus the battle between the villages seemed to me to be not only a symbolic dramatization of the battle of love and hate, the struggle with ambivalency towards the object, but also a genuine work of dramatic art, in which the actual process by which the world is created, for all of us, is poetically represented.

The battle over communicating the private vision, when the battleground is the evaluation of the body products, has a peculiar poignancy. In challenging the accepted objective view and claiming the right to make others share their vision, there is a danger which is perhaps the sticking point in the development of many who would otherwise be creative people. For to win this battle, when fought on this field, would mean to seduce the world to madness, to denial of the difference between cleanliness and dirt, organization and chaos. Thus in one sense the battle is a very practical one; it is over what is a suitable and convenient stuff for symbols to be made of; but at the same time it is also a battle over the painful recognition that, if the lovely stuff is to convey the lovely feelings, there must be work done on the material.

In the first version of this paper, I described how this boy had one day suddenly recited to me a long poem he said he had learnt at school; he made me write it all down on two successive days. (I have not been able to trace the poem and have quoted it as he gave it to me.)

> 'A parrot from the Spanish Main
> Full young and early caged, came o'er
> With bright wings to the bleak domain
> Of Mulla's shore.
> To spicey groves where he had won
> His plumage of resplendent hue
> His native fruits and skies and sun
> He bade adieu.
> For these he changed the smoke of turf
> A heathery land and misty sky
> And turned on rocks and raging surf
> His golden eye.
> But petted in our climate cold
> He lived and chattered many a day
> Until with age from green and gold
> His wings grew grey.
> At last when blind and seeming dumb
> He scolded, laughed, and spoke no more
> A Spanish stranger chanced to come
> To Mulla's shore.
> He hailed the bird in Spanish speech
> The bird in Spanish speech replied
> Flapped joyously around the cage
> Dropped down and died.'

I had added the comment:

The boy was obviously delighted with the poem and said he was going to set it to music. He denied that it was sad. The significance, in the transference, of the stranger who spoke his language, was shown by a dream; he had fallen on frozen ground and someone, associated with me, was helping him up and going to take him to a warmer climate. In this connection it is interesting that Eissler, in trying to find an analogy to explain an aspect of schizophrenics' positive response to his treatment, describes the reactions of a castaway in foreign land and says:[20]

'But this castaway will never forget the sounds of his mother tongue, and even after decades of not having heard it the first sounds of it will create in him an amazing reaction.'

When I tried to consider what was the experience in this boy's life which corresponded with the early caging of the parrot, the history of his feeding difficulties was clearly relevant; for this boy, like the parrot, had had in general a very good home and been much loved.

When I originally sent the second version of this paper to Melanie Klein (including the postscript about the girl patient Ruth), I received this answer.

'24 February, 1953

Dear Marion,

I am very sorry that I have had to delay so long my answer to your Notes. I agree with you conclusion that it is a great source of anxiety that there could be earliest desires implying a pouring out of urine, faeces, etc, a total "letting go", i.e. a complete regression; that is very interesting and I can confirm it from my experience. It is also very interesting that such "letting go" means a total obliteration of discrimination between the various body products and that such regression would seem to the more developed ego like a "bursting into bits".

I also agree with your conclusion that there is a mourning for such early experiences or states of mind, and I found your suggestion, that genital maturity implies a successfully accomplished work of mourning for pre-genital total orgastic experiences interesting. I often found that there is a mourning for the lost baby self but – and here I come to some points where I differ from you – the feeling that these early experiences were so blissful is bound up with idealisation of that baby-self and its relations, because I believe that when the baby experiences them they are by no means free from anxieties and conflicts. In order to make my point clear I should like rather to speak in those terms in which I have so often described early processes. The pouring out of love and hatred, urine, faeces, products of the body, parts of the self, parts of the ego, implies a projecting out first of all into the mother. Miss Freud's saying that a baby "wants to love his mother with all his bodily powers" is another way of saying that his desires from all sources – oral, urethral, anal – are first of all related to the mother. Such desires are bound up with love and hatred and that is the way in which he loves her. Such processes of projection have been more recently described by myself and others as projective identification, and are abound up with splitting, with falling into bits. The dangers implied in an ejaculatory projection of that kind are a losing of the ego into the other person, "the total merging" and a fear of not being able to retrieve it. This is a cause of great ego disturbance. Now one of the main reasons why this process becomes excessive and is felt by the adult, as well as in some cases by the baby not only as a blissful but also as a terrifying experience is due to the fact that aggressive phantasies and impulses play such an important part in it and therefore the feeling that the object into whom such projection has taken place – first of all the mother – will retaliate in kind. The danger of regression to such an early stage besides the one on which you remark implies being subject to uncontrollable omnipotent impulses dangerous to the self and to the object because of the admixture with aggression. That regression would also imply a disintegration of the ego, a falling into bits, and all the dangers implied in excessive early projective processes. Introjection is another of those dangers bound up with excessive projective identification since that person into whom destructive projection takes place would not only retaliate and intrude into the self but is also introjected as a dangerous object. I believe therefore that it is essential for the therapeutic effect to connect the fear of surging up, pouring out, etc. with the dangers I have just mentioned, ultimately with aggressive and sadistic impulses which are part of it. I have no doubt that you analyse the sadism in the child you refer to, but the specific material you mention in your Notes needs, in my view, to be interpreted together with those points which I have now enumerated.

One more word about terms: you speak repeatedly of "excited" body products, "excited" giving, etc. I find the term "excited" vague and therefore misleading. Is it meant to be libidinal, or libidinal plus aggressive? I found it simpler and clearer to describe libidinal and aggressive urges in the old terms.

As I told you on the telephone I see no reason why you should not insert your Notes into the paper but that really is a matter to discuss with the Editors, and so would not risk altering your conclusions. I have found out that there is still four weeks' time to do so, and I hope that will give you the possibility of making the changes you would like.

I have now nearly got over the effects of my 'flu and if this beautiful weather continues I think we shall all feel much better soon.

The next Study Circle will be on Wednesday, 11th March, at
8.15 p.m.

          Love from
          Melanie'

Regarding my use of the word 'illusion', I had studied Christopher
Caudwell's *Illusion and Reality* before beginning my training, so was
particularly interested when D. W. Winnicott introduced ideas about
it in his paper on 'Primitive Emotional Development'.

I have also noticed (1985) that the word 'regression' does not
appear in my paper, though it does in D. W. Winnicott's important
footnote, added when I showed him the paper in manuscript. I
remembered also that, during the time when Melanie Klein was
supervising my work with Simon, and quite a long time before
writing this paper, I had once said to her tentatively that it might be
necessary sometimes to go back in order to come forward and that
she had agreed. This seems odd now, the fact that I put forward the
idea so diffidently, when so much has been discussed since about
benign kinds of regression. I also remember battling with the idea of
possible premature ego development and, sometime later, when
talking to Martin James, he said that he had found it necessary to
develop the same idea through his own close observations of infants.

References

1 Milner, M. (1952) Aspects of Symbolism in Comprehension of the Not-
self. *International Journal of Psycho-Analysis* 33: 181–95.
2 Milner, M. (1952) The Role of Illusion in Symbol Formation. In M.
Klein, P. Heimann, S. Isaacs, and J. Riviere (eds) *New Directions in
Psycho-Analysis*. London: Tavistock.
3 Jones, E. (1948) *Papers on Psycho-Analysis*. London: Balliere, Tindall, &
Cox.
4 Klein, M. (1948) *Contributions to Psycho-Analysis, 1921–45*. London:
Hogarth.
5 Read, H. (1951) Psycho-analysis and the Problem of Aesthetic Value.
International Journal of Psycho-Analysis 32.
6 Fenichel, O. (1946) *The Psycho-Analytic Theory of Neurosis*. London:
Kegan Paul.
7 Read, H. (1951)
8 Wordsworth, W. (1798) Preface to *Lyrical Ballads*. London: Longman
(1800).

9 I have had to omit some of the play in the middle of the session for reasons of space. It was connected with the theme of the previous months, in which there had been only one village, which he had continually bombed and burnt. I had interpreted it as partly an attempt to gain reassurance about his attacks on his mother's body, by acting them out in this comparatively harmless way and with my approval; I had also linked it with the aggression he had actually shown when his mother was pregnant.

10 Milner, M. (1950) *On Not Being Able to Paint*. London: Heinemann.

11 Scott, W. C. M. (1949) The Body Scheme in Psychotherapy. *British Journal of Medical Psychology* 22: 137–43.

12 Winnicott, D. W. (1945) Primitive Emotional Development. *International Journal of Psycho-Analysis* 26: 152–3. (1948) Pediatrics and Psychiatry. *Britsh Journal of Medical Psychology* 21: 209–40.

13 Winnicott, in a private communication, states that he does not entirely agree with Scott's restatement of his view, as quoted above. He adds the following modification:

'I agree with Scott's comment only if he is looking back at early infancy, starting from the adult (or child). Regression is a painful and precarious business partly because the individual regressing goes back with experiences of forward emotional development and with more or less knowledge in his pocket. For the person regressed there must be a denial of "evil union" and of "evil me" and "evil you" when an "ideal union" between "good self" and "good mother" is being lived (in the highly specialized therapeutic environment provided, or in the insane state).

This begs the whole question, however, of the earliest stages of an individual's emotional development studied there and then. For an infant, at the start, there is no good or bad, only a not yet de-fused object. One could think of separation as the cause of the first *idea* of union; before this there's union but no *idea* of union, and here the terms good and bad have no function. For union of this kind, so important for the founding of the mental health of the individual, the mother's active adaptation is an absolute necessity, an active adaptation to the infant's needs which can only come about through the mother's devotion to the infant.

Less than good enough adaptation on the part of a mother to her infant's needs at this very early stage leads (it seems to me) to the premature ego-development, the precocious abandonment of illusion of which M. Milner writes in this paper.'

14 Sharpe, E. (1937) *Dream Analysis*. London: Hogarth.

15 Heimann, P. (1950) On Counter Transference. *International Journal of Psycho-Analysis* 31: 81–4.

16 Berenson, B. (1950) *Aesthetics and History*. London: Constable.

17 Rank, O. (1932) *Art and Artists*. New York: Knopf.

18 Caudwell, C. (1937) *Illusion and Reality*. London: Lawrence & Wishart.

19 Unfortunately I was not able, before writing this paper, to read Susan Langer's *Philosophy in a New Key* (1942, Cambridge, Mass: Harvard University Press), which was a detailed discussion of the nature and function of symbolism, as it was not yet published in England and I could not obtain a copy. Had I been able to obtain the book in time I would have made specific reference to some of Langer's statements about speech and symbolism. Particularly relevant to my problem is her emphasis on the advantages of small sounds made with part of one's own body as a medium for symbol formation. One of these advantages is the intrinsic unimportance, in their own right, of these sounds. This relates to my point about the effectiveness of the toys as a medium for thought and communication being due to their pliability, that is, that their real qualities are unimportant for practical expedient living, so they can be given arbitrary or conventional meanings and thus be used as a language. I would also like to have elaborated on the relation of Langer's conception of the function of symbols to Jung's *Psychological Types* (1933, London: Kegan Paul), and to have considered the bearing of both on the material presented here.

20 Eissler (1951) An Unknown Autobiographical Letter by Freud and a Short Comment. *International Journal of Psycho-Analysis* 32: 319–24.

1955: The communication of primary sensual experience

The yell of joy

I have already written something about these two patients, the one called Ruth in the postscript to 'The Role of Illusion in Symbol Formation' (see Chapter 9) and Susan, whose experience with toys I have already described (see Chapter 6), although here she is called 'Miss A'. In this paper I tried to combine something of what I had learnt from both Ruth and Susan through their drawings.

The aim of this paper is to present some drawings from two patients of mine – a child, Ruth, and an adult, Miss A, both suffering from acute social anxieties. Ruth's drawings were made between the ages of 10 and 13, Miss A's when she was 28; Ruth's were all made during the sessions, Miss A's mostly between the sessions. Miss A made over 4,000 drawings during a period of about nine months, when she was in an extremely regressed state. She said she did not think while drawing what she was drawing.

In discussing the drawings I shall not be talking about the reparative aspect of them, but about the light they throw on the specific problem of how love and joy is to be expressed, communicated. I shall be talking about the interplay betwen the wish to communicate, to share feelings, and the strivings after primary narcissistic states; and how this interplay is shown in the drawings, in the specific fields, both of anal erotism and that part of oral erotism which has to do with the use of the voice and facial expression.

Both these patients made drawings showing something special

happening to the body boundary; it is either blurred or multiple or radiant or luminous: for instance, a duck (*Figure 3*) drawn by Miss A

Figure 3

and representing herself. Miss A told me that she had, at the age of 20, experienced very intense sensations spreading over her body, which made her feel luminous and transparent. She said that other people noticed something happening in her and said she looked beautiful; she insisted that whatever it was that happened, it had nothing to do with sexuality. She also drew very many flower-like shapes radiating from the centre, the centre being occasionally a mouth, as in *Figure 4* (p. 116), or an eye. Although she described the luminous states as having to do with 'beauty', she seemed uncertain whether they sprang from love or hate. In fact she remembered saying at the time that love and hate were the same thing, but no one had understood her. When I said that perhaps she had meant that the love and the hate oscillated so quickly that she could not distinguish them, she said, 'Yes, of course I meant that.'

Figure 4

Figure 5 shows one of her drawings made in the session, and it does in fact oscillate between being a full face with a lock of hair down the middle and two profiles facing each other. Clifford Scott has discussed oscillation phenomena in terms of the swing between love and hate. When Miss A made this drawing I began to consider whether the fact that it oscillates between one face and two might not mean that it represents the swing between: on the one hand, the wish for the discriminated state, recognition of separateness, and therefore experience of the series – instinct tension, need, demand, satisfaction; and, on the other hand, the wish for fusion, oneness, the oceanic

116

Figure 5

Figure 6

Figure 7

feeling, or the state of cosmic bliss. The term cosmic bliss is Scott's, but I believe Miss A had her own 'word' for it ('word' in inverted commas since her drawings can be looked upon as a primitive ideographic language); I think *Figure 6* (p. 117) is her word for cosmic bliss. If this is true then one might say that what the full face pole of the oscillation means to her is depicted in this drawing: clearly it has also to do with the satisfied sleep.

Scott uses the term 'catastrophic chaos' for the opposite of cosmic bliss, and *Figure 7* (p. 117) shows, I suggest, a visual equivalent of such a concept, for this patient had been given ECT with disastrous results, and this drawing does seem to represent her phantasy of the fit. It does therefore represent the other half of the pole from the primary unity, because for her this is what happens when she faces duality and object relationship. Repressed memories of screaming are important in her analysis; and in this drawing the focus of feeling is clearly the mouth. She says that since the ECT her hands no longer feel like hands, and this is interesting, since a scream is a kind of hand – it reaches out and bridges space. I have evidence that the fit does partly represent a scream, also that she has great uncertainty whether the scream is one of maximum joy or maximum pain and hate.

Ruth shows how the striving to bridge space can be expressed by the kiss (*Figure 8*), and she deals with the boundary problem by giving the boy and girl only one boundary between the two of them. This drawing also oscillates; it is hard to see it steadily as two profiles, interest flickers from one to the other. It is almost as if a bite were taken out of one or the other so that the bitten one becomes merely background. Thus the oscillation here seems to be whether to kiss or to bite.

Miss A did another oscillating drawing (*Figure 9*, p. 120), in which the top profile, the non-oscillating one, has a multiple boundary (Miss A continually told me that since the ECT she had had no boundary to her head, she could not tell where it stopped; also that she had no face). *Figure 10* (p. 120) is a tracing of the oscillating part so that it can be seen more clearly; in it there are three overlapping circles, which oscillate between the central full face (eyes, nose, mouth) and at least two faces in profile which also themselves oscillate. Owing to the overlap of the circles there is only one nose – either one of the profiles can have it or the other, but not both. There is a third possibility, however – if neither has it, the profiles become no longer perfect circles, but much nearer the reality of the human profile. Thus I think that the perfect circle here represents the undifferentiated state, and to become human one has as it were to take a bite out of the circle, that is to limit perfection. *Figure 11*

Figure 8

(p. 121) shows one of Miss A's drawings which, as I see it, is vividly expressive of her need for an extremely protective environment if the dawning differentiated consciousness of duality is to emerge without catastrophe.

Miss A is not yet well; but the child made a very good recovery, and I am showing some of her drawings because she seemed to me to be struggling with some of the same problems as Miss A, though not so ill. The drawings chosen are to illustrate how the strength of her desire for the undifferentiated oceanic state (which is fulfilled temporarily in the orgasm) affected her social relations and made her terrified of showing maximum joyful appreciation. I think the material indicates how, in the longing for the oceanic state, there is fear that the longed-for total lack of differentiation will be achieved and will spread to the various body openings; thus there will be confusion between them and their products, with socially disastrous results. *Figure 12* (p. 122) shows the first of her drawings which expressed for me the essence of this problem.

After the first two days of analysis Ruth had refused to speak to me in the sessions, for ten months; all direct verbal communication had been by writing notes, usually on lavatory paper, and dropping them down behind her for me to pick up; though she also sang songs, wrote messages and poetry on the walls, and scribbled and drew pictures. But although she had persistently refused to speak to me in the playroom, she had repeatedly, on leaving, turned back at

119

Figure 9

Figure 10

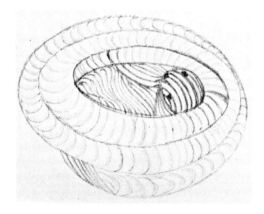

Figure 11

my gate and shouted, with the utmost intensity, 'Good-bye Stinker!' Also she had persisted in secretly writing, both on my gate and front porch, in indelible pencil, 'Stinker lives here.'

All this time she had been attacking me physically in every possible way; but interpretations of this behaviour in terms of aggression for not receiving the love that she wanted had had no effect. It was only gradually that she made me see that the crucial battle was over how she was to communicate her love, how she was to convey her pleasure, not her anger. Thus she made me see that she was the little black dog who wanted to wag her tail, who wanted to use her bottom rather than her top to express appreciation.

When in the tenth month Ruth suddenly began to talk, it was after I had interpreted her fear that the breath that came out of her mouth when she spoke would stink like the gas which came out of her bottom. Before this she had drawn on the wall a picture of herself, as an infant, with her father, they were saying 'Hello' to each other. Thus I was now able to show her that her acute anxiety in the early months of analysis had been linked with her fear of her inability to locate the stinker in herself, to decide that it lived in her bottom and not in her top, and with the fear of having her appreciative noise, her 'Hello, Daddy' rejected because it came from her bottom, was a tail-wagging and not a tongue-wagging. In fact it is the fear of her wish for the undifferentiated state in which there is no difference between her bottom and her top. And perhaps no difference between the love gift and the person it is given to; for after her thirteenth birthday, when grumbling over the difficulty of deciding what to say in 'Thank you' letters, I found she had scribbled on the paper, 'Dear Smell, I hope you're well.'

121

Figure 12

After drawing on the walls she had gradually settled down to drawing on paper and then to painting. But here a ritual began. At the end of each session in which she painted she tried to hurl the paint water full in my face. Interpretations in terms of aggression did not stop this; but when I interpreted in terms of the problem of the tail-wagging, it did stop, and also the type of drawing changed. After months of drawing and painting, either just faces, or isolated figures like fashion-plates, she now produced a picture filling the whole paper; it was of a fountain made with free brush movements and no previous drawing. (It is not shown here as it needs reproduction in colour.) I saw this picture as marking the accomplishment of mourning for a double loss; one, the having to give up the use of her own body product, her urine, as a medium for expressing her appreciation and joy in loving; and two, the having to give up the joy she had once had of feeling she was actually urinating on to her mother, which also meant into her mother. In fact she had now accepted symbols, both for the loving urination (and defaecation) and for the object of it. She had accepted the paper instead of my skin and the paint and paint water instead of urine and faeces; also at the same time she had now accepted the disillusion that the lovely bodily mess was not literally as lovely as the feelings experienced in making it.

Later she drew several pictures of boys expressing appreciation of

Figure 13

girls by a wolf whistle; *Figure 13* is one in which the nipple itself is shown as the object of appreciation. So here it was possible to show her more clearly how the love-call, love poem, serenade, which uses breath for the communication of feeling, had had its earlier versions in the stink from the stinker, and in the wetting which was a silent version of the loving shout or yell.

Now she became able to paint a picture showing the use of the whole body, rather than its products, for the expression of joyful feelings; she painted a gay and graceful dancing girl, all in colour. Following this it eventually became possible to interpret the inhibition of her masturbation, and she began to experiment at nights and tell me about it: she also began to tell me of conscious day-dreams about her father's penis. At this time her main pre-occupation was that she wanted to talk what she called gibberish to me, but was too frightened. Finally she forced herself to try, and succeeded in singing to me what she called a gibberish song. It began with nonsense syllables and ended with 'Hey-bo, Ho-bo, mine's the best by far-bo'; 'Bobo' was her name for her genital and I interpreted this song as standing for the yell of joy and triumph in the climax of her masturbatory dance. I also interpreted how frightened she was of letting me hear it, because it was linked with day-dreams about her father, and so stood for triumphing over mother and sisters and me; it was the triumphant claim that 'her's was the best by far-bo.'

Miss A, I think, also showed the same kind of problem when she produced a drawing which was half woman, half 'cello (*Figure 14*, p. 124); for here the multiple boundary suggests the orgastic oceanic state, but the shape of it suggests a female genital. Thus the drawing

123

Figure 14

seems to me to introduce the idea of the connection between musical sound and masturbation; that is the link between genital sensual experience and the cry of joy by which it is made known to the world. (This patient is deeply musical but can hardly listen to concerts for fear that she will scream or perhaps wet herself.) She has an inhibition of genital orgasm, and when the drawings were made suffered acute vaginismus and frigidity.

For Miss A the idea that she might want to scream in the session was utterly terrifying. She did however one day produce a drawing which, in the original, can be seen as using the blackness of the pencil to its maximum intensity (*Figure 15*); it shows a piano-like form and a piercing nail. Thus the drawing can be seen as depicting the intensity of her struggle against the all-out yell or scream; and it makes the link between the all-out yell and the all-out mess, the blackness of the faecal marks having become the silent representative

124

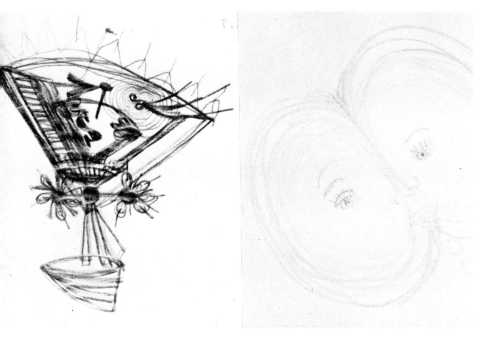

Figure 15   *Figure 16*

of the repressed yell, as well as standing for the intensity of the anal feelings in their own right.

Miss A also did a drawing showing explicitly the confusion between mouth and anus (*Figure 16*), and also another (*Figure 17*, p. 126) showing, I suggest, the effect of this confusion in the inhibition of the use of the mouth and the face for the expression of feeling; for the little creature in the drawing has a bound-up face. She also did many drawings (*Figure 18*, p. 127, is an example) in which both the idealization of the faeces is expressed, as shown here by the halo, and also her sense of the hypocrisy of her apparent submission to the social evaluation of them, for she said that the right-hand figure was a devil and full of pretence.

There was one drawing (*Figure 19*, p. 127), often repeated, which showed a dancing figure; it never had any feet, only breast-like shapes, and it always seems to be trying to reach backwards to its own anus. Miss A also produced a whole series of drawings in which it seems to me that she is trying to sort out what my child patient would call 'the stinker' from 'the stink'; that is to sort out the psychic reality of the sensual experience in the urethra and anus, while

125

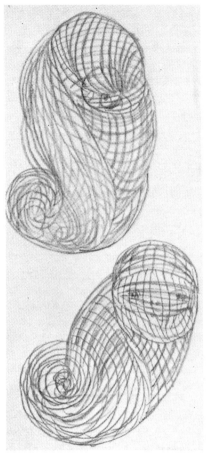

Figure 17

urinating and defaecating from the actual products of these organs –
and from the external object which stimulates these organs to loving
or hateful activity. I think they also show the stages by which
transfer of interest occurs from the anus, as an instrument for the
expression of communication of, feeling, to the face. *Figures 20–25*,
pp. 128–9, show a few selected examples from the series.

They were made at first entirely in thick brown paint, and started
with leaf-like dancing faecal shapes whirling round a circular centre
(*Figure 20*). Gradually the shapes coalesce into something approaching a
dancing human figure (*Figures 21* and *22*). But now a second element
appears – she used two colours here, brown and yellow (*Figures 23*),
and it begins to look like a dancing couple. And now the doubleness
theme is developed so that *Figure 24* shows a mask-like shape in

Figure 18

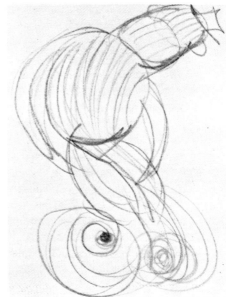

Figure 19

which the empty spaces have become eyes and mouths – and they have expression. There were many similar drawings, sometimes like a plate, sometimes like a mask. In fact Miss A seemed to be developing the idea of something in front and something behind, and the something behind is peeping through, it is lively. And now this theme again branches out into two directions. One series becomes a jug-like shape with holes (*Figure 25*), the idea of a container and a contained. But then the jug shape itself becomes face-like (*Figure 26*, p. 130) though also with plate-like qualities. In fact something very intense, full of complex human feeling, is beginning to shine through. And finally she gives the drawing a name. She says, 'It's my mother.'

Looking at it now, I seem to have left out of this paper a very important part of Ruth's play (perhaps because it did not include a drawing) in which she would repeatedly make as if to throw a brick through the playroom window. I had tried interpreting this in terms of various aspects of her aggression towards me, but this had made no difference. One day I happened to mention it to Clifford Scott, who said, 'Doesn't she want to know whether her first intercourse will hurt?' I said this to her, and after that there were no more brick-throwing gestures.

Figure 20

Figure 21

Figure 22

Figure 24

Figure 23

Figure 25

Figure 26

Attending to the background

Some time after giving this last paper it was suggested to me that a further study of some of the drawings shown there, made by Ruth and Susan, would be useful. Apparently I did not send this new study for publication and it is not even dated but I do feel it contains many hints of what I was learning from my patients and myself during these years. I therefore feel it should be published here as a contribution to the main thread of this book, though in a shortened form and modified order.

When I tried to clarify the wider context in which I was seeing some of the drawings, I could see in many of them aspects of the awareness of an undifferentiated background, whether inner or outer, and the relation of this to the rhythms of bodily experiences.

What I have called the oscillating drawings are those in which the attention of the viewer swings from one profile to another, with the other becoming, recurrently, only the background, taken for

130

granted. Susan (Miss A) made many forms of this symbol. But there are other drawings in which there is no oscillation, though there is a depicted background, for instance the 'Man in the Moon' picture (*Figure 6*) where the background is a holding one, made by the form of the moon; but since the man in it seems to be asleep one could try saying that here is depicted the extreme state of unawareness of the outer background, though the inner one may be present in the consciousness of the sleeping man, in the form of the dream-screen background to a dream; if so it appears to be a happy dream, judging by the smile on the face of the man. But Susan's association to the moon was that it sucks up the earth.

In the 'Baby Seal' picture (*Figure 11*, p. 121) the holding environment or background is again shown but here what is contained in it is no longer asleep. Also, although the baby looks cosy there is a hint of a python in the encircling coils, as if the background were not entirely to be trusted to give the baby enough space to breathe; it might even be crushed in the coils. And here arose the question, what do the rhythmic lines on both the serpent-like coil and the baby really represent? I now guessed that they stood for the basic body rhythms, the rhythmic pulse of breathing and the heart-beat, both the baby's and the mother's, with a smaller rhythm for the baby's, also the rhythm of being rocked in one's mother's arms.

In the 'Cello Woman' (*Figure 14*, p. 124) there is also the rhythmic line forming a kind of nest; and, since the theme of music comes in, there could be some connection with the spreading of flatus, both in sound and smell (cf. Ruth's play about 'Stinker lives here'). Clearly too there is some masturbatory reference.

In 'Piano and Dagger' (*Figure 15*, p. 125) rhythm also appears in the alternating black and white keys of the piano. But here it looks as if the pressure of frustrated instinct, which could lead to a scream (symbolized visually by the dagger) is coming in as part of what was one of Susan's problems, the inability to play the piano, since the ECT. Also I thought this pointed, not only to the body rhythms of masturbation, as well as of speech, but also to the rhythms of walking, running, dancing. For, according to Susan, her mother said she had not let either of her daughters walk till they were 2 years old, so that their legs would be straight. If only partially true this meant that Susan must often have been strapped in her pram while all the time longing to experiment with independence. Thus it seemed likely that the energy of such blocked longings could only go into masturbatory activities, and angry ones at that; hence, I thought, the piercing dagger directed towards the helpless body form that seems to be lying on top of the piano.

Associated with the theme of music-making was not only the idea of sounds produced by the mouth, or the anus, but also, I thought, memories of the musical sounds of urinating into the pot, in contrast with the silence of using a nappy. I even wondered whether the flowing lines surrounding the 'Cello Woman', like ripples in a pond, could also reflect the body sensations of the flowing, expanding warmth produced when the urine spreads through the nappy, a self-created warm pool, even a memory that could be merged with the actual warm holding background given by the mother's lap and arms.

Included in this question of what is symbolized by the rhythmic puddle of lines, like ripples in water, there must be also, as I have said, the idea of the ebb and flow of breathing. However, since the them of music is being discussed, there is not only its rhythmic aspect to be considered but also the fact that the sound of it, like the air it permeates, is without a spatial boundary. Here I thought of how Susan had said that after the ECT she felt she had no boundaries, everything was her so the bombs were bound to fall on her.

In the first paragraph of the 'Yell of Joy' paper I had said that it was to do with the interplay between the wish to communicate, to share feelings, and the striving after what I there called primary narcissistic states. I now wanted to restate this in terms of an unease about the adequacy of the concept of primary narcissism in this context. Certainly there was here, I thought, a partial to-and-fro interplay between the wish for active encounter with the outside world, with the 'other' and the wish to retreat into a world of non-encounter, a state in which one does not want to be bothered with demands from the environment, which is known to be there but is needed only in a supplying and holding role; it should have no needs of its own.[1]

Whatever the word used to describe the non-encounter state, there is also certainly a problem to do with the transition process from this state to the one of full encounter.[2] In all of Susan's oscillating pictures there is, because of their visual structure, no smooth transition from one view to the other; in fact, as I have said in the paper, in *Figures 9* and *10* (p. 120), when one side is seen as a profile there is a bit taken out of the other. Certainly, to be disturbed when in a state of reverie or deeply concentrated play can feel to be a shock, a sudden shrinking or lessening of one's size, because of the jerk into full consciousness of separateness and realistic encounter. By contrast, in *Figure 5* (p. 117), where the oscillation is between two profiles separated by a lock of hair and one full face with the lock of hair down the middle, the lock of hair does in fact create a space between the two profiles and there is no 'biting' in the oscillation. It is interesting that this drawing was done by Susan during the session and a long time after the other ones shown in the paper. Thus it seemed to me now that this drawing could be seen as expressing her belief that, as a result of a long period of analysis, she and I, patient and analyst, would eventually be able to meet face to face with a breathing space between us and hence room for spontaneity and growth.

It was interesting that, years later, Susan became able to play, not only on paper, but in a direct relation to me and in the loaded situation of saying goodbye at the door; she had suddenly seized my hand on an ordinary day (hand-shaking was usually for the beginning and end of holidays) and said, with a twinkle in her eye and a party voice, 'Goodbye, *so* glad to have met you.'

By contrast with her new sense of relaxed freedom to play in relationship, the profile head, at the top of *Figure 9*, all surrounded by spikes, suggests a state of expected persecution (from the background) and a need for aggressive defence which is far indeed from the state of confidence and trust in which play alone is possible.

There is another aspect of the drawings, that is the humour in them. There is certainly humour in *Figure 3* (p. 115), 'Duck with a Hat on', but here I think the fun in it has a marked defensive quality, for I had come to see that the hat and the beak together create dangerous-looking crocodile jaws.

There is also a background of humour in the mocking submission of the devil in *Figure 18*, which is drawn just beside what looks like a foetal dragon or winged tadpole. Here I speculated whether the winged tadpole with its halo did not stand for the intensity of the creative potential that she was aware of in herself. I wondered also whether the halo (a symbol that she often used again) could not stand for the manic phase of the creative swing, like the full circle face in the overlapping circles drawings, the phase in which the opposites are temporarily transcended, self and other, seer and seen, are fused into one harmonious whole. In these terms too her little devil's pretence of submission, playing at humility, suggested to me the possibility of the healthful beginning of recognizing what is perhaps an inevitable split in the ego (as Freud suggested in his last unfinished paper),[3] something that I thought Susan could have been partly aware of when she used to grumble that the amount of social conformity that she did manage to achieve was 'only behaving', that is not truly spontaneous. It was almost as if she were claiming that everybody's adult living should be always as carefree and spontaneous as the infant state where the mother provides all the caring. But the recognition that social living does require a learned adaptation that is not spontaneous and yet that the spontaneity need not be totally denied and repudiated seemed to me to be shown in the many mask forms she produced (for instance *Figure 24*). In many of them there seemed to be something lively and mischievous peeping through.

From this standpoint too one could try looking at Ruth's painting of the fountain as depicting a growing sense of the abundance of the uprising source of life in her. And this in its turn, surely closely linked with her sense of the flow of love given to her, through the years of analysis, the experience of having the analyst's exclusive attention to her play in the analytic session. For she did say, shortly before she stopped, that her analysis was the best thing that had ever happened to her.

As for Susan's pictures (*Figures 20* and *21*, p. 128) of whirling, leaf-like shapes with something emerging from a centre which is at first an empty (that is undifferentiated) core, I came to look at this as perhaps depicting that very inner matrix from which emerges the awareness of feelings. It was as if she were depicting the 'booming, buzzing confusion' of what the inner matrix, the as-yet undifferentiated inner experience of the body, feels like when first faced and out of which crystallizes an image, an impulse or a wish, if this initial chaos can be tolerated.

Figure 12 (p. 122) suggests that what might be about to emerge could be pretty fierce.

In the picture Susan called 'My Mother' (*Figure 26*, p. 130), which in its coloured form is a beautiful work of art, she did seem to be showing that, through the work of making the drawings and bringing them to me she had at least glimpsed the possibility of moving beyond the phase where the 'other' is taken for granted, as only background, to the phase of recognizing me as mother, as a whole person, and existing in my own right. For the picture is full of complex feeling; though based on a jug-form, it is half like a lion but also half human, the animal and the human seem to be integrated; and there is also both joy and sadness, for there are tears in the eyes but the mouth is smiling, although the head is full of holes. This it really did seem to me to represent, if only momentarily achieved, a restored self and a restored object, both in their wholeness of encompassing the opposites of feeling. It also seemed to be a very subtle portrait of my own state of mind throughout many phases in the battle of the analysis.

In short, it is a face that has an inside; for the eyes are shown as not just peeping out on the world as in the 'Baby Seal', unaware of what is behind them, but now are in contact both with the outer world and the inner one, and this in contrast with what Susan said about her state after the ECT, that she was 'shot forward' and 'no longer behind her eyes'. Thus this drawing, since the face is still partly a jug (and is a development of other jug drawings she did) seemed to depict, not only the idea of the feeding breast, but also the growing concept of herself as a container, including the idea of the self as open to its own body sources. Thus the picture did suggest to me that, in making it, she was showing that she had become able, at times at least, to make use of me as a mother substitute who has worked through the sadness of being a separate person,[4] enough to allow her, my analytic child, a space in which to be; in contrast with her actual mother who had never reached this stage, who had therefore been more like a python, crushing her daughter's separate individuality by not reliably recognizing its existence.

It semed to me also that in some of these drawings not only is there a struggle to achieve a recognition of space, both an inner space, and a surrounding space, or a space between two, but also there is depicted a struggle with time. For I began to see how the oscillation of the two profiles emphasizes by its very oscillation, which happens in time, the passing of time, and therefore the basic biological rhythms, (inbreathe–outbreathe, fullness–emptiness, hunger–satiation, and so on) which in fact do organize time. However, in many of these oscillating pictures, as I have said, the viewer experiences an uneasy rhythm, a sudden jerk from one view to the other, so they could perhaps be depicting a state of fighting against the biological rhythms? By contrast, Ruth's little black dog picture with his wagging (oscillating) tail, wagging in time, is perhaps nearest to depicting the idea of a natural rhythm.

As for the way in which play branches out into the cultural phenomena of celebration, both these patients liked drawing flags – Union Jacks – which I did come to see as likely to be expressing their intuition of the orgiastic fusion of the opposites, of self and other, and the joy in this, the mutual celebration of joy in differences by an act of merging,[5] as well as symbolizing the inner parents eventually allowed to come together.

In this connection too, I thought that Ruth's water-colour picture of a girl dancing was not only an accepted day-dream of satisfying exhibitionist desires, but also an intuition of a state when the whole body feels flooded with consciousness, every bit of the body felt to be cathected even to the fingertips, nothing held back, in fact, 'soul and body meet again'.

Clearly too, this theme relates to orgiastic experiences and therefore, I thought, to the spreading, radiating lines in many of Susan's drawings. Although in these particular ones the waves seem

135

to be externalized, in other drawings, made later than these, she used another symbol, an open flower form, which she would put in various parts of the body of whatever she happened to be drawing – usually it was a duck.

The spreading puddle theme could also be seen in terms of the process by which the psyche lets itself dissolve; for this reminded me of how the boy, Simon, had liked to fill a tin with all sorts of ingredients (calling it 'the fire cup') and melt them down to an undifferentiated whole. Especially too, how he would light a whole bundle of candles and let them burn down into a soft puddle of wax (see Chapter 9).

Thus it seemed to me that he really did know something about the need for a recurrent psychic loss of his masculine assertive consciousness, as when he would often melt the lead soldier, saying, 'There has to be a victim, a sacrifice'. I even came to see this as, amongst other things, standing for his intuition that, in creative process, there does have to be the willingness recurrently to sacrifice, let go, the differentiating consciousness.

During the years before I wrote the 'Yell of Joy' paper, there had been many developments in the field of combined physiotherapy and psychotherapy on the subject of deliberate muscular relaxation; for instance, it has been observed (beginning with Darwin)[6] that directing attention to a particular muscle from inside does by itself cause the muscle to relax, apart from specific blocks to do with repressed fantasies, memories, or feelings, which as Reich pointed out,[7] tend in their turn to emerge into consciousness when the relaxation is achieved.

So I came to wonder whether Susan's drawings of open flower forms, as well as the spreading radiating lines, might not be her ways of trying to communicate the sensations of muscular relaxation.

In conclusion, I can say that, through these patients' play with a pliable medium, I had been able to watch something of the process by which they externalized, threw out of themselves on to the paper, marks which, because of the pliable character of the medium, could take on an infinite variety of shape and thus provide a feedback, a basis for communication, both with the analyst and with themselves. I had come to see how the medium, for instance, paint, by its special qualities of spreadability and the way it allows one colour to mix up with another and so make a new one, and because it does not intrude its demands, but just waits, submitting to things done to it, waits for the painter to become more and more sensitive to its real qualities and capacities; by this means it does for the painter, I believed, some of the things that a good mother does for her baby.

I have tried to show how these two patients could be seen as having been able to externalize this inner encounter, through their willingness to enter into an active relation with the blankness of the paper, as well as through the pliable medium of paint, chalk, water. Also, in the light of Susan's later drawings and my analysis of them, I had come to see how the drawings shown here did foreshadow the later working through of the problems they symbolized, but now in relation to the more complex reality of encounter with me, the analyst, as a whole person. Thus it could be said that, in order to achieve this, it had first been necessary for her to go through the stage of relating to me as the primary substances of the media she used, substances which, by their pliability, gave her something near to the illusions of primary omnipotence, for here I remembered Simon's insistence that I was his 'lovely stuff' that he had made.

I have also tried to show ways in which I have come to make use of the symbols Susan offered me, not only the oscillating profiles, but also a simpler form, that shown in the centre of *Figure 10* (p. 120), the overlapping of two circles, and use it as the basis of a model for thinking about the relation between two persons, about the need for an area of overlap in which there is a partial fusion of interest, a bit of common ground.

In short, over the years, I have been discovering more and more, both in my patients and in myself, about the mind's capacities for making deliberate contact with its own background, and the sometimes startling effects of this meeting of mind and body; included in the term background there is not only the background of inner space, but also that of inner silence that is the background to all noise, and that can bring with it, when it is made contact with, the silencing of the inner chatter of daily preoccupations together with the deep sense of renewal of vital energies (Ruth's fountain?).

Thus, included in this I found myself more and more attending to the varying qualities of the silences, between me and my patient, within the sessions.

Viewers' comments on a patient's drawings (1960–65)

Off and on during the following years I tried out an experimental study, asking various analysts and some non-analysts to visit me, individually, and (with promises of anonymity) give me their spontaneous responses to certain selected drawings from those made by Susan. I had the idea that these viewers' responses might perhaps reveal certain ideas not yet formulated in recognized psychoanalytic theory, as well as revealing something of the basic approaches of the various psychoanalytic groups.

I did not get to the stage of making a paper of my findings because I became absorbed by feeling the need to write a whole book about the part Susan's drawings played in her analysis, a book that was eventually published in 1969 under the title of *The Hands of the Living God*. However, I feel that some of the viewers' comments on the drawings shown in the first section of this chapter may throw interesting light on the different approaches of analysts from different theoretical backgrounds as well as helping me in my own thinking.

My choice of viewers was rather haphazard; often I asked someone I happened to be talking to if I thought he or she might be interested. There is only one of the Anna Freud viewers because, owing to the group divisions, I knew very few of this group. Some of the viewers must have heard or read my original 'Yell of Joy' paper and so knew something about the patient while others did not. As for the order in which the drawings were shown, I let the viewers pick those they were most interested in out of a pile. In this third section I have put the comments on the drawings in the order in which Susan did them whereas in the first section of this chapter their order was determined by the idea I was trying to formulate.

I have also added four drawings not shown in the 'Yell of Joy' paper, one, that I called the 'Post-ECT Drawing' (*Figure 27*), was made a few days after she had had the ECT in November 1943, and the first night in the house of the people who were going to give her a home and had arranged for her to come to me for analysis. However, she did not in fact bring it to me, or tell me about it, till nearly nine years later in January 1952 and after she had made all the drawings shown here.

The second one I have added is called 'Man Exhibiting his Buttocks' (*Figure 28*, p. 141), made a few months after she first began to draw, in June 1950. I have to put it in because of the great contrast of mood, from the, as I saw it, agonized despair of the 'Post-ECT Drawing' compared with this quality of bland mockery, as well as for its anal theme. Incidentally it is the first of her drawings to show the overlapping circles motif that was to be used many times. It also reminded me of the bottoms-up little pigs in her play with the toys.

The third one, called 'Spider Creating its Web' (*Figure 36*, p. 156), seemed important enough to be included because of the very interesting viewers' comments. The fourth drawing is called 'Geometric Head' (*Figure 40*, p. 161).

Post-ECT drawing

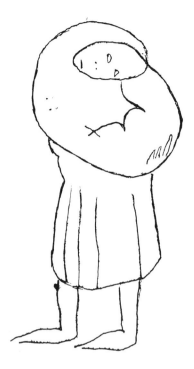

Figure 27   Post-ECT drawing

INDEPENDENTS

D.W.D. (male)
It is terribly sad, as if that which envelops one is felt to be not really stably based in itself – or perhaps it is felt to be not anchored in something which is safely based in itself.

T.E.F. (female)
No good trying to hold her own heart, as if she had it in her arms.

Y.G.H. (male)
Womb-like cradle, arms undifferentiated, folds of inside of the womb. Embracing arms as a protection, womb-like, being held by arms which, at this moment, is more important to her than breasts; it's being carried.

L.G.H. (female)
The mother and child are one so that personal identity has been lost. Also, with the head on one side, there is someone's view of the world at an odd angle.

JUNGIAN

S.E.P. (female)
Dreadful, utterly defeated, somehow carrying her own head; arms or breasts encircle the head.

KLEINIAN

A.K.L. (female)
Head jammed into her body, she's both the womb and the baby inside the womb, the ECT as a huge trauma preventing her either staying inside or being born. Very great anxiety about being in a world of bits and pieces, both the internal mother and herself in bits, very great confusion which bits are hers and which bits are mother's. So squashed, any attempt at integration brings squashing.

S.O.P. (female)
Almost enfolding herself . . . what a face, how terrible.

A.K.L. (female)
All to do with the quest for safety, stability. Here there is folding in, she never had her mother's safe arms, the arm itself is life going on. The quest for eternal life as the only stability. Every stage means a giving up, that is accepting mortality; all change, like beginning menstruation, or menopause, any development leads to death. There's such an idealization of life in the womb. If not pushed out by the children inside, its paradise, which is then projected into mother's womb phantasies, and heaven . . . in reality one lives in one's children, there's continuity and 'eternal life'.

Being born means being shot out, either by another baby or by father's penis. Shot out of the inner world, mother, womb, eternal life, shot out into space. Safety is in the inner world mother. When shot out and taken to the breast there is no protection.

NON-ANALYSTS

T.S.T. (painter and head of an art school/male)
Very good, amazingly good, frightfully good, requires no comment. Absolutely original.

Man exhibiting his buttocks

KLEINIAN

N.R.S. (male)
Basically something hostile and omnipotent, ridiculing and yet helpless, shitting, but, by the drawing, it becomes idealized, into 'Look how clever I am!' A denial of basic impotence to communicate. Has movement in it.

NON–ANALYST

N.G.H. (writer, teacher of psychology of art/male)
A reproduction of primitive sexual experiences, eyes transplanted to tail, looking is done with bottom.

Figure 28 Man exhibiting his buttocks

Devils, chrysalises
(Named 'devils' and 'chrysalises' by the patient)

ANNA FREUDIAN

A.D.L. (female)
These are attempts to conceptualize confusion, all these lines, very obsessional, the supportive skeleton that obsessional thinking is for containing psychosis. Her chief idea is merging.

INDEPENDENTS

L.G.R. (female)
Like Leonardo da Vinci, hair-waves. Terribly concerned with drawing the value of little bits, say, of herself, because lovingly drawn, though not yet put together and become anything. Feeling psychoanalysis as a place where she can treasure little bits, fragmented bits of herself, things you have to face losing, hair, (waves?), theme of Faust, sold her soul to the devil for love of her psychotherapist and the quick reward, too proud to become as a child.

JUNGIAN

S.E.F. (female)
So alive, so near to people.

L.M.N. (male)
So intensely organized although only bits.

Figure 29   Devils, chrysalises

142

KLEINIAN

A.L.M. (female)
Entirely inside mother's body, conceived of as in pieces, some of them hostile, herself in pieces, one may be an angel, when she idealizes and makes a saint of them, that is the real devil.

N.R.S. (male)
Like primitive persecutory ju–ju, or food, hidden, seeds, coconuts, most unusual, all very well-formed stools, hair, and faeces, the mutilated objects inside, very minute scrutiny to find the objects they contain, heads and hair, very strange, so different for obsessional doodling, very paranoid, a very ill person.

NON–ANALYSTS

T.S.T. (painter and art teacher/male)
Would be proud of these himself, their origin not obvious, not a single one is stupid, by no means. They show a great urge to express, and not observation so much as integrity of feeling.

R.R.S. (painter and art teacher/female)
The most intense and the most obscure, such vitality.

N.Z.O. (painter and professor of painting/male)
Very good artistically, originality . . . able to produce form, nothing accidental.

Baby seal (p. 144)

INDEPENDENTS

L.G.H. (female)
The foetus, seeking to start again with the analyst. She has her eye on me, schizoids do that. Whatever she has got inside, a sort of nexus of consciousness almost guiding her through the ups and downs of being ill and trying to turn illness into something creative. A centre of awareness that guides one's way through, like 'Who dreams the dream?' And, in terms of the foetus, question of whether to be the baby or find the inner eye.

A.E.F. (female)
Rather nice, (laughs) intrauterine, of course, on couch and well held. The nest is a bit bowel like.

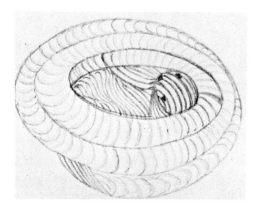

Figure 30   Baby seal

D.T.U. (male)
Smug, has a quality of being pleasant, starts off as a sensuous experience but allowed to have a development into a kind of integrated object built up out of small experiences; a suggestion of an animal's face and paw so the whole thing in the end could be an animal with a long tail curled round itself and therefore seen to be protected and comfortable.

Y.G.H. (male)
In something shell-like which one imagines could be become a prison, but it looks cosy inside.

JUNGIAN

S.E.F. (female)
Beautifully comfortable, shut in, not ready to come out.

D.K.L. (female)
Kundilini snake, coiled up energy.

L.M.N. (male)
The awakening self, very intense, Jung would say enveloped in the snake that eats itself.

KLEINIAN

A.K.L. (female)
Quest for safety, stability, never had mother's safe arms.

S.O.P. (female)
Wrapped up in its couch, pathetic.

NON–ANALYST

N.Z.O. (professor of painting/male)
Very sensitive, interfolding shape, like a snake curled up. Very three-dimensional but the space is ambiguous. Where the head comes there is a disturbance in the quiet folding – in, suddenly a disturbance, a distortion of space, it's no longer a coil, suddenly there is a jerk, the space is destroyed, the coil turns into a sudden wall.
   There is beauty in the cavity, a place to rest, but one is uncomfortable with the outside, the coil gets lost, both inside and at the bottom end, the animal is flat, a flattening.
[1986 comment: I noticed that what this painter perceived, although he had no experience of psychoanalysis, was the trauma hidden in the formal qualities of the picture, the sudden jerk, the disturbance of space.]

Z.L.M. (painter/male)
Just a symbol, a creature lost in the labyrinth of its own body, captive there.

N.G.H. (writer on art/male)
Rather beautiful, very striking, some animal in a phallic womb.

T.S.T. (painter and teacher of painting/male)
Snake curled up, very clever, wonderful, not a single line superfluous, very like, close to, a mad woman's drawing he has seen.

Profile Madonna (p. 146)

INDEPENDENTS

Y.G.H. (male)
There are two centres, one in the head and one in the middle, from which she is organizing herself. There is a condensation of breast, buttocks, anus, genital. It is ambiguous what is defending and what is defended against.

35 (viewer's name lost, probably Independent)
Cruelty of a hail of little bullets, children are contained in the uterus structure but the uterus is armed and violent, the top face is smiling

145

Figure 31   Profile Madonna

but also armed. Could be that she has something beautiful inside which she has to defend.

L.G.H. (female)
She is trying to discover who she is, and other people, in her inner world, so quick changes of identification.

I.N.D. (male)
It shows stages of development of the breast theme, the breasts put in as babies' heads.

146

T.E.F. (female)
Doesn't see it as oscillating, never can, thinks feelings don't oscillate, they happen both at once.

JUNGIAN

S.E.F. (female)
The top half shows a sort of pride. The bottom half terribly imprisoned, like the inner world. Also multiple breasts.

KLEINIAN

A.K.L. (female)
Each breast has an eye, one very sly. The smug sun-face is sly too, it is mother inviting her to be tortured, saying, 'I only want you to come to the breast to be tortured'. And the profile Madonna who turns away her head doesn't know what these torturing breasts are doing. Also the quest for safety from all this hypocrisy, duplicity, torturing.

N.R.S. (male)
Much less hope here than in the 'leaf' drawings, a strong feeling of 'going under', of being trapped in a kind of 'Iron Maiden'. She is more and more inside her objects.

A.L.M. (female)
The idealized pregnant mother with the baby inside the breast. The breast is herself; whatever she does to mother is always from inside. She has put herself inside the breast and the mother does not seem to mind because the mother's face is peaceful. There is progress because the baby's head is integrated and the mother's breast integrated. Her ideal is of projective identification, of putting her head right inside mother's breast, with her eyes open, with the feeling that it does not destroy or disintegrate mother. The lower half suggests the idea that after each feed she leaves a part of herself in mother's breast, but she is then jealous of her twin in the breast and bites its nose off.

It is much more integrated because it shows separate well-defined parts of herself not a mass of fragments.

S.D.P. (female)
Much confusing of breasts and buttocks, a half-way stage from fusion, moving towards differentiation.

NON–ANALYSTS

R.R.F. (painter/female)
Is very much aware of the other person going on down below, yes, it
does oscillate. There's a metallic breast shield like the thing Salome
wears.

Z.L.M. (teacher of painting/male)
Spikes as coat of armour, helmet – there is an oscillating phenomenon
when recalling people visually in one's mind, one recalls the side face
and the full face, Picasso represented both at once.

   Oscillation depends on a time factor – Chinese symbol for life also
oscillates.

B.A.L. (teacher of languages/male)
It's like her children, longing for motherhood . . . also is original.

Mouth in centre of flower

INDEPENDENTS

D.T.U. (male)
The breast eye view of a child. Or the penis's view of a female genital
with the mouth put instead of the vagina. There's a bit of a shock in
it because of this sexual mouth in it which contrasts with the purity
of the flower. There is repetition which is shown in the petals,
something which goes on and on. The word orgasm hovers. The
mouth is put in to put us off and only she can know what it is? A
nothingness, an abstraction, not a penis or a vagina, a stillness that
belongs to an equal amount of movement both ways?

A.E.F. (female)
All going back to the same thing, round and round. Could say that,
as a flower, it is something that had opened up. It's more to do with
feelings and also perhaps trying to prevent an explosion.

L.G.H. (female)
The mouth centre, deflowered, to do with blossoming out and
flowering . . . but by keeping split between body and head these
patients really believe they are immortal. It goes with a phantasy of
an utter ruthless invasion of themselves, because the life they are
withdrawn from is one that means some penetration of their inner
world.

Figure 32   Mouth in centre of flower

Y.G.H. (male)

These explosions like hand grenades, what does the centre of the flowers signify? And the shapes? Something which in its original form was a centre and a periphery, so it can be expressed by a face of a child, or a womb-like shape with a child in the middle – which is birth of a new self out of a primary matrix, occurring sometimes explosively, sometimes a check on it.

Chaccras, the first one to awaken, is said to be in the perineum, behind the anus, at the base of the spine – and one in the solar plexus and one at the top of the head. Sees these as corporeal centres of

149

generation of energy which at times she will feel irradiated by and she's terrified of, it's got all tangled up with some sort of internalized web of false. . . .

There's no father, no real male principle apart from the hand grenades going off.

It would be easier for her to be the spectator of father and mother tearing each other to pieces, the drawings suggest she has not used that experience.

JUNGIAN

S.E.F. (female)
A nightmare thing that goes on growing and growing.

KLEINIAN

N.R.S. (male)
Most unpleasant, a sort of Venus fly-trap, some attempt at idealization, all meant to be explosive but gets very unpleasant feeling of vortex, of going in.

NON–ANALYST

Z.L.M. (teacher of painting/male)
Flower, mouth, spider all incongruous.

N.Z.O. (painter and professor of painting/male)
Some kind of shyness, trying to hide something.

N.G.H. (writer on art and teacher/male)
Much more sick, defensive, and aggressive oral genital. Repulsive smug pinched look of mouth dangerous . . . and pubic hairs – spikes going out. If decoration was more sweet would find it more sick. A very well-drawn genital mouth but horrible, like a meat-eating plant with a trap.

Duck with a hat on

INDEPENDENTS

D.H.O. (male)
The ultimate deception is in a duck, what does it hide? One of those [drawings] designed not to give away what it's about. Teeth hidden in the outline making the outline less determined. We are allowed to see something which looks like a couple of breasts. It's quite

Figure 33   Duck with a hat on

amusing, which applies only to the deception element. What surprises is that the things which look like breasts are allowed to show so much.

L.G.H. (female)
The duck is me, it can go on water and on dry land, can survive both in the conscious and unconscious.

A.E.F. (female)
Breasts are inside. There's a condensation of lower extremities into the tail; there's a wide open–toothed mouth made of the hat and the beak.

JUNGIAN

S.E.F. (female)
Defended with teeth all over, two breasts or eggs inside.

151

KLEINIAN

A.L.M. (female)
A fellow devil(?) Is it the smug mother out to torture her? No good to talk to them of envy as they feel it is the breast doing it all. Their reality is that the breasts are out to mock and torture, it's me mocking, laughing at her.

NON-ANALYST

N.Z.O. (professor and teacher of painting/male)
Beautiful drawing, a duck as a point of departure with some idea of an old lady – 'old duck' – affection – interesting unity of rhythm, breaking all the forms with zigzag lines.

By this formal trick achieves spontaneity. Two eggs. Two breasts. Has she some envy? Has freshness, originality.

N.G.H. (writer and critic of painting/male)
Lovely drawing. Two bosoms in the wrong place but this is not upsetting – restfulness is folded in, like a paisley design, showing artistic sensibility – the hat is a vagina, a lovely one with feathers.

'Leaves' whirling round – Catherine wheel
(Made in hospital because of holiday   August 1950.)

INDEPENDENTS

D.T.O. (male)
Unintegrated state tending towards integration from unintegration.

A.E.F. (female)
A flatus explosion. Are the faecal things split into bits but also, in each brush stroke, there is a miniature hand.

D.N.O. (male)
Thank god for the limited paper, without that would be utterly exhausted. If no limit, then all she can do with her impulses is exhaust herself [but] within this [frame] of the paper this little thing, central, can exist – lke the wheel of Krishna, symbol of basic unity (Krishna and Arjuna). What's healthy is that seeing is not self-observation but self-expression, not preconsciously organized. It's like a child who has come into the room with dirty feet and hands. It's about not having someone to pick one up; if there was there would be no need for all this.

152

KLEINIAN

D.R.S. (male)
More lively, more seed shapes, more hope for growing.

NON–ANALYST

D.N.O. (writer and teacher on psychology of art/male)
There is a definite scattering but it still holds together, whirling flakes – highly decorative, it's come off, not schizophrenic, stable (must have been hard not to have the thing run away). Very integrated, not a sharp separation in the middle, much movement, not stiff or superimposed line. The tearing and connecting well put together, no break in the tension, it does spread to picture edge, less defended, great simple boldness of imagination, use of simple brush strokes, spikes scattered around.

R.R.S. (painter and teacher of painting/female)
Where did she start? Enjoys the way the blobs made with the brush stroke move around.

Z.L.M. (painter and teacher of art/male)
Shows her talent, some violence but controlled and very beautiful, white spots well conceived, spaces which result from brush strokes which coagulate as one goes in, convincingly not scatteringly to a

Figure 34 'Leaves' whirling round – Catherine wheel

centre, with a loosenes of organization which still holds together marvellously, no stiffness of brush.

Chinese dragon
(Made in hospital in brown paint during August holiday)

INDEPENDENTS

D.T.O. (male)
An integrated phenomenon.

D.N.O. (male)
Oh, very beautiful! Here things are beginning to have a relationship; first real attempt at seeing that gestures are a property of the body, an alphabet. Something of joy in this. Still a little manic and paranoid but that doesn't matter. Also the image is striking here. A very good representation of aggression which fends one off, like barbed wire, yet not really hostile. Satisfying, something to do with personalization and religious sensibility.

A.E.F. (female)
A devil [laughs] a fit of rage, a punch coming out, an explosion, perhaps of flatus.

Y.G.H. (male)
Like a Chinese ideogram, implied movement, rather ferocious,

Figure 35   Chinese dragon

154

warrior creature on top and tremendously dynamic. Not clear whether these elements are going to topple and fall or turn against each other. Whether to find a dynamic synthesis with each other or all going to turn extremely nasty.

JUNGIAN

S.E.F. (female)
So angry and fierce, as though it had bitten off the rest of itself.

NON-ANALYST

N.G.H. (writer and teacher of psychology of art/male)
Everything has been sucked into the animal in the centre, very good, full of movement, yet the sign itself extremely stable. Here's the good fit, the counterpart of the bad fit – enormous strength and movement and *not* persecuted, compare 'Yell of Joy' which is tongue and mouth and throat.

Spider creating its web (p. 156)

INDEPENDENT

Y.G.H. (male)
Often there seems to be a figure caught in a web or a wheel, a wheel in so many, crab-like sometimes, caught in ambiguity, so often vivaciousness of the strokes, something either generating or imprisoning itself/mandalas. The centre generating all this remains itself imprisoned. It's as if the periphery of the mandala which is very radiant and ecstatic has come to imprison and yet, at the same time, is, paradoxically, the centre which is generating remains itself imprisoned – as though a sun or source of light from which all this radiates has somehow been darkened by itself – like lighthouse capable of generating light all round it and yet there is a fuse inside so that the light the lighthouse-keeper reads by has gone out.
  Of course one takes for granted the anal-faecal part of all this.

Figure 36   Spider creating its web

My mother
(Painted in blue and brown)

INDEPENDENT

D.N.O. (male)
The personalizing process making a person out of the disparate elements – to do with quietness and sadness. A beginning of inwardness, taking the risk of being a person, the manic defence of being mad(?) has got to be. Ideal image of the depressive position, a sad self with all paranoid elements bounded with a boundary. An attempt at self-containment, but if so, is unapproachably sad, so that to be bounded into oneself means to accept that there will never be communication. The mess that compels others to be involved with one.

Figure 37   My mother

KLEINIAN

A.L.M. (female)
Mother is mostly a womb, beginning to recognize that this womb has human qualities but full of holes that she has bitten out of it. A very depressed mother. That mother is still a womb or a breast become a womb, so she gets inside. Here is the depressive sorrow for mother, sorrow with mother, harmony with mother, a harmonious picture, a self identified with a mother full of tears who is altered by being fused with me (as analyst). Understanding and wisdom shown in the eyes.

NON-ANALYST

T.S.T. (painter and art teacher/male)
Damned good, should be framed and kept. A sort of magical mask, very, very powerfully magical, very, very beautiful, rather pure magic, white magic, not at all satanic.

Y.S.T. (housewife and art teacher/female)
Primitive like a totem pole, wonderful, gorgeous colours, so free and so marvellous to stop at that, not to spoil it.

E.L.M. (painter/female)
Terrific humour in it.

N.S.T. (Painter and writer on art/male)
Very beautiful, very remarkable.

Z.L.M. (painte and art teacher/male)
As if occupied with clarifying what is background and what is not, so there is an indecision about it. It's an important step if things of the background become foreground.

T.D.E. (art critic/male)
Expects more aggressive destruction. So rhythmically unified. Would even say it was the product of an art student; excellent design.

Piano and dagger

INDEPENDENTS

D.N.O. (male)
Don't understand it, too sophisticated. To do with anger and lack of

Figure 38   Piano and dagger

a body, everything happening in the head. . . . Punch and Judy Show, primal scene, a tremendous need for forgiveness. Someone watching someone else; people really looking for a state of grace. In a paroxysm of intense guilt and pain and need for forgiveness, but there is nobody in her world that is worthy of it; people create God because no other human being can put one in a state of grace.

This is personally held madness, saying 'I am mad . . . this is madness'.

D.T.U. (male)
This ship is not a ship, a collection of symbols, breasts, piano, lamps. Sensuous experience in the making, rather freer than what could be expected; a prickly mess.

Dancing figure among leaves
(Brown paint)

INDEPENDENT

A.E.F. (female)
Things trying to come together, broken off bits, some suggest something inside, enfolded which might open.

NON–ANALYST

N.G.H. (writer and teacher of psychology of art/male)
Shows her talent, some violence but controlled and very beautiful, white spots well conceived, spaces which result from brush strokes which coagulate as one goes in, convincingly, not scatteringly, to a centre, with a looseness of organization which still holds together marvellously, no stiffness of brush.

Figure 39   Dancing figure among leaves

Geometric head

INDEPENDENTS

T.E.F. (female)
A robot, defending herself, not human.

Y.G.H. (male)
More disturbing, no sense of generating a focus of power at the same time as a focus of serenity. As if potentialities temporarily held in a

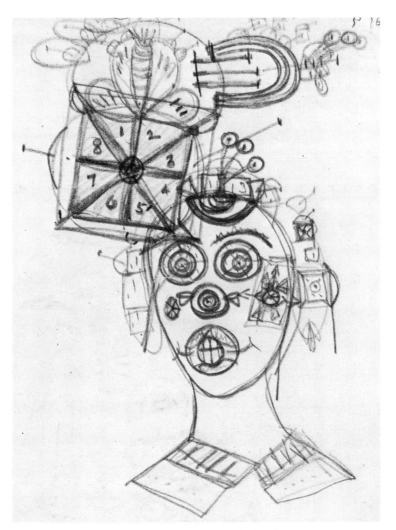

Figure 40 Geometric head

161

clock-like fixity; feels would rather have the ambiguity (of some of the others) than this kind of crystallization held together by pins and framed up.

L.G.H. (female)
Gadgets, to do with ECT. Now through art, she is trying to work back through the ECT experience to the situation where she could have said 'No.' She feels she could not accept the value of her little alone opinion. She feels that God let her down and she made a pact with the devil to deal with her despair.
 The gadgets equated with God and so lost to humanity. What should have been human has become machines or parts of machines.

A.E.F. (female)
She's mechanized things; it's to do with sound. Is her circle (outside the square flag shape) something to do with abstraction and her brain working? As opposed to anal feelings? Could be a tremendous attempt at thinking [but] with a rejection of all these conscious ideas of order and conceptualization.

JUNGIAN

S.E.F. (female)
Very, very dreadful, the mechanical, non-human, everything gone mechanical, eyes, ears, mouth. And there's a clock thing impinging, but also, outside, and a magnet.

KLEINIAN

N.R.S. (male)
More contempt than horror, for people who think they know everything, tell fortunes, mechanistic.

A.K.L. (female)
In all previous ones there was a certain integration because she felt faced with the object only out to torture her. Now there is fragmentation starting in order not to feel. The face is the breast, but disintegrated, and the bits put together in a perverse, bizarre way, therefore not so persecuting; there is dismantling and the shapes put together in a different way.

S.O.P. (female)
Ghastly thing, gated mouth, clock . . . she can't speak to the world nor communicate with her inside.

162

N.G.H. (writer on psychology of art/male)
A mad face, could it be a clock? . . . the insect phallus again, become almost a vagina . . . a terrible picture . . . a pinning down instead of an exploding . . . there's a magnet like a croquet hoop. Things must hold together up here in the head. There is horror in the stereotyped rings of mouth, eyes, nose.

T.E.F (sculptor/female)
What was the person has turned into a calculating machine but because she is still a person she can't do the job and is left with neither.

Viewers' general comments

INDEPENDENTS

D.Y.Z. (female)
[This is the consultant who interviewed Susan in 1950 and later went through all the drawings.]
There is much to do with ego-nuclei, the ego is a projection of a surface, there are very few drawings of hands, many eyes, very few ears. Feet are often represented by the curious curved metal shapes.

There are wandering penises and breasts, what is animating them? There is much confusion, she is asking – are ears, eyes, vaginas, like mouths? The problem of part objects standing for whole ones, which means losing both. It's to do with the problem of whole object perception, including contiguity, all the parts belonging to the same person, as well as continuity, continuing existence in time, and discovery of the objects inside as well as outside.

T.E.F. (female)
[This viewer, who did not say very much at the time, except that she never could see the oscillations in those drawings which seemed to me to oscillate, asked for a second viewing and then posted me the following comments.]
There is the discharge theme in the exploding flowers, release of tension, tightness, holding.

The overlapping circles is to do with her feeling of a bit of common ground between me (analyst) and her; it is two people with partially shared experience, as against complete merging, that is the delusion of unity.

There are only two extremes: either I know everything because I am her and she is me, for instance the duck, or, I must know nothing because that would mean I eat her.

In the drawings she explodes herself, throws herself out on to the paper where I have to hold all the bits; that's the only way I can help her, it may be enough, or perhaps it won't.

I (the duck) eat her, and she, the duck, eats me, all is confusion.

All I do is part of her, my hands taking the drawings, my eyes, my brain that understands, she does it all. Not just that she creates me, she is me.

There is no room for concern with pleasure, only for survival; the to-and-fro movement to fuse with me and break with me; all conveying the absoluteness of her world-destroying, me-destroying movement (if free).

If her mother had the same delusion, then the pictures are showing not only the patient's delusion (of no separateness) but also her mother's, as experienced by her. So, the problem of separating out her madness from her mother's.

One of her purposes is to drive me mad (with all these mad drawings) and prove that I, mother, she, are all one, and that separateness does not exist.

Being in the world means having her own craziness and letting other people have theirs.

Every line, dot, and squiggle, is a part of her body, not just a symbol.

She is expressing over and over again the failure of fusion, after separation, the failure to restore the prenatal state.

JUNGIAN

L.M.N. (male)
Sees all these flower shapes as integrating centres around the mouth or an anus-mouth.

Feels there is very much a person there, very organized in her tastes, from childhood. The analyst has to catch a bit of what's exploded out, (perhaps cough or light a match), there are many attempts at focusing a centre all over the place, clocks, flags. Mandalas do form in psychotics but blow up, not a sign of achieved integration.

Explosions, central source of energy in perineal areas.

KLEINIAN

N.R.S. (male)
So much anal sadistic, implosive, masturbatory, voyeurism . . . in direction of ridiculing; all very delicately balanced whether to

deteriorate or able to see object as attractive, either possession or envious contempt . . . wish to rescue object.

Mouth-anus cheeks buttocks not such vicious mockery, sucking each other, more hopeful.

In retrospect I found the responses of T.E.F. (p. 163) to the drawings very relevant for I remembered again Susan's panic about the bombs, because she felt she was everything. These comments also brought in the concept of delusion as compared with that of illusion that I had been so concerned with.

As for her artistic gift, one particular question came to me now about the 'Post-ECT Drawing'. I asked myself, how was it that this girl, who said, when she came to me, that since the ECT she had lost all her feelings, how was it then that she could have produced a drawing so acutely full of feelings? And not only that but also made with such originality and authenticity of artistic invention?

As for the delay of nearly nine years in bringing it to me, I guessed that it was only after all these years, including the last two during which she had done hundreds of drawings in addition to those shown here, that she became able to face the agony and despair depicted in it. But this does not answer the question of how it was that such a marked artistic gift had emerged when she felt so much else had been destroyed.

I could not find out whether she had drawn much as a child; all she could remember was liking to draw pictures of furniture from catalogues.

As I have said, I did not continue with this pilot experiment; instead I stowed away all the comments for further scrutiny, which in fact I did not manage to achieve until now (1986), the reason being the urge to study all the drawings myself, in the light of the actual day-to-day analysis, hence the book *The Hands of the Living God* (1969).

Central to my decision to write the book was the fact that there had come a day, nine years after her first beginning to draw in the analysis (again nine years!) that she had come to her session saying she had just found a note in her diary (for 8 January) saying 'I am in the world for the first time for 16 years'. Then, on 31 January she had brought me a written account of how she was feeling. This is what she said:

'It is very difficult to communicate things which although we are aware of so clearly in our minds, are somehow not transferable into words – and yet the awareness is unmistakable – the awareness of a reality that I have not been in contact with for 16 years.

The shock of the realisation that one could have been unconscious for so long a time seems almost to send one into unconsciousness again.

Maybe it will [that is, shock her back into unconsciousness again] – I do not know – but it is something to have become conscious again even for a few minutes.

With it, in its relief, I have at the same moment a realisation of my conduct during the years. These, since I was not aware at the time, went by unobserved. But now, in a split second, it seems I have to take responsibility for what I have done since I gave up my life in 194[?].

I can remember them now as years of blackness. Blackness in mind and heart. Being unaware of oneself and consequently of other people makes it impossible to observe and question one's own actions, so one behaves as one will, with no consideration for anybody or anything. This realisation is awful to be conscious of. Not only has one violated the sense concerning others, but one has also gone against any duty to oneself and one's own integrity – and if you believe in God then it is intensely against Him that you have turned – and your predestined self, the self you know not of, the self which thinks and grows regardless of conscious choice, this you have had to put out of existence. This is of course impossible, one is not so strong, after all, but it is possible to reject and thereby stultify growth. I have done that, so help me God.'

Here I noted particularly her phrase 'the self which thinks and grows regardless of conscious choice'. It seems as if, although now able to accept a bigger self than her conscious ego, she was not yet able to fit into her self-model the idea that she could relate herself to it, by conscious choice; in fact that there could be, must be, a co-operation between her conscious and unconscious functioning. She ends with:

'To adjust oneself in consciousness, in however small a measure, is a great task, a life's work no doubt; but, instead of it being gradual, the realisation that is, if it comes suddenly it seems too much to be called upon to bear.'

I quoted this writing of hers, in the book I came to write about her, and tried to show how the drawings led up to this final discovery that the world was once more outside her and that she was in it, a small bit of it, but not the whole world.

166

References: The Yell of Joy

This paper was originally published as Milner, M. (1956) The Communication of Primary Sensual Experience: The Yell of Joy. *International Journal of Psycho-Analysis* 37: 278–89. Previously read at the Nineteenth International Psycho-Analytical Congress, Geneva, 24–28 July, 1955.

Darwin, C. (1934) *The Expression of the Emotions in Man and Animals.* London: Watts (Thinkers' Library).

Ferenczi, S. (1938) *Thalassa: A Theory of Genitality.* New York: *Psycho-Analytic Quarterly* Inc.

Scott, W. C. M. (1949) The Body Scheme in Psychotherapy. *British Journal of Medical Psychology* 22: 139–50.

Scott, W. C. M. (1954) Libidinal and Aggressive instincts. *International Journal of Psycho-Analysis* 35: 234–37.

Scott, W. C. M. (1955) A Note on Blathering. *International Journal of Psycho-Analysis* 36: 348–49.

Searl, N. (1933) The Psychology of Screaming. *International Journal of Psycho-Analysis* 14.

Sharpe, E. (1950) Psycho-Physical Problems Revealed in Language: An Examination of Metaphor. In *Collected Papers on Psycho-Analysis.* London: Hogarth.

References: Attending to the background

1 Balint, M. (1952) *Primary Love and Psychoanalytic Technique.* London: Hogarth Press.

2 Winnicott, D. W. (1951) Transititional Objects and Transitional Phenomena. In (1958) *Collected Papers.* London: Tavistock, p. 221.

3 Freud, S. (1938) Splitting of the Ego in the Process of Defence (unfinished paper). In *Standard Edition,* vol. XXIII. London: Hogarth Press.

4 Klein, M. (1934) Depressive Position. A Contribution to the Psychogenesis of Manic Depression. In *Contributions to Psychoanalysis.* London: Hogarth Press.

5 Ferenczi, S. (1938) *Thalassa: A Theory of Genitality.* New York: *Psycho-Analytic Quarterly* Inc.

6 Darwin, C. (1934) *The Expression of the Emotions in Man and Animals.* London: Watts (Thinkers' Library).

7 Reich, W. (1945) *Character Analysis.* London: Vision Press.

11

1956: The sense in nonsense
(Freud and Blake's *Job*)

In 1956 Peggy Volkov, editor of the educational magazine *The New Era,* arranged a weekend when a Freudian, a Jungian, and an Adlerian were asked to give papers on what they felt their particular viewpoint could offer to schoolteachers.[1] I chose to talk about Blake's *Illustrations to the Book of Job*, feeling it was the only possible way of presenting what I really wanted to say.

I remember now (1986) that I had sent a copy of this paper to Melanie Klein and that she had written back saying that she liked it, but why had I not mentioned the Depressive Position? I might have answered, but doubt if I did, first that I did not think it was the kind of paper for which technical terms would have been appropriate, and second that the Depressive Position is actually described, I should have thought, in Blake's quoting the text 'And the Lord turned the captivity of Job when he prayed for his friends'. However, the illustration (xviii) containing this text is not included in my paper.

'Without contraries is no progression.'

> William Blake, *The Marriage of
> Heaven and Hell*, 1790)

When I tried to think how psychoanalytic ideas could best be put into a form that would make any sort of bridge between the experiences of the teacher and the experiences in the consulting room, I remembered Blake's *Illustrations to the Book of Job*. It is now ten years since it first occurred to me that this series of engravings seemed to be dealing with the same kinds of facts about human beings that I had been trying to understand during five years' study of the system of education in schools. I had had the idea then that there was something being left out of the system and that it was something to do with the problem of psychic creativity; but that is also the theme of Blake's illustrations. Thus I have come to look on Blake's *Job* as the story of what goes on in all of us, when we become sterile and doubt our creative capacities, doubt our powers to love and to work; and also a story of the battle we all have to go through, to a greater or less degree and whether we know it or not, in learning how to become able to love and to work.

Freud was also concerned with the story of the battle, in fact it emerges as the central theme of his researches; and the essential fact about Freud is that he invented a new instrument for the study of this battle. He discovered that, in a setting in which it is understood that a person can, as far as the listener is concerned, say exactly what comes into his head, without bothering that it should be polite, or even whether it makes sense, then what he says will gradually be seen to be making a sense of its own, a hidden sense that the person had never guessed was there.

The problem of how the facts about human growth, which the use of this instrument revealed, can be made available for education is a vast one; thus the attempt I am making here to indicate something of the implications of these facts is necessarily very limited in its scope, both on account of space, and because I can give only my own personal belief about what is most relevant for teachers, both in Freud's work and in the work of his followers. These beliefs are based on fifteen years of clinical practice with patients, together with reading about the findings of others who are using the same instrument and who are struggling to formulate what they have seen in terms of a scientific body of knowledge. It is owing to the difficulty of the kind of language that analysts have developed, for the sake of convenience in talking amongst themselves, that I am trying to present what I want to say in this different language, the language of the Bible.

In this article, therefore, I am going to give a brief description of Blake's version of the Job story, as shown in pictures, for the sake of those who are not familiar with them;[2] and then I will attempt to describe certain ways in which what Blake is saying in visual and poetic symbols could be restated, both in terms of current Freudian theory and also in terms of what Freudian theory may be developing towards. Since I believe that a work of art is something that, through its manifold symbolism, speaks to each in his own tongue, I make no claim that what I see in it is what everyone must see in it, for it is

Figure 42   (vi) Satan smiting Job

Figure 41   (v) Job gives his last crust to a
                   beggar

obvious that each must make his own interpretation.[3]

Blake's *Job* consists of a series of twenty-one engravings, with texts from the Bible and various linear designs set around the margins.[4] The first picture shows Job with his wife and family all praying under a spreading tree, surrounded by his flocks, while musical instruments hang unused upon the tree. The second picture also shows the family scene; but up above, instead of the tree there is God the Father enthroned with angels, God the Father having the same face as Job: and Satan is shown leaping in before the throne. The third picture shows Satan destroying the sons and daughters and their children; the fourth shows messengers bringing news of the disaster to Job and his wife who sit alone. The fifth (*Figure 41*) again shows the Deity on his throne, but looking rather insecure, and Satan beneath him is holding a nozzle which belches flame in the direction of Job's head; whilst Job, having lost everything, is sitting beside his wife and offering his last crust to a begger. In the sixth (*Figure 42*), God has disappeared and Satan dominates the picture; he stands astride the prostrate body of Job, still directing the fiery jet against him, but now with all the force behind it of the thunderous clouds which fill the sky. The text says, *'And smote Job with sore boils.'*

In (vii) Satan has gone, but the battle with Job's friends begins. Job is shown, utterly weak but still patient. His wife and his friends join

Figure 43   (xii) Arrival of Elihu

Figure 44   (xv) Behemoth and Leviathan

in lamentations and their pity finally undermines his control, so that in (viii) his rage breaks out and he begins to curse the day he was born, his wife and friends now speechless before his grief. In (ix) one of the comforters, Eliphaz, is shown revealing his own vision of God, here shown as a stern commanding immovable figure above the clouds. In (x) Job still maintains his innocence but his friends point accusing fingers at him and his wife argues with him. In (xi) the God Job has called upon appears, but in demonic form and his friends have now turned into devils, they are pulling him down into the fires of the pit.

This is the crisis of the descent of his spirit, now the recovery begins. For in (xii) (*Figure 43*) Elihu appears and there are now many stars in the sky; and in (xiii) God appears to Job and his wife in the whirlwind. (xiv) is the famous picture 'When the Morning Stars sang together', the starry heavens of (xii) have now become peopled with seraphim and below them is again the figure of God with the face of Job, no longer enthroned but with his arms outspread as if creating the world. Beneath the clouds are Job and his wife and his friends, now all looking upwards. In (xv) (*Figure 44*) God is reclining amongst the stars and pointing downwards, directing the attention of Job and his wife and friends to an enclosed circle in which are the two monsters, Behemoth and Leviathan. In (xvi) Satan is shown being cast out from heaven, and in (xvii) the Deity has gone, but the figure of Christ is shown, standing beside Job and his wife and blessing them. In (xviii) Job prays for his friends, and instead of God with the face of Job the sky is filled with the sun, and Job is in an attitude of worship; (xix) is the opposite of (iii) in that here Job and his wife are shown receiving charity; and (xx) shows Job for the first time within his own house, surrounded by three daughters, and on the walls there are paintings. The final picture (xxi) is the same as (i); Job is here once again under the tree with his wife and sons and daughters, surrounded by his flocks. But they are no longer praying, they are now all standing up and playing upon the instruments which had before hung unused upon the tree.

Having given this brief description of the pictures I will now comment upon them, in the light of the marginal texts. I am not quoting all the texts, for reasons of space, but have selected those that seem, for me, to throw most light on the pictures.

The nature of Job's error

The first question is, what is the exact nature of Job's sin, as depicted by Blake – sin being defined, as clearly Blake meant it to be defined, as that which cuts us off from creative power? I think the answer is given in one of the texts to the first picture and elaborated throughout the whole series. *'There was a man . . . whose name was Job, and that man was perfect and upright.'* Surely here is the answer, no man can be perfect, therefore he is denying his human nature. But how does he get the idea that he is perfect? It seems to be because his conscious intention is good, he *'feared God and eschewed evil'*. Thus he is shown persistently denying that there could be any evil in himself; and he is shown as able to do this because he believes only in the conscious life, he believes that because his conscious intention is good and solely devoted to the worship and service to God, therefore he must be good. But in (ii) Blake shows Job's inner world (that which is above is within, says Blake elsewhere) and here is the exact opposite of Job's idea of himself as perfect – for here destructiveness, in the person of Satan, leaps in and demands expression.

But what is the cause of the destructiveness, since Job was shown in (i) as having everything he could possibly want? I think the answer is that in the first picture Blake is describing both the earliest state of infancy, which feels like a wholeness, but a wholeness which is inevitably lost through growing experience of the frustration of the instinctive life: and, at the same time, the attempt to return to that

172

state through conscious submission to an imposed moral law. Thus he seems to be depicting the same idea of the first state of infancy that Freud talks about; the state before the child is able to distinguish between himself and the world in terms of actuality, when all goodness seems to be part of oneself, when the heaven of one's mother's arms seems to be one's own creation, all heaven is ours and all power. This concept would explain why God the Father bears the face of Job. But this state does not last, it is a kind of dream life, says Freud; and he says that, when we do wake from this first state, it is so hard to give up the original feeling of omnipotence that we project its memory outwards on to an omnipotent external father, and then reincorporate it in the form of an almighty father 'up above' – that is inside. So Blake puts as his text for the first picture, *'Our Father which art in Heaven . . .'* By perfect obedience to the will of this heavenly father, we come to feel that we can regain vicariously our original estate; we feel we can become one with our father in heaven. But with such obedience there also goes rebellion, even though unrecognized, for it seems we do not give up our wilfulness so easily; and our destructive rage at the loss of our original heaven, if unrecognized, is split off and put into an outside evil thing, so that it is not we who wish to destroy, it is 'Satan' or his equivalents. And so, in the third picture, Blake shows Satan filling the sky, towering over the dead and dying bodies of Job's sons and daughters and their children and the crashing timbers of their house. So also in the fourth picture the news of the disaster is brought to Job and his wife; that is he has not seen it happening, because he as yet quite unconscious of the depth of destruction going on within him. And it is then, in (v), that Blake shows Job, having lost all he has, giving his last crust to a beggar; and the God within, whose face is still the face of Job, almost pulled down off his throne, as Job is given into the power of his own Satanic destructiveness. What did Blake mean by this special twist he gives to the story, by showing the beginning of Job's inner downfall, after the loss of all his children and possessions, as coming at the moment when he shares his last crust with a beggar? Why is this the moment when God gives Satan the power to afflict his body and his soul? Certainly Blake's making this the crucial moment in Job's downfall is a reversal of conventional views on Christian charity. But Blake, of all people, would not disparage charity in general. Why, therefore, does he show Job as given into the power of Satan by such an act? It seems to me that Blake meant to show that Job is in the power of his own satanic rage just because it is still unrecognized, just because he is desperately attempting to defend himself, by philanthropy, from recognizing his own primitive lust

173

for possession, and the rage when this is frustrated. So it seems that it is this, the unconscious hypocrisy of the act, that brings about the inner disaster and that finally leads him into the depths.

Descent to the depths

In the next picture (vi) showing Job prostrate upon the earth, with Satan standing astride his body, pouring down the fiery vial of the tempest upon his head, Job is still consciously the perfect obedient servant of his God. *'The Lord gave and the Lord hath taken away, blessed be the Name of the Lord.'* But consciously he does now recognize that he was helpless as an infant, not omnipotent: *'Naked came I out of my mother's womb and naked shall I return thither.'* A Freudian could say that this is the beginning of his becoming able to recognize a fundamental fact: the fact that his initial feeling of wholeness, unity with the universe, was only made possible because he had a mother there, separate from himself and therefore able to nourish and protect him from the hurtful impacts of that universe. But he does not yet recognize his anger at having eventually to give up both that protection and also the illusion that he did not need it because he thought he did it all himself. He does not yet recognize his anger, but his body breaks out in boils.

In this picture Job's head is reared backwards, so that he sees neither Satan standing over his loins, nor his wife weeping at his feet, whom he seems to be repudiating with a gesture of his hands; although there is a stream of light flowing from his feet up her kneeling thighs, while his own face is in darkness. All this suggests that Job's inner battle is also affecting his sexual powers, the lack of creativeness shown in the first picture is also a sexual impotency. So it seems that in his ideal of his own perfection he is repudiating his sexuality and all that is to do with the flesh, since he is shown straining to avert his gaze from his own body, as well as from his wife. Here Freudians would say that the denied rages of his infancy at the loss of the first feeling of total possession of his mother have now made him doubt the goodness of his own sexual love; for the nozzle of fire wielded by Satan clearly has a phallic significance. Thus his love for a woman must be repudiated because his first love for a woman (his mother) was too much mixed with unrecognized anger: anger which included the rage at discovering that he himself was not God the Father, and that his real father also had rights.

It is in (vii) that his friends' lamentations for his plight finally undermine his control, and in (viii) that he breaks into that magnificent flood of poetry by which, in the Bible story, he curses the day he was born. Blake quotes: *'Lo let that night be solitary and let no joyful voice come therein: Let the day perish wherein I was born.'* Thus the anger, when it does come to expression, is half turned against himself, it is half suicidal; but it is also an attack upon his parents for ever causing him to be born. His friends and wife now bury their faces at the sight of his grief and remain silent beside him for *'seven days and seven nights'*.

In the next picture (ix) he is shown getting slightly nearer to recognizing that the cause of his trouble is within himself, for he is shown looking upwards (that is inwards) for the first time. And what he sees, through the vision of Eliphaz, is what Freud would call the persecuting super-ego – a terrifying figure, not an indwelling spirit of love, life, action, but an angry sternly commanding God, with arms bound, remaining aloof and taking no part in creation but sternly judging with a fierce half-dark light blazing from him, one who *'putteth no trust in his Saints and his Angels he chargeth with folly'*. Job can see this terrifying vision through another's eyes, but he does not yet see that his own God can be unjust, because of containing the satanic element within himself that he has had to deny; although this understanding is hinted at in the text: *'Shall mortal man be more just than God? Shall a man be more pure than his Maker?'*

In (x) he still maintains his own innocence and that his God is just *'Though he slay me yet will I trust in him'*. In fact he tries to defend himself against knowing that his own internal father-God can contain destructive aspects by feeling that the destructiveness comes from his friends, it is they who are wrongfully pointing accusing fingers at him: *'The just upright man is laughed to scorn'*, says the text. He is indeed far from seeing that Eliphaz's fierce God is also his own, and even farther from seeing that this stern God of accusation and vengeance is his own creation, fashioned out of his own anger at all that has frustrated his instinctual desires. Instead he is in a state of confusion, he pleads his own weakness, even makes an attempt at placation and pleads for mercy: *'Man that is born of a woman is of few days and full of trouble . . . , And dost thou open thine eyes upon such a one and bringest me into judgment with thee.'* In (xi) when the God he has called upon appears as the Devil, Job himself is again prostrate, once more turning his face away; but now it is the looming closeness of the body of the Devil that he is trying to fend off with his hands. He feels himself the helpless victim of the evil thing; no goodness remains anywhere, his friends have become demons pulling him down into the fire of the abyss – and his Satanic God, with cloven hoof and a huge serpent entwined about him, but still wearing the face of Job himself, presses down from above, entirely obliterating all else. In fact, as the text says, this is a dream. And presiding over all Blake has put a double shape which commentators identify as the tables of stone of the Mosiac Law.

The texts show here how Job's battle of the spirit expresses itself in bodily symptoms: *'My bones are pierced in me in the night season and my sinews take no rest.'* And he now oscillates between belief in a persecuting God and a saving one: *'Why do you persecute me as God . . . I know that my Redeemer liveth.'* At the same time he has become confused about the distinction between what is good and what is evil: *'Satan himself is transformed into an Angel of Light'*.

This then is where the reliance on conscious obedience to the moral law imposed from above has landed him, this is the final outcome of believing in the letter of the law and denying the inner unconscious realities of instinctive human nature. For this picture may be compared with the first, where Job was the omnipotent lord of all he saw, everything was his and God was in his image; whereas here it is the Devil that is in his image and he is utterly helpless before him. *'Who opposeth and exalteth himself above all that is called God or is worshipped'*, says the text. And Freud would say it is this very idea of omnipotence which explains why Job has had to set up such a wholesale defence against knowing the bad in himself, against knowing the difference between himself at his best and himself at his worst. For if one is omnipotent for good one can also be omnipotent for evil.

Recovery

In the next picture (xii) showing the beginning of Job's recovery, a new figure appears, Elihu; he stands in the bleak landscape before the dreary group of Job and his wife and his friends, he comes in like a dancer, one hand pointing to the many stars that now appear in the sky, the other directed towards the friends. The clues as to what Elihu means to Blake are in the texts.

(1) Job is beginning to discover that conscious processes are not the only kind there are or the only wisdom, but that understanding can come through looking at his dreams, that his dreams are telling him something:

'In a dream, in a vision of the night . . .
Then he openeth the ears of men and sealeth their instruction.'

176

(2) Also he is realizing something about his mind and its limitations, beginning to realize that his thoughts and wishes are not omnipotent and therefore that he is not responsible for everything that happens, either for good or for evil:

'Look upon the heavens and behold the clouds which are higher than thou'
'If thou sinnest what doest thou against him . . .'
'Or if thou be righteous what givest thou unto him.'

And if his thoughts and wishes are not omnipotent, neither the constructive nor the destructive, then he will have more courage to face the bad ones.

(3) He is also discovering that all he has been through is not accidental and pointless, but that the living force within him, which is more than his conscious mind, is doing something, striving after something:

'Lo all these things worketh God oftentimes with Man to bring back his Soul from the pit to be enlightened with the light of the living.'

(4) And at last he is beginning to recognize the mind's capacity for being aware of itself, the seeing part at last separated from the judging and commanding and interfering part:

'For his eyes are upon the ways of Man and he observeth all his goings.'

And it is a very young capacity of the mind as compared with the countless generations of blind living.

'I am Young and ye are very Old wherefore I was afraid.'

Thus I think Elihu seems to stand for a new kind of awareness; for in Job's eyes is that inward look, as if he were just daring to let himself see an immense expanse of new possibilities. But his friends have that blank expression which people show when unconscious processes are mentioned but they still believe that conscious ones are all there are. And Blake also seems to be saying that it is through relationship with a person that such a capacity develops: '*If there be with him an Interpreter One among a Thousand.*' Job has also discovered something about his body, for in the marginal drawings his sleeping figure is shown with streams of spirits emanating from his hands and feet as well as his head, and ascending to the stars.

In the next four pictures I think Job is shown beginning to test in his own experience the new idea that Elihu has given him. Having taken the momentous step of becoming able to be aware that his conscious thought is not all there is, he now revaluates his position with regard to powers outside him. In (xiii) where God speaks from the whirlwind it seems that he and his wife face their own smallness before the powers of nature outside them: for God is here shown no longer separated from them by the belt of clouds. And the texts show the beginnings of the capacity to accept ignorance (a theme also developed in (xiv)), a capacity which, Freud would suggest, begins with the first momentous questionings of childhood. For, having discovered that he is not the omnipotent lord of the world, nor did he make it, the child then must ask, who did make it, and who made him. *'Hath the rain a Father and who hath begotten the drops of the dew'*, says the text. But it is not the dew that the child is most concerned with, it is himself, and what made him. Above the picture Blake has put the text, *'Who is this that darkeneth council by words without knowledge'*: and below it, *'Then the Lord answered Job out of the whirlwind.'* A Freudian would see implicit in this picture a reference to the child's problem of coming to believe in the real creative forces, both in himself and the universe; a problem which has as its centre his anger at having to face the fact of that union of his parents which created him. In addition there is also I think a hint of the child's anger – not God's – the child's protest against an education that fails to show him how all growth and creation are the result of the interplay and integration of opposites.

And then comes (xiv), 'The Morning Stars', a picture so full of profound meaning, but essentially I think a statement of what happens when the spirit no longer stands aloof, like Eliphaz's God, but is spread out to embrace and give itself to the whole of the external world. When anyone discovers how to stop seeing the world with the narrow focused attention of expediency, stops interfering and trying to use it for his own purposes, then says Blake, something like a miracle can happen, the whole world can become transfigured. *'That he may withdraw Man from his purpose and hide Pride from Man'*, said the Elihu picture: *'Canst thou bind the sweet influences of Pleiades, or loose the bands of Orion'*, says the Morning Stars picture. And Blake implies that such experiences are also something to do with accepting one's own dual nature, the male and female aspects of the psyche; for under the spreading arms of the Deity with the face of Job are shown the sun god and the moon goddess, one on each side. And Freud would add that it is something to do with coming to accept, emotionally as well as intellectually, the fact that each of us was created by a father and a mother, and there was joy in that creation – or there was meant to be.

In fact 'The Morning Stars' seems to be a picture of a particular kind of imaginative concentration, both very active and very still, a widespread contemplative attention which gives of itself, of its own essence, to what it sees, a state which brings a joy that Blake tries to express by the interlinked shouting seraphim: a state which is sometimes spoken of in Freudian language as one of 'cosmic bliss'. And Blake seems to be saying that it is a state of mind which does create the world anew, and oneself in it, not cut off and isolated but essentially part of it. In fact I think he is saying that perception of the external world itself is a creative act, an act of imagination; without the imagination we would not in fact see what is there to be seen. And it is surely a state that is known at moments, to all of us, in childhood, but so often entirely lost in the purpose-driven life of adulthood; although we can find it again either actively or vicariously, through the arts.

But these high moments do not last. In the next picture (xv) it seems that the principle of simple, non-interfering awareness, represented by Elihu, is directed, not towards the outer world but towards nature within. Instead of the moment of cosmic bliss, of union with creation in which everything is linked in joy and ecstasy, there is the picture of Job and his wife and friends peering down to where the hand of God is pointing. And it points to the two monsters, Behemoth and Leviathan; Behemoth, half elephant, half rhinoceros, standing upon the ground, Leviathan, a kind of spiny sea serpent lying on its back in the water in what looks like an agony of suffering or even about to expire.

In fact, with his new-found power of seeing, Job does now look inwards and tries to understand what has been happening to him. And what he sees are these two great beasts, the life power within himself in its most primitive forms. The texts say: *'Of Behemoth he saith he is chief of the ways of God.'* Does not this mean that although Behemoth is shown as a great ungainly monster he is also one of the prime sources of the creative energy? The text for Leviathan says: *'He is King over all the children of Pride.'* And both have a suffering look, a look of blind unseeing eyes, as if to express the idea of energy not yet aware of itself.

Freudians tend to look on the basic energies of man as two-fold and argue about what names to give them. Blake also seems to be showing them as two-fold and here calls them Behemoth and Leviathan. The fact that Leviathan (although called 'he' in the texts), is represented in such a passive position, lying on its back, half drowning, with an expression of what might be either an agony or ecstasy of submission, suggests an idea of femaleness; while Behemoth is shown as full of a heavy bull-like power. There is also further evidence that Leviathan represents the female aspect of energy in that it is shown as half sea serpent; for in 'The Morning Stars' picture the moon goddess on the left is shown driving a team of sea serpents, in contrast with the sun god's team of horses. Perhaps the fact that Leviathan looks as if expiring is also meant to express the thought that the 'female' way of functioning has not been given sufficient recognition by Job, an idea which is certainly developed further in the last picture but one, where Job's daughters are given 'inheritance among their brethren.'

The next picture shows the results of awareness. *'Hell is naked before him and destruction has no covering.'* Satan is being cast out; and the texts show that when Satan is cast out so also is the belief in the omnipotence of the conscious intellect. *'It is higher than Heaven what canst thou do, It is deeper than Hell what canst thou know?'* Also: *Canst thou by searching find out God, Canst thou find out the Almighty to perfection.'* So Job has now become able to tolerate ignorance. And apparently, as he recognizes his own denied rage it is no longer split off into a satanic power before whom he is helpless; since he no longer thinks he is the perfect upright man because his conscious intentions are upright, he no longer feels his own accusing conscience as something not himself. *'The accuser of our brethren is cast down'*, says the text. So it seems that seeing has become separated from judging, awareness has replaced condemnation. *'Thou hast fulfilled the judgment of the wicked.'*

I have said that this is the last picture in which the God with the face of Job appears: this seems to mean that Job can now stop the compulsion to worship himself. It seems that he has now no need to create such a central image of himself as God in order to counterbalance its opposite, the denied knowledge of his own capacity for ruthless destructiveness. He no longer needs to protect himself from the terrible grief and shame of knowing that he is capable, in the secret depths of his heart, of wishing to destroy those he loves most when they frustrate him; because, in recognizing the destructiveness he has also brought in another force that has power to control it. *'Even the devils are subject to us thro thy name'*, says the text. And, if this is a picture of becoming able to dispense with his concern for the perfection or otherwise of his own image of himself, it throws light on a text that Blake put beside the earlier picture (xi), where Job's God appears as the Devil. *'. . . yet in my flesh shall I see God whom I shall see for myself . . . though consumed be my wrought image.'* For here I think Blake indicates that the process of getting rid of the wrought image of oneself is something that accompanies the discovery of the new kind of power over destructiveness. The Satan that is cast out would thus be a composite symbol; he stands partly for primitive destructiveness in the face of frustration, but also for the 'wrought image' of the righteous self-hood, this virtuous self-image created as a defence against the pains of knowing how much we can hate what we love: but a defence which only makes us more vulnerable. For, if others do not agree about our perfections, if they criticize, then we become more angry, an anger which covers fear of being in fact the opposite of perfect – of being utterly worthless.

It is in the next picture (xvii) that Jesus actually appears, standing upon the earth beside the kneeling Job and his wife and blessing them. Clearly it is an intensely real experience, for the text in this picture says: *'I have heard thee with the hearing of the Ear but now my Eye seeth thee.'* Also it is an essential part of Job's recovery: *'He bringeth down to the Grave and bringeth up.'* It seems that Job no longer needs the omnipotent father God commanding from above-within and identified with the 'wrought image' of himself, for he has found a kind of control that is inherent, part of what is controlled, not separated and split off. He has found a power that transcends the duality of controller and controlled. *'And that day ye shall know that I am in my Father and you in me and I in you'*, says the text. Thus the psyche is surely no longer split into a part which orders and a part which obeys – or rebels. And the resulting control of instinct is based on love rather than fear. *'He that loveth me shall be loved of my Father and I will love him and manifest myself unto him.'* But again Blake emphasizes that it is accepting the truth that is the redeeming force: *'And the Father shall give you another comforter . . . even the spirit of truth.'* Thus he seems to be saying that when all the disillusion at discovering oneself a separate body, at loss of belief in omnipotence and at the discovery of dependence, is accepted, mourned for, and the mourning itself not denied, in all its suffering and anger and tears, then something new happens, to do with the transcending of the separateness of the separate body – through the imagination.

The popular view of the Freudian concept of the unconscious is that it contains only the bad things, the hates and lustfulness that we do not like to admit in ourselves. But any practising analyst knows also how strong is the repression of love. *'O Human Imagination! O Divine Body I have crucified!'* says Blake elsewhere. There is no doubt that Blake is saying that we do in fact continually crucify our imagination, kill our capacity for the imaginative understanding of others, and for two reasons. It is partly because such understanding can bring pain and responsibility; but it is also due to our clinging to those principles of logical thought which require a duality, a split between subject and object, between seer and seen. Certainly, we do have to make that split if we are to emerge from the dependence of babyhood and manage the practical necessities of our lives; but where this principle fails is when it is given more than its rights in our relations with our fellow men. Thus Blake, since he clearly uses the figure of Jesus to stand for what he calls imagination, is making claims for this other kind of thinking which is not based upon the duality of formal logic – subject-object. Hence also Satan is used as a symbol of the isolation (bringing hate) which results from this way of thinking that insists on the complete self-sufficiency of the conscious individual ego.[5] In fact, he also stands for that reliance on the exclusively logical mental activity which separates itself from what it looks at and also from its unconscious roots; a reliance which Blake considers as a kind of sleep, from which we shall wake up. As yet there is hardly any logic for this other kind of thinking, although the phrases, 'the logic of irrationality', 'the sense in nonsense', do show that the problem is increasingly coming to the fore in current philosophical thinking, as well as in psychoanalysis; in fact a psychoanalyst can now say, 'We are poor indeed if we are only sane' with some hope of being understood.[6]

And Blake seems to suggest that this second kind of thinking which is non-interfering, non-assertive, is also a wide embracing kind which does not primarily concern itself with boundaries; he shows this by the position of the arms of Elihu, and of the Deity after the appearance of Elihu, wide-stretched arms in contrast with the tightly bound ones emphasizing the separateness of Eliphaz's God. Also in the marginal drawings for the Elihu picture the spirits which emanate from Job's sleeping body reach out of the universe; as if Blake wishes to indicate that a process is here going on which undoes the over-fixed separation between self and other, self and the universe.

In the next picture (xviii) Job is praying for his friends. Having discovered how to face his own destructiveness, the unredeemed animal nature within him, he now has to face the real nastiness in other people; not the omnipotent nastiness derived from his own fears of himself, as when he saw them as demons, but their real nastiness, their actual accusations and criticisms and failure to understand him. And Blake suggests that the facing of this problem is crucial for the restoring of Job's creative powers; for he puts, for the first time, a palette and brushes in the marginal drawings, also ripe ears of corn. And Job is standing facing a stone altar from which rises a flame that forms a background to the upper part of his body and outstretched arms. In the earlier pictures fire has always been associated with Satan; now it is as if all the passion of Job's instinctive life has become concentrated into a single flame of imaginative concentration. Thus the centre of his being is no longer his own private wish-fulfilling idea of himself, it has become something not private at all but shared by everyone, something symbolized for Blake by the sun. *'For he maketh his sun to shine on the Evil and the Good and sendeth rain on the just and the unjust'*, says the text. So Job can now give to his friends the same wide understanding that he can give to the primitive within himself; and the result is that he is now freed from the necessity to protect himself continually against them in a hard defensive armour of possessions and rights: *'And the Lord turned the captivity of Job when he prayed for his friends.'*

The next picture (xix), in which Job is shown accepting charity, goes back to that early critical moment when Job lost everything, but denied his sorrow and rage by splitting it off and feeling that it was someone else suffering the pains of loss, not himself; when he shared his bread with a beggar and Satan gained power over his body and soul. For here he is accepting help, not giving it, able to wait and be dependent upon the goodwill of others, able to be empty and in need without either becoming angry and destructive or having to give charity out of essentially selfish motives, in order to bolster up the belief in his own self-righteousness. *'The Lord maketh poor and maketh rich'*, *'Who provideth for the raven his food when his young ones cry unto God'*, say the texts. And it is is this acceptance of dependence and his own low estate which leads directly to the next picture of the full freeing of his creative imagination.

In (xx) Job is shown for the first time in his house, and his arms are outstretched in the same position as the creator in 'The Morning Stars' and the Whirlwind. On the walls to the right and the left, are two pictures of destruction, reminiscent of the earlier ones but not identical, and in the middle is a repetition of the God of the Whirlwind. In fact, Blake seems to be emphasizing, through the fact that the destruction is in pictures on the inner walls of his house, that they are imagined acts of violence, not real ones. I think this means that Job has now become able to face the destruction that he has done in his secret thoughts and to realize how, in his early belief in the omnipotence of thought, he felt he had really destroyed those he loved and so had had to build up the wrought image of his own perfection to compensate. Thus in spirit he has now become able to encompass all the manifestations of the primitive energy; the violence of the inner whirlwind is no longer denied, shut out, so its energy can now be enchannelled for creative ends. And grouped around him are his three daughters; it is they who are restored to him, his sons do not appear till the next and final picture of his restored external life. The marginal drawings are of musical instruments and the leaves and fruit and delicate tendrils of the vine. And the texts say: *'There were not found Women fair as the Daughters of Job in all the Land and their Father gave them inheritance among their brethren.'* I think that here Blake means to show that the acceptance of what he calls the female principle within the psyche, equally with the male, is necessary if the full creativity of the human spirit is to be established. This would throw light on the fact that in the picture where Satan smites Job with boils, Job is shown repudiating his wife; and also why, in the stage of recovery depicted in 'The Morning Stars', the moon goddess on God's left is given equal prominence with the sun god on the right. In fact it looks as if Blake means to say that the need to suffer, in the biblical sense, to permit, if not recognized and given psychic expression, if denied and crowded out by the need to dominate and control by force, will still find its own perverted expression in physical suffering, in bodily pains and enforced dependence upon others, like the enforced helplessness of Job under Satan's trampling feet. Here a Freudian would say that the drawings also indicate how Job's relation to the mother within him has been restored, since it is the mother who is the first to disillusion and so becomes the first object of the infant's wrath.

In the last picture (xxi) in which Job is once more under the tree with his wife and sons and daughters, now all are playing upon their instruments, they are again surrounded by their flocks, and the sun and moon are again on each side of the great tree; but this time the sun on the right and the moon on the left. This is the reverse of the first picture, and is an example of that use of right–left symbolism by Blake, which I have had to omit from this interpretation.

What exactly is Blake saying? Many things, some of which a Freudian can corroborate from clinical experience, and also probably many other things which we shall not fully understand for a long time to come.

(1) I think he is saying that the necessary restrictions of society do produce destructive rage, rage that we have to give up so many primary pleasures in learning to live with others, to work and take our turn and not demand more than our fair share. He is saying that this rage can be dealt with if it is recognized and allowed for, but if it is unrecognized then it can lead to internal and external disaster.

184

(2) He is saying that the primitive in ourselves which responds to frustration with anger and destructiveness, can in fact be dealt with in a different way; there is another force making for control, which is other than that of ordering and forbidding and punishments for disobedience.

(3) He is saying also that the traditional idea about how the primitive in us can be reformed, contains a deep pitfall. He is saying that the traditional method of setting up a standard of moral attitudes, to be consciously copied, and then exhorting people to set to work to copy, is full of dangers. Here, I think, he does not mean that there should be no social rules, that a certain deliberate patterning of behaviour is not necessary, for the sake of convenience; otherwise social living would become impossible. But what he does seem to be saying is that if this obedience to social rules is thought of as more than that, if it is thought of in terms of the acquisition of virtuous qualities and as a means to self-righteousness, then we are in danger, both of spiritual sterility and of inner disaster. In fact he is saying that our pride in our virtues is as much a cause of creative sterility as our denial of our vices, for pride in virtue is still concerned with the 'wrought image', it is still Satanic.

(4) He is saying that when our aim is to know the worst about ourselves, not in order to wallow in it, but just to know, to know the truth, then this new force enters into the inner situation, and the cave-man within becomes tameable, even redeemed. For the primary bodily delights and omnipotent illusion of infancy, whose loss can stir such pain and rage, can be rediscovered in a new imaginative synthesis of body and mind, of self and 'other'.

This is what Blake seems to me to be saying. Is it revolutionary? I think so. I think these ideas are still revolutionary, in spite of the fact that they were already formulated 2,000 years ago in the Sermon on the Mount and elsewhere in the Gospels. *'Blessed are they that mourn, for they shall be comforted.'*

And Blake seems to be saying this in terms of a male–female duality. He says that this idea that we can make ourselves grow spiritually, improve ourselves, by consciously following a pattern or model, is a result of a one-sided way of thinking, a way which he calls male; a way that tries to feel it is all there is, ignoring that there is also another way, which he calls 'female'; hence the picture of a Father-in-Heaven but no Mother-in-Heaven, and the idea of Job as a successful patriarch.

185

And Freud also is concerned with the growth of the spirit; he is concerned fundamentally with the growth of the power to love. For if one looked for a single sentence in which Freud epitomized his findings I think it would be 'A man who doubts his own love, may, or rather must, doubt every lesser thing.' And all his writings do in fact show how it became clear to him that learning how to love means learning how to mourn; that is it means learning how to tolerate separation, the loss of what one loves, either temporarily or permanently, without either denying the love, saying the grapes were sour or that love does not matter, or the love turning to hate. Thus learning how to love is learning how to manage the pain and primitive response of anger when the love is frustrated. And he showed how this learning to accept separation from what one loves applies internally, how it applies to the awareness of the separation between what we are and what we would like to be, the gap between our ideals and our actuality. He showed also how it applies to the problems of physical growth and the fact that, in growing to adulthood and old age, we have to leave behind some of our past joys which were only physically possible for infancy or for youth. In fact, psychoanalysis insists that we must be allowed and allow ourselves our griefs, otherwise our joys will be stunted; it is saying that the capacity to mourn is an essential part of our humanity, and an essential condition of psychic growth.

Thus I think that Blake is maintaining what all psychoanalytic experience confirms: that change of heart, growth of spirit, does not come about in the same way as that by which we alter our material surroundings, it does not come from purposeful activity, by having an ideal or plan and then working directly to achieve it. For it seems that the laws of growth of the heart are not even the same as the laws of growth of what we call the mind, those laws of learning by which mental and physical skills are acquired, something which can in fact be done by working to a plan. For it seems that true change of heart, growth to maturity of feeling, only comes about through facing the psychic pain of the recognition of the opposites in ourselves, the pain of the difference between how nice we would like to be and how nasty we often are. In fact psychoanalytic experience seems to be indicating more and more that change of heart is initiated by those moments when we manage just to look at the pain, feel it, embrace it, not trying to get rid of it, or remove ourselves from it, as we would if it were something outside us giving us pain. Thus there seems to be a fundamental paradox here, change of heart seems to come only when we give up trying to change. Apparently it cannot come by striving to conform to any pattern, however exalted, the very striving to escape from what we do not like in ourselves only drives us deeper in.

Thus psychoanalysis, which began with an attempt to cure neurotic symptoms, has become increasingly concerned with problems of character and personality: with the change in character and growth in stature which seems to have as its starting-point those moments when the patient is able to look at his sins, defects, weakness, without either trying to whitewash them nor trying to alter them in order that they themselves may become more admirable people. They are in fact moments in which hopelessness about oneself is accepted; and it is this which seems to enable the redeeming force to come into play. In fact it seems that when one can just look at the gap between the ideal and the actuality in oneself, see both the ideal and the failure to live up to it in one moment of vision, without either turning against the ideal and becoming cynical, nor trying to alter oneself to fit it, then the ideal and the actuality seem to enter into relation with each other and produce something new; and the result is nothing to do with self-righteousness or being pleased with oneself for having lived up to the ideal.

The relevance for education

Uses of authority

I think the fact that Freud discovered how the one-sidedness of reliance on the logical conscious reasoning power could be redressed, in the experience of the analytic session, through learning how not to interfere and control thoughts according to a preconceived order, has certainly led to some confused ideas about order and freedom in education. The fact that both the struggle against having to give up one's infantile feelings of omnipotence and the battle for spontaneity of the instincts is felt, at least in a patriarchal society, as a fight against the father, led some pioneers in education to think that if there were no authority in schools the pupils would all grow up free from neurotic restraints and inhibitions. This did not happen and I think for the following reason.

A wider reading of Freud's conception emphasizes the fact that the conflict with the father or father substitute is only the battleground for a more general fight; that is between nature inside man, his instinctive desires, and nature outside him, the objective facts to which he is compelled to adjust if he is to stay alive. But man, by becoming a social animal has, to a large extent, substituted the compulsion of society for the compulsion of nature. Thus through the emergence of society, including the family, he has become less the slave of nature, more free in the external conflict with nature, than the animals; yet by so doing he has become more torn by internal conflict and revolt against that very order which is the condition of his material freedom. Thus a most profound problem of society is that the instinctive needs of human beings, if unordered, unintegrated, are themselves disruptive of that very external stability which they need if they are to be satisfied. And this is why the task of the educationist is so difficult, since the teacher, as also the parent in the role of teacher, cannot help being partly a disillusioner. The teacher represents that society which refuses to accept the primary instinctive ways of showing love and demands that substitute ways be learnt, however painfully. 'An infant wants to love his mother with all his bodily powers', says Anna Freud. But that infant, in growing to be a child, has to learn to tolerate the rejection of his primary ways of loving; he has to learn to give his love to parents, to society, in highly sophisticated ways which take much learning: in speech, not babble; in writing, not scribbling and smearing; in ability to wait, not impulsiveness; in social manners, not the abandonment of the puppy. And in order to learn at all the child also has to climb down from the original heights of omnipotence, to discover how little he knows, where once he felt he knew everything, how little he can do, where once he felt he could do everything. However skilfully this process of disillusion is accomplished it seems there is always pain in it – for the child – and somewhere, however hidden, some degree of hate. Thus it is that good teachers understand (intuitively, if not explicitly), that their task is to help the children with their hate, help them to accept it, recognize it, not shut it away so that it becomes a hidden Satan; which means that the teachers have come to terms with their own hate, so that, although disillusioners, they are also merciful.

Uses of hard work

In this sense the public examination is not essentially a test of what a child knows; it is an initiation ceremony intended to give a public recognition to our power to take pains, to undergo pains, labour, for the sake of something we value. In face the Freudian viewpoint sees work well done, whether school work or earning a living, as essentially part of the struggle to come to believe in, and have good grounds for believing in, one's power to love. Also it sees, as a result of clinical experience (with the so-called 'normal' as well as with those who know they are not), that the inner structure of the unconscious part of our psyche is essentially animistic. That is we build up our inner world on the basis of our relationships to people we have loved and hated, we carry these people about with us and what we do, we do for them – or in conflict with them. And it seems that it is through these internalized people that we carry on our earliest relationships, developing and enriching them throughout life; even when these first loved people no longer exist in the external world, we find external representatives of them both in new people who enter our lives, and in all our interests and the causes that we seek to serve. And because these internal people contain something of ourselves, they contain, represent, the love and the hate which we first felt for the outside people, so we go on throughout our lives, continually discovering more of ourselves and more of the world, in developing our relationships to them through their substitutes. And not only do they represent the original objects of our love and our hate, they also are felt as helping or hindering figures working within us, and in this sense they become identified with our own powers.

In the Job story Blake's identification of the helping figures with the capacity for becoming aware sems to express the same idea of the essentially personal quality of the structure of the inner world. So also in psychoanalysis the curative process seems to occur because the patient, by continual experience of the not-interfering, not-judging, truth-seeking attitude of the analyst, is eventually able to 'take the analyst inside'; that is he becomes more aware of and able to make use of the same spirit of truth within himself.

I think that the idea that, however impersonal our activities may seem to be, they are fundamentally to do with people, should be fruitful for teachers. For instance, the extent to which the staff of any school are used by the children as the dramatis personae of their own inner dramas can, at times, be a source of irritation or mystification, if the teachers have not understood the inevitability of the process; it may give them anxiety to discover they are temporarily being used to play the part of Satan, or of the demons that Job's friends became: or it may bring undue gratification or embarrassment when they seem to be cast for the role of Elihu or Christ.

What else is Blake saying that is relevant for education? Something about the one-sidedness of Job's approach to life as being to do with an underestimation of the importance of the image-making capacity of the mind; for in the 'Job with his Daughters' picture, Job is surrounded by obviously self-created images. (In another picture Blake made of Job, one not included in the final series, Job is shown

189

surrounded by the three figures of Painting, Poetry, and Music.) Freud discovered the same thing, that it was by attending to what his patients freely imagined rather than to their conscious reasoning, that they were helped towards a freeing of their powers. The application of this to education is already being worked out in many recent experiments. One particular way is by offering to teachers vacation courses in which they themselves can be helped to experience the astounding quality of the untapped capacities of the creative imagination in each one of them; particularly in those who have never had it interfered with by a teaching that believes only in the power of a split mind working to an imposed pattern, a teaching which fears that spontaneity means only chaos, or that the freeing of the imagination only means giving over the control to Satan.

Uses of absentmindedness

Blake is also saying something about the importance of the occasions when the free imagination interacts with perception and produces moments of vision in which the external world is transfigured. For the Freudian these are the moments when there is a temporary fusion of inner and outer, an undoing of the split between self and not-self, seer and seen; and it seems likely that these are the crucial moments which initiate the growth of new enthusiasms, the finding of new loves, moments when what Blake calls each man's poetic genius 'creates' the world for us, by finding the familiar in the unfamiliar, moments when the imagination catches fire and lights up a whole new vista of possibilities of relationship with the outside world. Thus they are moments of falling in love, which need not only be with a person, but can be also with a skill or a subject or a medium, with words or clay or sounds or stone. They are moments when the 'Spirit bloweth where it listeth' (Like Blake's God in the Whirlwind); they cannot be induced, either by the teacher or the child. But they can be allowed for; and, if psychoanalytic experience is right, they are most likely to occur in a particular kind of setting, one in which there is not too great fear of a tyrannical authority, so that the spontaneous life is either denied, or expressed in defiant rebellion; nor yet too much license, which would mean that the child is kept too busy with unshared responsibility for his own aggression to dare to give his imagination its head; in fact, in a setting in which it is safe, sometimes, to be absent-minded.

If one were to use Blake's work to form the basis of a prophecy, and attempt to point the direction in which further psychological discoveries will become of use for education, I would suggest the following: they will be to do with a deeper understanding of the creative relation to the internal spontaneous forces, making for wholeness.

References

1 Milner, M. (1956) The Sense in Nonsense (Freud and Blake's *Job*). In *Freud, Jung, and Adler: Their Relevance to the Teacher's Life and Work. The New Era* January: 1–13.
2 I am not here concerned with the problem of Blake's position as a visual artist, but only with the depths of his understanding, as a poet of human nature.
3 In trying to come to my own conclusions I have made much use of Wicksteed's commentary but I am not discussing Blake's extensive use of right–left symbolism, which is carefully studied by Wicksteed. (Joseph Wicksteed (1910) *Blake's 'Vision of the Book of Job': A Study*. London: Dent.)
4 The version I am describing is the fourth and final version (published 1826). Blake engraved this version and added texts from the Bible and marginal drawings, after he had made other versions in water-colour. There are various modern editions which can be obtained at most public libraries.
5 I am greatly indebted to Kathleen Raine, Blake scholar as well as poet, for reading this paper and introducing me to Blake's use, in his works, of the concept of Satan; also for making comments which, for me, emphasize the difficulties that arise when the same words 'ego' and 'self' are used to mean quite different ideas, by different schools of thought; although it is beyond the scope of this paper to try and sort out these difficulties.
6 Winnicott, D. W. (1945) Primitive Emotional Development in *Collected Papers* (1958), London: Tavistock, p. 150 and (1965) The Effect of Psychosis in Family Life in *The Family and Individual Development*, London: Tavistock, p. 61.

12

1956: Psychoanalysis and art

In 1956 I was asked to give a lecture to a public audience at London's Friends' House on psychoanalysis and art, as part of the Freud centenary celebrations.[1] Here I once more decided to make use of some of Susan's drawings (see Chapter 6) and, again, some of Blake's *Illustrations to the Book of Job*.

What is art? And what is genius in art? When I set out to prepare this lecture I intended to try to select out of writings on art, both by analysts and non-analysts, whatever might point the direction towards an answer to these questions. I read many books and technical papers on both sides. On the non-analysts' side, for instance, I read Berenson, Kenneth Clarke, William Empson, Gombrich, Susanne Langer, Maritain, André Malraux, and Herbert Read. On the analysts' side I read Freud, Ernest Jones, Ella Sharpe, Anna Freud, Melanie Klein, Balint, Fairbairn, Kris, Hanna Segal, Rycroft, and many others. I also read two who are not analysts but who are identified with the analytic approach – Ehrenzweig and Adrian Stokes. Of course I soon found what an enormous task of digestion I had set myself. Instead of my mind being full of ideas about what art is, it felt a complete blank, so that it seemed quite impossible to achieve any sifting of the various ideas presented by all these writers. Gradually, however, after many weeks, instead of fighting the blankness I became able to accept it. And then I found that certain ideas about what I had read began to emerge of their own accord.

The first one came from the non-analytic side, from Herbert

Read's latest book *Icon and Idea*, where he says that the great painters, sculptors, poets, and musicians make conquests of consciousness that are afterwards occupied by the mind in widest commonality.[2] He also says that art is finding (rather than seeking) new symbols to signify new areas of sensibility. The next idea came from the analytic side, from Ernst Kris's book *Psychoanalytic Explorations in Art*.[3] In this book he tells how, in the sixteenth century for the first time in history, a work of art was considered as a projection of an inner image; for in a contemporary guidebook it was said that a Michelangelo unfinished block was better than the finished one, because it came nearer the state of conception. Hence, says Kris, it is not nearness to reality but nearness to the artist's psychic life that becomes the test of the value of the work of art. Then I found myself haunted by another phrase from the group of non-analytic writers. It was, 'the sovereign awakening of creative subjectivity to itself'. I recognized this as from the French Catholic philosopher Maritain; so I turned to his book *Creative Intuition in Art and Poetry*, where he develops the theme that, as compared with Eastern art, Western art has progressively laid stress on the artist's self.[4] In its last phase, he says, it has plunged deeply into the incommunicable world of creative subjectivity. Here I found my sense of confusion and despairing emptiness had gone, for I felt this phrase 'creative subjectivity' contained a central idea from which to approach the subject of art.

Maritain goes on to talk about the modern painter having become less and less interested in what the painting is of, the something in the outside world that the painting is to be a picture of, and more and more interested in the actual painting. This, he says, has been described as a turning away from nature in favour of an interest in themselves, in their own subjectivity. But, he adds, all this, though true, is only a half-truth. He says that what we see in great modern painting is more interest than ever in nature, but in a different way. He says that the painters are men who, seeking after themselves, are by the same stroke carried along beyond the natural appearance of things in desperate search of a deeper reality. Thus the conquest by brush and palette of this unnameable something is enough for a man to offer up his entire life. And, he says, it is so because creative subjectivity cannot awaken to itself except in communing with things. Thus he maintains, the relation with nature has been changed but has not been abolished.

Now here, in Maritain's description of what the modern artist is doing, we also get a hint of how he is doing it. For Maritain is saying that it is only through the relation to things that it can happen; by 'things' he means all that is outside the self. Here Freud would have agreed with him. Maritain goes on to try to decribe the creative act itself. He says that at the root of the creative act there must be a quite peculiar mental process without parallel in logical reason, a process through which things and the self are grasped together by means of a kind of experience of knowledge which has no conceptual expression and is shown only in the artist's work. He calls this process creative or poetic intuition. And he goes on to say that in poetic intuition, objective reality, and subjectivity, the world and the whole of the soul co-exist inseparably. He says; 'At that moment sense and sensation are brought back to the heart, blood to the spirit, passion to intuition.' And he adds that this particular intellectual process, which has no parallel in logical reason, is not really a process of liberation from reason because reason possesses a life both deeper and less conscious than its articulate logical life. In poetry, he says, we enter a nocturnal empire, a primeval activity of the intellect which, far beyond concepts and logic, exercises itself in vital connections between imagination and emotion. So here is something else that it does – or a different way of describing the bringing back of blood to the spirit; this time it is bringing together imagination and feeling. Note also that he talks of reason as having a life deeper and less conscious than its articulate logical life. (By 'articulate' I think he intends to convey the ordinary dictionary meaning, which is both 'verbalized' and 'organized together'.)

Now, this word 'articulate' brought me back again to the analytic side, to a writer who knows about the process of analysis from direct experience, although not himself an analyst; to Ehrenzweig and his book *The Psycho-Analysis of Artistic Vision and Hearing*.[5] For here Ehrenzweig talks about what he calls the 'articulating tendency' of the surface mind, and the fact that we tend, for the most part, to notice compact, simple, precise forms, at the same time eliminating vague, incoherent, inarticulate forms from our perception. He points out how both William James and Freud, independently of each other, drew attention to the articulating tendency of our surface perception. So, he says, did the *Gestalt* psychologists; they used the term '*Gestalt* tendency' to describe how we tend to perceive in terms of compactness and coherence – how we like to see a pattern, find one, even in chaos. Ehrenzweig goes on to tell of how the *Gestalt* psychologists take art as a supreme manifestation of the human mind's striving towards articulate *Gestalt*; but he thinks this theory has led to a failure to appreciate some of the most fundamental aspects of art; that is what he called in a recent broadcast talk 'the role of the creative accident'. He also reminds us that Freud not only noticed the articulating tendency of our observing mind but also found that ideas coming from the lower layers of the mind, like our dream visions, tend to be inarticulate; they appear to our observing mind as altogether chaotic and difficult to grasp; and not only our night dreams but also our day-dreams have this elusive quality. Of course we do not really need an expert to tell us this. We have only to try to take a look at our own day-dreams, reveries, moments of absent-mindedness, to know that we do, ordinarily, think on two different levels, in an oscillating rhythm, and that when we return from the absent-minded phase it is not always easy to say what we have been thinking. In fact, it must be clear to anyone who looks inwards that our mental life does progress with a movement rather like a porpoise. (The old cartoons of the Loch Ness monster perhaps give the best graphic picture of it.)

Ehrenzweig points out how Otto Rank maintained that artistic creativeness involves a cyclical displacement of mental energy between two different levels; yet he considered the inarticulate phase preceding the emergence of ideas as mere interruption of consciousness, emptiness of vision. Here Ehrenzweig refers to William James, and how he said that the creative state wrongly appears as an emptiness of consciousness only because we cannot grasp its fluid content in the definite perceptions of the surface mind. Ehrenzweig concludes that any act of creativeness requires a temporary, cyclical paralysis of the surface attention. He gives an example of such temporary paralysis from an artist sketching in his background forms in a state of diffused attention, a state by which he looks at figure and background in one glance; an impossible task, says Ehrenzweig, from the point of view of *Gestalt* theory. he also talks of the particular technique needed to get hold of the visions filling the creative mind (during the alleged lapse of consciousness), as a kind of absent-minded watchfulness. (Thus may, by the way, be compared with Freud's description of the kind of attention required of the analyst.) Ehrenzweig also discusses that particular class of people who have forgone the attempt to relate their visions to surface perception – the mystics. He says that when the mystic returns to surface consciousness he has the memory of deeply significant visions but without a trace of definite imagery. Thus the mystic's vision does not appear to him as mere emptiness, and he does not try to project a more elaborate pattern into it, as Freud says we do when we unconsciously give to our night dreams some sort of secondary shape and communicability.

Ehrenzweig goes on to point out how Freud also talked about the mystical state, a state which he described as a feeling of being one with the universe. Freud called it oceanic (a term borrowed from a friend), and he admitted that he had never had it himself. He explained it as a regression to the early infantile state of consciousness, to the state when the child's ego is not yet differentiated from the surrounding external world. Hence, says Ehrenzweig, Freud is claiming that the feeling of union is no mere illusion, but the correct description of a memory of an infantile state otherwise inaccessible to direct introspection. Ehrenzweig adds a futher explanation, one based on Freud's own discoveries about the form of thinking in dreams. He says that the mystic feeling is explained by our rational surface mind's incapacity to visualize the inarticulate images of the depth mind, and his central point is that the creative process takes place in these gaps in our surface mind's activity. He goes on to point out how these rhythms of the mind can be seen as a series; it ranges from the rapid oscillations of everyday thinking and perception to the slower cycle of waking and sleeping and to the even slower double rhythm of the creative activity in which the submerged phase may be sometimes extremely protracted.

What Ehrenzweig does, I think, imply but not state is what Maritain states so clearly; that is that this process which goes on in the gaps essentially involves an undoing of that split into subject and object which is the very basis of our logical thinking. Ehrenzweig says that it also follows that the depth mind can do things that the surface mind cannot do. It can encompass a complexity of relationships that is quite beyond the capacity of the surface mind. He talks of this as the unconscious sense of form, and says it can only be reached by the diffused, wide stare, not by the narrow focus of ordinary attention. He maintains that it is this wide focus which makes it possible for the artist to get closer to a more primitive vision of the world, a vision which can appear confused and chaotic to the adult mind but is not really so; it is not chaotic, only more generalized. He also offers evidence that the perception of time relations in the depth mind is different from that of the surface mind. He says that the depth mind is not, for instance, limited by the surface mind's preference for time relations which only go one way; in fact, it can perceive time relations backwards just as easily as forwards.

These ideas of Ehrenzweig interested me very much, especially the emphasis on the wide diffused stare of attention. For when I first began, thirty years ago, to try to observe from inside – that is introspectively – the effect of different ways of looking at the outside world, I discovered that it was just this wide focus of attention that made the world seem most intensely real and significant.

The state of mind which analysts describe as a repetition of the infant's feelings in its mother's arms, the state which Freud called oceanic, is thus being regarded by certain writers on art as an essential part of the creative process. But it is not the oceanic feeling by itself, for that would be the mystic's state; it is rather the oceanic state in a cyclic oscillation with the activity of what Ehrenzweig calls the surface mind, with that activity in which 'things' and the self, as Maritain puts it, are grasped separately, not together. And the cyclic oscillation is not just passively experienced but actively used, with the intent to make something, produce something.

Figure 45

Figure 45 shows a doodle drawing made by a patient in analysis (see Chapter 6). She had had some experiences near to those that mystics talk about, though she had not called them mystical. This drawing will give you the opportunity of observing in yourselves a moment of oscillating perception; when you look steadily at it you will see that it alternates between being a single face seen from the front, with a lock of hair down the middle, and two faces looking at each other, seen in profile. *Figure 46* shows another of this patient's drawings; the top face is uncertain about its boundary and the lower part of the drawing oscillates between being one full face, round like the sun, and two profiles. *Figure 47* is a tracing of the lower half so that it can be seen more clearly. My interpretation of this drawing is that the full face does represent the state of feeling of oneness with the universe, the undivided state, while the profiles represent the phase of separation, of twoness, of differentiation of oneself from others.

Figure 46

Figure 47

Now I will turn to another writer, also a non-analyst, but deeply identified with the psychoanalytic approach, one who has written many highly interesting studies of works of art – Adrian Stokes.[6] I will quote what he says, not about the state of mind in which a work of art is produced, but about the work of art itself. Stokes talks of a work of art as an individual separate object, differentiated yet made of undifferentiated material, something that suggests an entirely separate entity yet having a pulse in common and joined to the heart of things. He says that this is what the artist strives to recreate, a sense of fusion, thus renewing the oceanic feeling but combined with object 'otherness'. And he says that it is from this state of fusion in which ideas are interchangeable that the poetic identifications flow.

At this point, instead of seeking further amongst the writings of analysts or non-analysts, I am going to do what Freud himself, in 1932, advised one to do, when science seemed not yet able to provide an answer to a problem.[7] He said, 'Ask the poets'; but the subject he was searching for light upon at that moment was not art but femininity. So I am going to remind you of a work of art which combines the vision of two poets; the one ancient Hebrew, the other late-eighteenth- and early-nineteenth-century English. It is Blake's *Illustrations to the Book of Job.*

This work of Blake's (I am talking of the final version, published in 1826) consists of twenty-one engravings with texts from the Bible and linear drawings set around the margins. You remember the story of Job, the perfect and upright man; how Satan appears before God and says it's all very well for Job to be so good when he has everything he could possibly want, but what if he really suffered, would he be so good then? So God gives Satan permission to plague Job in every possible way short of killing him. *Figure 48* for instance, shows Satan killing Job's sons and daughters (iii). And you remember how Job at first bears all patiently, but finally succumbs and curses the day he was born. And then when Job has reached the depths of despair a new figure appears, Elihu; after this Job gradually climbs back to his original estate – but with a difference. Now Blake has made it quite clear that he is using this ancient story in a special way in order to say something about the stultification of creative expression in the arts. In the first picture (*Figure 49*) of Job with his wife and family, surrounded by his flocks, they are all shown grouped under a spreading tree upon which hang musical instruments, unused. Job is reading from a book and one of the texts says, '*The letter killeth, the spirit giveth life*'. The last picture (*Figure 50*), showing Job with his family and flocks restored to him, has the same design, but now they are all singing or playing upon their instruments (xxi).

199

Figure 48 (iii) Satan smiting Job's sons and daughters

Figure 49 (i) Job with his wife and family

Figure 50 (xxi) Job with his family restored

Figure 51 (xx) Job with his daughters

And the picture immediately before the last (*Figure 51*) is of Job in his own house with paintings upon the walls, and grouped around him are his three daughters (xx). The texts say, '*There were not found women fair as the daughters of Job in all the land and their father gave them inheritance among their brethren.*' Blake also makes it quite clear what the three daughters signify, because in another picture (not included in the Job series) Job is shown surrounded by the three allegorical figures of Painting, Poetry, and Music.

The first eleven pictures of Blake's version show the gradual stages of Job's downfall and descent to the depths – from the second picture, where Satan appears before the throne of God (and God has the same face as Job), up to the climax (*Figure 52*), where the God Job has called upon appears, but as a demon, though still with the face of Job himself (xi). Then come the stages of recovery, beginning with the advent of Elihu (xii: *Figure 53*).

If one asks, 'What is Blake' view about why Job had to go through such torment?' the answer is clear. There is no doubt from Blake's choice of texts throughout the series that, for him, the nature of Job's error was two-fold. In the first place his mistake was that he thought he was perfect because his conscious intention was perfect; Job lived, as he thought, in perfect obedience to his God according to the letter of the law. And he could do this because he thought that what he was conscious of in himself was all there was; so he is shown persistently denying that there could be any evil in himself just because his conscious intention is not evil. But Blake is quite clear that in Job's inner world there is evil; 'that which is above is within', says Blake elsewhere. So in the second picture (*Figure 54*) Job's inner world is shown above his head and in it is Satan, the principle of destruction, leaping in and demanding expression.

In the second place, Blake seems to be saying that there is a mistake in Job's whole attitude of mind in respect of what Blake seems to call maleness and femaleness; for he clearly shows that he thinks Job's attitude is one-sidedly male. Thus Job is shown not only as obeying the letter of the law and thinking that is all there is, but also as a successful patriarch, a man of power; and the idea that he is leaving something out of count, to which Blake gives the name of female, is expressed in various ways. For instance (*Figure 55*), when Satan stands astride him, smiting him with boils, Job is shown repudiating his wife, who kneels weeping at his feet (vi). If we are interested in the dark side of consciousness as containing, amongst other things, all those wishes that we have repudiated because they are incompatible with our standards and idea of ourselves, then we could certainly find plenty to say here about the conflicts in a man as

Figure 52 (xi) God appears, as a demon

Figure 53 (xii) Arrival of Elihu

Figure 54 (ii) Satan leaps in before the Throne

Figure 55 (vi) Satan smiting Job with boils

a man (Job here standing for all men) about women as women. But if we are also interested in the nature of the processes in the dark side of consciousness, as I am here, then I think it is clear that the figure of Job's wife does also stand for an unadmitted way of functioning in himself. I think this is a legitimate interpretation in the light of the ideas expressed in the pictures of the recovery. For not only is there the picture of the restoring of Job's daughters before his sons, there is also in the famous 'Morning Stars' picture (*Figure 56*; the third after the appearance of Elihu – xiv), the moon goddess (driving a team of serpents) given equal prominence with the sun god driving a team of horses. Also there is an interesting recurrent theme of the position of the arms in the pictures of the recovery, both those of the Deity and of Job. They gradually become spread out in a wide, embracing gesture; and this is surely significant in connection with that wide-focused, wide-embracing kind of attention which Ehrenzweig claims is characteristic of the functioning of what he calls the depth mind. By contrast (*Figure 57*), there is Blake's picture of the God of Job's friend Eliphaz, as seen by Job in a dream; you will notice the arms are tightly bound, not wide-embracing (ix).

Most interesting of all, perhaps, to the psychoanalyst if not to the artist, is the picture after 'The Morning Stars' (xv: the fourth after the arrival of Elihu, *Figure 58*). In it the Deity is shown lying on a cloud, and drawing the attention of Job and his wife and friends to what is obviously an inner world – because enclosed in a circle – but this time down below. In it are the two monsters, Behemoth and Leviathan. What did Blake mean by this picture? Like all poetic symbolism, it must have manifold meaning. But as I see it and in the setting of the problem of creativeness, we are back on the theme of the two levels of the mind — the surface or conscious mind and the depth or unconscious mind. For Behemoth seems to be standing on the land, though looking rather angry about it; and Leviathan is certainly half submerged in water, and looks as if about to go under, though whether in a swoon of agony or ecstasy it is hard to say. The fact that Blake shows the Leviathan figure, the figure related to the depths, as half serpent, suggests that he does think of Leviathan as related to, if not identical with, a primitive form of the female aspect of the psyche; for it is the moon goddess who drives serpents. However, as against my theory, I must admit that Blake calls Leviathan 'he', and puts the text, 'Of Leviathan he said, he is King over all the children of pride'; but perhaps this is not as contradictory to my argument as appears at first sight. Certainly in this picture Blake seems to be showing his idea of the basic human energies in their most primitive form, for both creatures have a look of blind, unseeing eyes, as if to express the idea of energy not yet aware of itself. Thus it seems to me that Blake is developing in these pictures, following the arrival of Elihu, an idea of the same kind of happening in human development as that described by Maritain when he talks of 'the awakening of creative subjectivity to itself'. Also Blake seems to be saying that this awakening comes through the acceptance of, equally with the male, what he seems to look upon as the female phase of mental functioning; also that the full experience of this female phase means a willingness to accept a temporary submergence below the surface consciousness.

Blake also implies, I think, that this phase or state that he calls female is not concerned primarily with the boundaries that mark off the self from the rest of the world. For in the marginal drawings of the Elihu picture the spirits which emanate from Job's sleeping body reach out to the stars; as if Blake wished to indicate that the process is here going on which undoes the over-fixed separation between self and other, self and the universe. Thus it seems that having once achieved the sense of separate existence, it is then necessary to be continually undoing it again, in a cyclic oscillation, if psychic sterility is to be avoided.

This idea of undoing a separation is also developed in the seventeenth picture of the series (*Figure 59*). Here Christ appears standing on the ground beside Job and his wife, and blessing them, while the friends shrink away in terror. Several of the texts here are form the Gospels. One of them says, 'I and my Father are one'; also 'And that day ye shall know that I am in my Father and you in me and I in you'.

If one asks the question, 'Why does Blake bring the figure of Christ into the Job story?' I think the answer is quite clear. He does it because he really does feel that the teachings of Christ have something to do with creative process, whether in art or science. For instance, in his poem *Jerusalem* he says, 'I know of no other Christianity and of no other Gospel than the liberty both of mind and body to exercise the Divine Arts of Imagination. . . . The Apostles knew of no other Gospel . . . O ye Religious, discountenance every one among you who shall pretend to despise Art and Science.'

Also in the same poem he says:

'O Human Imagination! O Divine Body I have crucified!'

Thus he certainly does seem to be saying that this state of oneness has something to do with creative process, both in science and art; and also that the working of this creative power requires an active surrender of the purposive, controlling, deliberative mind. 'That he

Figure 56 (xiv) The Morning Stars sang together

Figure 57 (ix) The God of Eliphaz

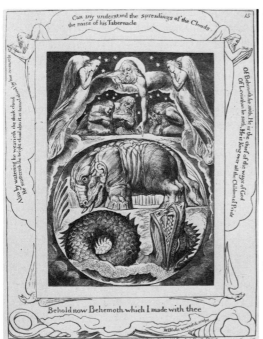

Figure 58 (xv) Behemoth and Leviathan

Figure 59 (xvii) Christ blessing Job and his wife

may withdraw Man from his purpose and hide Pride from Man', says one of the texts to the Elihu picture. You will notice that I said 'active surrender', for it is not a blind surrender; as André Malraux says in his book, *The Voices of Silence*, art is certainly not a complete capitulation to the unconscious.[8] Thus in the light of these pictures I think there is no doubt what Blake thought about the flowering of creative process. He is saying it depends on giving equal validity to a state of mind which is attentive and receptive to what is happening (symbolized by the female), equally with the state that tries to force what happens into a preconceived idea or pattern. But let no one suppose that because it is that it is therefore easy; it is an ordeal, what Maritain calls the 'inner ordeal of creative freedom', when discussing Chardin's words, 'He who has not felt the difficulties of his art does nothing that counts'. And there is discipline involved, though not the kind that is imposed from above by practice in following rules. It is rather a struggling to let something happen in relation to a chosen material, that malleable bit of external world which can be shaped. And it is by this struggle with the material that the conscious mind disciplines the chaotic forces in the creative depths.

Some such conception of the nature of the creative process is also necessary, I think, for the full understanding of Freud's work and discoveries. For what he invented was, in fact, an instrument for the study of the psyche – and one that at the same time was an instrument of healing. For his patients the medium to be manipulated was a vocal sound, the action required of them was simply that they should talk – or, as a present-day analyst, Clifford Scott, has put it, make a noise – without trying to impose any standards of logic, order, politeness, or decency. And by this free talking, or free association as Freud called it, his patients began to discover what it was they really thought. They did it by gradually becoming able to hear what they said (like E. M. Forster's old lady who said, 'How can I know what I think till I see what I say'). Freud discovered that his role was simply to listen and try to help them see the implications of what they had said. And the result was, when things went well, that the patients began to be able to relate themselves more fully, both to the hidden creative roots of their existence, and to what is offered in the real world, and so became able to free their powers of loving and working. In fact, I think it could be said, although Freud himself did not say it in just this way, that what he found was this: that the people who came to him were in trouble over a failure to discover how to manage their own feelings and desires, because they were trying to manage them by means of a one-sided kind of thinking which did not, in fact, work.

They had been trying to solve problems of feeling by means of the kind of thinking which divides what we see from ourselves seeing it, the kind of thinking which we call logical and for which we have formulated laws – the primary laws of logic; such as, for instance, that a thing is what it is and is not what it is not; or that something cannot both be and not be at the same time. He found also that these people were intensely preoccupied and influenced in their feelings and behaviour, in an irrational way, by a different kind of thinking, a kind which did not work according to the laws of logic, a kind which Freud called unconscious phantasy. Thus it seemed as if they were trying to live their lives as though conscious, common-sense, logical thinking was all there was – for good or for ill – just as Job had done, and it was only when they found that they could not solve their problems by reasoning with themselves that Freud was called in to help. And it was then that he found, by attending to what they freely imagined rather than to their common-sense reasoning, that they were helped to a freeing of their powers.

But this other way of thinking (which Freud and psychoanalysts after him call phantasy), which is not based on making that rigid distinction between subjective and objective that logical thinking does, has some relation to what Maritain describes as the poetic activity. He talks of a margin of dreaming activity which many have murdered within themselves, by which the soul is known in the experience of the world and the world is known in the experience of the soul. He says that it is a knowledge which does not know itself, for such knowledge knows not in order to know but in order to produce. His central claim is that, apart from the process which tends to knowledge by means of concepts, there is also something which is preconceptual, not a mere way to the concept but another kind of germ which does not tend towards a concept to be formed. Such a thing is knowledge in act, a kind of inherent knowledge which, he says, is of the essence of poetry. But it is not only Maritain who talks about this inherent kind of knowing; descriptions of it can be found in poetry itself. For instance, Thomas Traherne in the seventeenth century wrote:

> 'It acts not from its centre to
>   Its object as remote,
> But present is, when it doth view,
>   Being with the Being it doth note.
>   Whatever it doth do,
> It doth not by another engine work,
> But by itself; which in the act doth lurk.'

('My Spirit')

Maritain also talks about the substance of man being obscure to himself; he knows not his own subjectivity, or if he does, only as a kind of propitious or enveloping night; he says subjectivity as such cannot be conceptualized, it is an unknowable abyss – which is perhaps what the Chinese say more concisely when they say:

'The Tao of which we speak is not the real Tao'

I hope these last quotations will give you some idea of the difficulty of talking logically about this other half of thinking, which Blake calls female and which he insists must be given 'equal inheritance' if there is not to be psychic sterility.

Now I want to go back to Job's other mistake, his denial of his own destructiveness. For this much is clear, to a Freudian at least: Job's perfect obedience left out of count all his rebellion and anger at not being himself as omnipotent as he once, as an infant, thought he was. Classical Freudian theory would say that, by perfect obedience, Job has tried to regain that lost omnipotence, tried to regain it by being one with God. A Freudian would say also that the state described in the text to the second picture (*Figure 54*), '*When the Almighty was yet with me. When my children were about me*', is a description of the original oceanic feeling of infancy when one had, as Freud said, 'the notion of limitless extension and oneness with the universe'. Thus Job's anger, as shown in the person of Satan, can be seen as his infantile destructive anger at being forced by the impacts of external reality to give up that feeling.

With this theme of destructiveness I want to go back to the subject of symbols and to Herbert Read's remark about art as the finding of symbols. For it is a fact that more and more analysts are now becoming concerned with the way in which symbols are created; and this includes, of course, the problem of the creation of concepts, for verbal concepts are only a special class of symbols. Analysts find that in their most deeply disturbed patients the process of symbol formation has been interfered with, or perhaps never properly established. And two ideas are emerging from this. First, that the achieving of a symbol (a symbol being seen as essentially a substitute) involves a mourning for the loss of that for which it is a substitute. Second, that the process of finding the substitute requires a temporary merging of the idea of the original thing with the idea of the substitute. Now, this idea of the experience of loss as an essential aspect of symbol formation does, I think, provide a bridge between Maritain's formulation and the psychoanalyst's. For Maritain, in talking about Dante, speaks of 'Some abiding despair in every great poet, a certain wound in him that has set free the creativeness'. What psychoanalysis is adding is that where there is such a wound or loss, then there is also, implicit or explicit, anger at the loss. There is certainly plenty of anger in Dante, expressed in the tortures he gives to the souls of the damned; also in Blake's pictures, such as the one of Satan destroying Job's sons and daughters.

At this stage in my argument I think the names that have been given to the two phases of the mind's oscillation become important. For instance, Ehrenzweig borrows from Nietzsche the terms Apollonian and Dionysian. He says that Greek tragedy grew from the Dionysian mysteries, expressive of fear, anguish, cravings for self-destruction, and mystic union with the universe. It is most interesting that he makes this link between self-destruction and mystic union (as religions have so often done) because it has a bearing on what Freud called the death instinct or Thanatos, which he postulated as the inescapable pair of the life instinct or Eros. Freudians, at least some of them, say that the so-called death instinct aims at self-destruction; but they do not, as a rule, go on to say that this self-destruction is perhaps a distorted, because frustrated, form of that self-surrender which is inherent in creative process. But Ehrenzweig says so, and I think that Blake implies it. Ehrenzweig thinks that Dionysian Thanatos is the chaotic life force which tries to break up individual existence, while Apollonian Eros is the form principle of differentiation which safeguards individual existence by moulding the Dionysian chaos into order and beauty. Incidentally, I should like to mention that Ehrenzweig follows up this idea about the ordering of the Dionysian chaos with a discussion on the nature of 'beauty' and 'style'. It is a discussion which is made rather confusing, though full of interesting observations, because he does not make it sufficiently clear that he is limiting the concepts of beauty and style to what can be talked about and analysed by the aesthetician. I think he has artificially restricted the meaning of these concepts in order to get round the undoubted difficulty that what he is talking about is something which cannot, in fact, be analysed without destroying it, but can only be appreciated. And this, I feel, is also my chief difficulty in this lecture; I am trying to talk about a state of mind that does in a sense stop being that state of mind as soon as we separate ourselves from it sufficiently to talk about it in logical terms.

This theme of Thanatos brings us to the theory of artistic creation developed by Melanie Klein and her followers, particularly Hanna Segal.[9] Ehrenzweig takes account of this work and describes it as conceiving the creative process as a primary, psychic disintegration, both of the self and of the image of what is loved in the external world, under the direct influence of the Thantos urges, together with an acceptance of this double destruction, an acceptance which allows the artist to rebuild both the destroyed self and the destroyed loved object in the aesthetic experience of art. This approach has been vividly illustrated in Adrian Stokes's recent book on Michelangelo. He describes how Michelangelo suffered acutely from anxiety and depression, and the central theme of the book is built round Michelangelo's own phrase 'That he lived on anxiety and death'. Stokes maintains that an artist of this type can do this because he can transmute anxiety and death into the sublime forms of his art. The book aims to show, says Herbert Read in his review of it, that the very greatness of Michelangelo's art is due to a superhuman effort to repair this tormented psyche. Of course, some critics will say that not all great artists had such tormented psyches, and that it is unwise to generalize about the nature of art from such an extreme case. If we turn to Blake again for light on this problem, he certainly has plenty to say about psychic torment as part of the state of psychic sterility if not as an inherent part of psychic creativity; as, for instance, in the picture of the climax of Job's descent when the God he has called upon appears as the devil, and his friends have become demons pulling him down into the fires of the pit.

Now, as I have said, the theme of denial of destructiveness, denial of Thanatos, seems to be one theme in Blake's *Job*, but only one, the other being to do with the repudiation of that state of mind which Blake calls female and which has something to do with the submergence of consciousness. Now, the difference between these two themes could perhaps be restated in terms of the difference between the content of unconscious thought processes and the form of them. Thus the content of our unconscious thoughts includes, according to Freud's discoveries, the history of the battle between our loving and our hating from earliest infancy. But, and this is what Ehrenzweig is saying, it is also the form of our unconscious thinking that must be considered in any attempt to find out what art is. Thus I think it is true to say that any attempt to explain art solely in terms of the history of wishes (that is in terms of the genesis of adult powers of loving from their earlier forms in infantile loving) seems to artists themselves, and to the sensitive art critic, to be leaving something out.

Here I wish to go back to Maritain who, in the same book from which I have already quoted, makes a direct attack on Freud. He says that the disregard of the poetic function by psychoanalysis is both a sign of the dullness of our times and is why the explanations of psychoanalysts have proved particularly unfortunate in the domain

210

of art – and, he adds, of religion. How can this criticism be answered? Or can it be answered at all? Perhaps what I have deduced from Blake's *Job*, and also what Ehrenzweig says about the relation of the surface mind to the depth mind, can point a direction from which an answer could come. For in these terms it looks as if Maritain is saying that any 'explanation' of art which is only in terms of the content of repressed wishes, what Gombrich calls the artists's complexes, leaves out what is essential and perhaps specific to art. It leaves out this deliberately fostered getting in touch with, not just hidden wishes but a different way of functioning; and a way of functioning which is essential if something new is to be created. This is why I think Gombrich said (in his Ernest Jones Lecture) that many people feel the attempt to deduce an artist's complexes from his work to be irrelevant.[10] And it is for this reason that I am not here going to discuss such famous writings as, for instance, Freud on Leonardo da Vinci nor Ella Sharpe on King Lear, nor even Ernest Jones on Hamlet. For in all these the emphasis is on the content of the wishes revealed, not on the specific processes which make it possible for the creative artist to embody the wishes in such meaningful symbols. But there are writings of analysts who do attempt to describe the nature of the specific process in the artist. Here I will mention again Kris's book, because this, although entirely psychoanalytic in approach, does provide a bridge in the direction of Maritain's conceptions. For Kris does come to a conclusion about the specific capacity of the artist. Like Ehrenzweig, he says it is to do with a special kind of interplay between two levels of functioning; but he puts this conclusion in technical terms and talks about 'a controlled regression of the ego to the primary process'. This is not the place to go into the meaning of the term 'primary process'; I only mention it in order to show that Kris does see the creative process as a deliberate reversion to a different, more childlike way of functioning. Incidentally, I think there are signs that a revision of the concept 'primary process' is already in the air, a revision that has been partly stimulated by the problems raised by the nature of art.

In my own attempts to study the nature of creative processes, I have become more and more aware of the anxiety which accompanies such deliberate reversion to a more primitive process. Ehrenzweig also emphasizes this as an essential part of creation, not only because of getting nearer to forbidden wishes, but just because the depth mind's way of working seems like chaos to the surface mind. Stokes also hints that it is the seemingly chaotic form of the depth mind, as well as fear of the destructive wishes, that contribute to the creative agonies of the artist; for he says, 'Art, if only by implication, bears

211

Figure 60   Copy of Christ picture   *Figure 61*   Copy of Eliphaz picture

witness to the world of depression and chaos overcome.'

About twelve years ago, when first beginning to study these pictures of Blake's, I felt a rather blind urge to get past the richness of the ideas and poetic thought portrayed in them, and to see more clearly the purely graphic formal qualities of feeling. So I made a rough copy of the Christ picture, using only the pattern of darks and .lights and leaving out all the linear detail (*Figure 60*). In spite of doing this, it was years before I could bring myself to face the, to me, intensely disturbing quality of the masses on the right, which seem to be breaking away from the circular forms surrounding the figure of Christ. In fact, not until writing this lecture did I really become able to face the full significance of the terror of the Christ figure shown by Job's friends. Now I can link it with the fears roused in the logical argumentative mind by the impact of the creative depths, and see that the anxiety is not something to be retreated from, but that it is inherent in the creative process itself. I also made a similar copy of the picture of Job's dream of the God of Eliphaz (*Figure 61*). Here the most striking thing to me, in the purely feeling aspect of the picture, was the great, dark, empty space above Job's dreaming head – a pregnant emptiness. And this idea of a pregnant emptiness leads on to another observation. It is that if this feeling of emptiness, of

212

something 'without form and void', can be deliberately accepted, not denied, then the sequel can be an intense richness and fullness of perception, a sense of the world newborn, a feeling which I think is what Blake has sought to express in his picture 'When the Morning Stars sang together' (*Figure 56*).

To go back to Maritain's criticism; I think the most relevant answer is given by Ehrenzweig (by implication). He talks of how Freud did, in fact, discover the inarticulate structure of the depth mind through his work on dreams; but he became so busy with the startling therapeutic results of translating the dreams' inarticulate thought into rational language that he did, in fact, neglect the importance of this very inarticulate structure of the unconscious processes which he had himself discovered. Ehrenzweig suggests that this neglect mattered little in clinical work, but it did matter when it came to aesthetics. In other words, Freud became so interested in the content of unconscious phantasies that he neglected their structural form, even though it was he who had first enunciated the laws of that form. Susanne Langer is one of the non-analytic writers who recognizes his achievement here. She points out that the first systematic study of what she calls the 'canons of symbolization' or 'the laws of non-discursive expressive form', as compared with the laws of logical or discursive form, was undertaken by Freud, and that their main logically disturbing features were named by him the principles of overdetermination, condensation, and ambivalence.

Maritain also grumbles at psychoanalysis for being concerned exclusively, he says, with what he calls the animal unconscious. I think there is a clear answer here. It was Rickman who said, in a public lecture in 1936, that man is a phantasying animal. Also Susanne Langer has maintained that what differentiates man from animals is the capacity to make and use symbols.[11] Obviously we do share with animals, and have brought with us from our animal inheritance, a vital interest in sex and sex organs; the race would not continue if we had not. And equally obviously, our sexual urges do come into conflict with the needs of society, as do also our aggressive urges. But, and this is the point, out of this conflict we have developed another capacity – that for symbol formation. Originally, so the biologists tell us, the titanic forces of the life force which at first reproduced itself only by the method of splitting did invent another way; it discovered that the bringing together of two creatures with different functions brought more variety in the offspring. Perhaps it would not be too far-fetched to say that the second greatest invention of nature's, after sexual reproduction, was the invention of the psychic process by which, not two different

213

organisms but two different ideas can come together and produce a new idea which yet contains some elements of both the original ideas; in fact, the invention of the power to make symbols.

Herbert Read said, in his Ernest Jones Lecture, that psycho-analysis had done incalculable service to art by showing that art is symbolization from the beginning, and that the process of symbolic transformation, which is fundamental to the creative process in art, is also biologically fundamental, thus proving that the artist's feeling that what he was doing was not just escapism was right.[12] It follows from this that what is most important about this thing we call a work of art, that is admittedly a symbol, is not the original primary unconscious wish or wishes that it symbolizes but the fact that a new thing has been created. A new bit of the outside world, which is not the original primary object of the wish, has been made interesting and significant. Thus the original tremendous primary drive to physical union with another living being has been able to transform itself into interest in every conceivable and inconceivable thing in the universe – by means of the process of symbolization.

I will try to summarize. The central idea of my paper is that the unconscious mind, by the very fact of its not clinging to the disctinction between self and other, seer and seen, can do things that the conscious logical mind cannot do. By being more sensitive to the samenesses rather than the differences between things, by being passionately concerned with finding 'the familiar in the unfamiliar' (which, by the way, Wordsworth says is the whole of the poet's business), it does just what Maritain says it does; it brings back blood to the spirit, passion to intuition. It provides the source for all renewal and rebirth, when old symbols have gone stale. It is, in fact, what Blake calls each man's poetic genius.

I have come to the conclusion that the discovery of the nature of this capacity, a discovery which can be described as the awakening of creative subjectivity to itself, is illustrated by Blake in the Job series beginning with the appearance of Elihu; also that Blake means to show that it is a very new development, as compared with the millions of years of blind living, when he puts in the margin of the Elihu picture the text, '*I am Young and ye are very Old wherefore I was afraid.*' And I think Blake is also implying the same idea when he brings the figure of Christ into his study of creative sterility. In fact, I think he implies, although he does not actually say so, that he believes that it is the creative contact with the unsplit 'depth' mind that Christ was talking about, in poetic terms, in such phrases as 'Take no thought for the morrow', and 'Consider the lilies of the field, they toil not neither do they spin'. So I would hazard a very rough guess as to the way in which it may be possible to formulate an answer to the question, 'What is art?', a guess that has grown out of my own experience of using the method Freud invented for observing unconscious processes. Can we say that it is to do with the capacity of the conscious mind to have the experience of co-operating with the unconscious depths, by means of the battle to express something with the chosen medium? If so, then perhaps it is true to say that the measure of genius in the arts is linked up with the extent to which the artist does succeed in co-operating with his unconscious mind by means of his medium.

References

1 This lecture was published as Milner, M. (1958) Psycho-Analysis and Art. In J. Sutherland (ed.) *Psycho-Analysis and Contemporary Thought*. London: Hogarth and British Institute of Psycho-Analysis.
2 Read, H. (1955) *Icon and Idea*. London: Faber & Faber.
3 Kris, E. (1953) *Psychoanalytic Explorations in Art*. London: Allen & Unwin.
4 Maritain, J. (1953) *Creative Intuition in Art and Poetry*. New York: McClelland.
5 Ehrenzweig, A. (1953) *The Psycho-Analysis of Artistic Vision and Hearing*. London: Routledge & Kegan Paul; (1956) 'The Mastery of Creative Anxiety'. *Art and Artists*. Berkeley, Calif: University of California; (1956) The Modern Artist and the Creative Accident'. *The Listener*, 12 January.
6 Stokes, A. (1955) 'Form in Art'. In M. Klein (ed.) *New Directions in Psycho-Analysis*. London: Tavistock; (1955) *Michelangelo: A Study in the Nature of Art*. London: Tavistock.
7 Freud, S. (1949) *Introductory Lectures on Psycho-Analysis (1930): Civilisation and its Discontents*. London: Hogarth.
8 Malraux, A. (1954). *The Voices of Silence*. London: Secker & Warburg.
9 Segal, H. (1955) 'The Psycho-Analytic Approach to Aesthetics'. In M. Klein (ed.) *New Directions in Psycho-Analysis*. London: Tavistock.
10 Gombrich, E. H. (1954) (Ernest Jones Lecture) Psycho-Analysis and the History of Art'. *International Journal of Psycho-Analysis* 35: 401–11.
11 Langer, S. (1953) *Feeling and Form*. London: Routledge & Kegan Paul; (1942) *Philosophy in a New Key*. Cambridge, Mass: Harvard University Press.
12 Read, H. (1951) (Ernest Jones Lecture) 'Psycho-Analysis and the Problem of Aesthetic Value, *International Journal of Psycho-Analysis* 32: 73–82.

----------------------------------- 13 -----------------------------------

1957: The ordering of chaos

In 1957 Masud Khan suggested a second edition of *On Not Being Able to Paint* with an introduction by Anna Freud, which she very kindly agreed to do, and an appendix by me.[1] I include this appendix here as it summarizes much of what I had been trying to formulate.

The ordering of chaos

The writing of this book turned out to be an attempt to discover, within the limits of a special field, something of the nature of the forces that bring order out of chaos. It was a study that had to do with the discovery of a different kind of integrative force than that which results from any attempt, of whatever nature, to copy a pre-existing ordered model. The question then arises, how is this different kind of integrating force to be talked about, whether in terms of scientific concepts in general, or in terms of those so far developed in the particular field of psychoanalysis. Also the question of the nature of the force or forces that produced the free drawings brought me to see that the other question, that with which this book began, of how psychic creativity works, had inevitably branched out into the second one; that is how is this capacity called psychic creativeness itself to be conceived, in what terms is it to be talked about? While writing the book I had assumed that I knew what I meant by 'psychic creativeness' and had not troubled to define it; then I had gradually discovered that I did not know precisely. But finally, as a result of this study, and also as a result of writing a clinical paper on aspects of symbol formation, I had found a definition which seemed to be at least a workable tool: that is that psychic creativeness is the capacity for making a symbol. Thus, creativeness in the arts is making a symbol for feeling and creativeness in science is making a symbol for knowing.

I want, in this chapter, to put forward the hypothesis that, from the point of view of psychic creativity at work, the logical terms in which the capacity for symbol formation is thought about are perhaps less important than the prelogical. I want to suggest that it is the terms in which we think, on the deeper non-verbal levels of the psyche, about this specifically human capacity for making symbols that in part determines the way the capacity works in us.

Thus the content of the free drawings seems to me to illustrate not only the anxieties associated with 'creative capacity', but also different ways of thinking about that capacity – and thinking about it in terms that are derived from those various bodily functions which become the centre of interest at different stages of infantile development.

The anal aspect of the parrot's egg

As the first edition of this book was planned more especially for the lay public I deliberately did not enlarge upon certain aspects of the material of the free drawings. At the time of writing it seemed possible to describe the oral aspects of the problems depicted in the drawings and to some extent the genital aspects; but the implications in terms of the so-called anal phase of development were omitted. This aspect, however, is obviously of great importance in any enquiry into ways of thinking about the human capacity to make things, whether material objects, or ideas, or both combined. It is clear that one cannot present a book for analysts which deals with the theme of, on the one hand, illusion, idealization, falling in love (transfiguration), and on the other, disillusion, falling out of love, denigration, without also talking about the child's idealization of and disillusion with what it gives as well as what it receives.

Since writing this book I have had much clinical material, from both adults and children, who were suffering from inhibition of the capacity to produce ideas, whether in logical verbal form or in non-logical artistic form. It was clear that these patients had an extremely idealized notion of what their products ought to be, and the task of objective evaluation of what they in fact produced appeared to be so disillusioning to them that they often gave up the attempt to produce anything. Attempts to interpret their difficulty led me to a

217

consideration of the whole problem of idealization and the extent to which it is in fact deluded. In so far as it applies to the human object it is obviously deluded, since no real object can ever be 'what the whole soul desired'. But my patients often produced idealizations, in their clinical material, which seemed to be an attempt on their part to externalize, to find a way of conceiving, thinking about, one particular aspect of their own creations: that is the experience of orgasm, whether genital or pregenital. And in this sense the idealization was surely not deluded, because by definition, the orgasm is a wonderful experience. (At least theoretically it is, although there may be many interfering factors preventing it reaching this stage.) Idealization is commonly talked about by analysts in terms of its use as a defence against ambivalence in the relationships to the object; my patients' material suggested that it can also be used as a way of symbolizing the genital or pregenital subjective experience of orgasm. And in this setting the concept of disillusion takes on a special meaning, especially in connection with the urge towards passivity and the blissful surrender to the body impulses (for which the word 'passivity' is perhaps really inappropriate, since it is more an active letting go). For this letting go seems to mean not only a letting go of all voluntary control of the muscles, it can also mean a letting go of the discriminating capacities which distinguish differences. Thus what patients experience as a dread of 'passivity' often turns out to be partly a dread not only of letting go the control of the sphincters, but also of a perceptual letting go, which would mean a return to an extreme of undifferentation between all the openings of the body and their products. Thus there is a dread of the total letting go of all the excited mess, faeces, urine, vomit, saliva, noise, flatus, no one differentiated from the other, a state of blissful transcending of boundaries, which, to the conscious ego, would be identified with madness. The dread is of a wish for the return to that state of infancy in which there was no discrimination between the orgastic giving of the body products and the products themselves. I suggest that it is this original lack of discrimination which is partly responsible for the later idealization of the body products; and the disillusion is then experienced when the real qualities of the intended love gift come to be perceived. I find clinical evidence which seems to show that, particularly in poets and artists who are inhibited in their work, there has been a catastrophic disillusion in the original discovery that their faeces are not as lively, as beautiful, as boundless, as the lovely feelings they had in the giving of them. Thus the infant's disillusion about its own omnipotence, its gradual discovery that it has not created the world by its own wishes, cannot be discussed fully without also considering its disillusion about the concrete bit of the outside world that it literally does create; that is, the infant's own body products. It follows that for patients whose fixation point is at this stage, the surrender of the consciously planning deliberative mind to the spontaneous creative force can be felt as a very dangerous undertaking; for such patients have not yet grown out of their unconscious hankering after a return to the blissful surrender to this all-out giving of infancy.

It is part of psychoanalytic theory that, when the infant has reached the stage of recognizing the loved mother as not created by the infant but as a person in her own right, from whom love is received and to whom love is to be given, then arises the problem of how the love is to be given, how it is to be communicated. And this stage leads eventually to the need to accept a different medium for the expression of feelings from the child's own body products; and also to the need to accept the necessity for work with that medium, since the beautiful mess does not make a picture or a poem all by itself. Thus it seems to me that in the analysis of the artist (whether potential or manifest) in any patient, the crucial battle is over the 'language' of love, that is to say, ultimately, over the way in which the orgasm, or the orgastic experiences, are to be symbolized. It certainly seems that the analysis of this primary identification of the living feeling experience of the body with the non-living material produced by the body would be likely to be critical for any artist (in the wide sense), since an artist's work is essentially concerned with the giving of life to the bit of 'dead' matter of the external world which is the chosen medium. For, in a sense, what the artist idealizes primarily, is his medium. He is in love with it; and this fact may also lead to difficulties through exaggerated ideas about what the medium can do. But if he loves it enough so that he submits himself to its real qualities, at the same time as imposing his will upon it, the finished product may eventually justify the idealization.

Thus the way in which it was found possible to help patients with a fixation point at this stage was, not by interpreting to them the phantastic nature of their idealizations, not by showing them their mistake in so idealizing their own body products; but by showing them that the idealization was not a delusion in so far as it referred to the intensity of their own orgastic sensations, it was only a delusion when they clung to the belief that the 'mess' was itself as beautiful as the feelings experienced in making it.

In the light of these considerations it became possible to see further into the meaning of the Parrot's Egg symbol. Thus the storm represents the parrot's angry disillusionment at realizing the need to give up the belief that everyone must literally see in the anal product (the egg) the beautiful feelings that went to produce it; that is at the need to give up the subjective valuation and accept the objective. Thus the battle is with the mother (Grey Lady), not only over the evaluation of the love gift, but also over what is a suitable and convenient stuff for symbols of love, love 'poems' to be made of. It seemed to me that the same theme is also elaborated in 'Queen Elizabeth and the Bashful Parrot', though with the emphasis this time on the pain of recognition that the faeces are in fact dead, for the symbol of the crosses in the background was associated with graves. The Dog–Cat picture (which was actually drawn in black and yellow) also, I think, illustrates the stage at which there is no differentation between 'dead' faeces and the 'living' feelings, since the dark shapes surrounding the anus–sun take the form of animals; that is they are felt to be living and do in fact (according to the associations) represent moods.

Infantile prototypes of creativity

It is basic to analytic theory that, after experience has forced us to realize, as infants, that we have not made everything, we transfer this belief to our parents and feel that at least they have. And then follow all the vicissitudes of discovery round about the themes of the parents' real physical creative powers. Some of the pain connected with these discoveries is shown in the content of the drawing 'Ape in the Garden of Eden'. In the main part of this book I discussed the subject of the aggression that results from the child's jealousy of the parents' love relation. What I did not mention was the masturbatory aspect of the child's relation to the parents' sexual life. It is a commonplace of psychoanalytic theory that the child has a phantasy of containing the parents inside him, in some sort of relationship, and a relationship which the child seeks to feel he or she can control omnipotently; and this phantasy serves as part of the child's way of coming to deal with the painful fact of recognizing an actual dependence upon the real parents. But this phantasy is not only intimately connected with masturbation, it also seems to serve as the child's pre-verbal symbol for thinking about its own creative capacities – at least when it has reached the stage of becoming aware of and accepting the parents' genital creative function, and has passed the stage of believing in an omnipotent fiat of creation. This means that doubts about the goodness of wishes towards the external

220

parents, doubts about the capacity to master such jealousy as the Angry Ape's, lead to doubts about the goodness of the real creative forces inside itself. It certainly does seem that in some patients the difficulty in coming to trust and have faith in the fact of the creative forces within themselves is intimately bound up with their unconscious conflicts over masturbation phantasies. Since these patients often have difficulty in achieving a masturbation phantasy in which they feel themselves to be conducting a benign intercourse, they do in fact feel themselves more likely to conduct a malevolent one, and so they come to feel they have no reason to trust in the goodness of the 'baby' which will result from that internal intercourse.

Clinical material suggests that the symbols used for thinking about the creative process in oneself are derived, variously, from the stages of interest in different aspects of bodily experience. It might be possible to work out in detail the kinds of symbols used at the different stages of development. Such a scheme would have to take into account, for instance, the stage at which to open one's eyes was felt to be a fiat of creation, a saying 'let there be light', which resulted in there being light; or the time when to open one's mouth was to create the nipple that filled it; or the time when the opening of one's bowels was not distinguished from the opening of one's eyes, so one really did believe one's faeces were the same as the world one saw, one felt oneself to be a dancing Siva creating the world; or the time when to masturbate was to create a heaven (or a hell) with the dance of one's own limbs. For there seems to have been a time when even the faculty of consciousness itself was felt to be entirely creative, to be aware of anything was simply to have made it; all one saw was one's own, as Traherne said, and it was one's own because one had made it. And in this setting it is Mother Nature who is the disillusioner, who seems to rob one of one's own creativity; it is nature that is responsible for the fact that one's faeces are such a small and stinking and dead bit of the world. So she can come to be felt, in certain settings, as the Blasting Witch who shrivels up the landscape; as well as the powerful but helpful Grey Lady of the Angry Parrot picture.

Changes in the sense of self

In this book I have tried to describe how, under the particular conditions of making the free drawings, something new, unexpected did in fact emerge. The phrase 'contemplative action' had seemed an appropriate description of the process: 'contemplative' to distinguish it from practical expedient action, 'action' to distinguish it from pure contemplation, to bring in the fact of the moving hand.

The essential thing about this contemplative mood, combined with action, was that it involved me in a giving up of the wish to make an exact reproduction of anything I had seen. Since obviously one cannot anyway produce a truly realistic copy of any object known in the external world, for marks on a two-dimensional surface can never be an exact reproduction of a three-dimensional object, it would seem that this was not a very difficult wish to give up. Nevertheless, in spite of my early discovery that no attempt to copy the appearance of objects was what my eye liked there was still a continual inner battle to be waged against the urge to attempt this mechanical copying; and this, in spite of years of experience of the fact that it was only when I had discarded this wish to copy that the resulting drawing or painting had any life in it, any of the sense of a living integrated structure existing in its own right. Of course I knew that many of the greatest artists said that they did copy nature, but I had begun to doubt whether this really meant what it seemed to mean. I began to suspect that they were in fact trying to describe the process of surrendering themselves to the deep spontaneous responses of nature within them, that were stimulated by the contact with nature outside them.

I have also tried to decribe how, whenever I was able to break free from the urge to make a mechanical copy and a new entity had appeared on my paper, then something else also had happened. The process always seemed to be accompanied by a feeling that the ordinary sense of self had temporarily disappeared, there had been a kind of blanking out of ordinary consciousness; even the awarenes of the blanking out had gone, so that it was only afterwards, when I returned to ordinary self-consciousness, that I remembered that there had been this phase of complete lack of self-consciousness.

In considering what might be the relation between this change of consciousness, the surrender of the wish to work to a copy and the sense of an 'independent life' in the result, I was reminded of two sets of ideas. On the one hand, there was all that analysts have to say about certain kinds of changes of consciousness, described variously as states of elation, as blankness, as oceanic feeling; and, on the other hand, the blankness, referred to in various mystical writings, including 'emptiness' as a beneficent state, which is, for example, the central concept in the *Tao Te Ching*.

Analysts have related experiences of this kind to the satisfied sleep of the infant at the mother's breast. Certainly such experiences, especially those to do with ecstasy and elation, can be fitted into a coherent scientific pattern by our so relating them. But may we not be missing something important if we look on them only as an end product, as a hallucinatory getting back to where we have never quite given up wanting to be? Is it not possible that blankness, lack of mindfulness, can also be the beginning of something, as the recognition of depression can be? Is it not possible that the blankness is a necessary prelude to a new integration? May not those moments be an essential recurring phase if there is to be a new psychic creation? May they not be moments in which there is a plunge into no-differentiation, which results (if all goes well) in a re-emerging into a new division of the me–not-me, one in which there is more of the 'me' in the 'not-me', and more of the 'not-me' in the 'me'?

I do not want to enter into a discussion of which of the psychic institutions, ego, super-ego, id, can be looked upon as responsible for the vitality and 'newness' of a good free drawing, but only to bring into focus the fact that there is some force or interplay of forces creating something new, and to suggest that the way we think about it in ourselves affects the way it works. And I want to suggest the possibility that a number of states of mind that are different from everyday conscious awareness may be in part an expression of the unconscious or half-conscious need to give this creativeness its freedom; they may be in part distorted forms of an essential and normal phenomenon. And perhaps some of the aggressive attitudes of children have a similar meaning. I have elsewhere described as a holy war such attempts of people to keep in touch with this inherent creativeness, a war that is also shown, I think, in the Angry Parrot's dilemma (see chapter 9).[2] For it seems to me that there may be an added reason for a child's violent defence of its own spontaneity; that not only are instincts arrogant and imperious, seeking their own satisfaction as soon as possible, not only is impulsive action pleasanter and easier than waiting; but also any rigid division into twoness, into awareness of the separateness of the 'me' and the 'not-me' (even though this is essential up to a point for the practical business of living), any copying of, obedience to, an imposed plan or standard, whether inner or outer, does necessarily interfere with this primary creativeness.

Rhythm, relaxation, and the orgasm

Rhythm and balance were essential ideas in the associations to the drawing 'If the Sun and Moon should doubt'. But the concept of rhythm presupposes a time factor, which cannot in fact be present in a drawing itself, though there is rhythm and therefore a time factor in the movements of hand and arm that make it; and also a time factor is implied in the contemplation of it, the contemplating eyes do move according to what are usually called the rhythms of the picture. A rhythm has a beginning and an end, but a picture, once it is painted, does not begin anywhere or end anywhere, all its elements co-exist simultaneously; in this sense perhaps it is true to say that a picture is timeless. But whatever the linguistic difficulties of using the word rhythm to describe an ingredient in pictures, the fact remains that the concept of rhythm must be included in any attempt at verbalization of the nature of the unconscious forces that produce a free drawing.

In the chapter on rhythm I have already discussed the idea that the inherent rhythmic capacity of the psycho-physical organism can become a source of order that is more stable than reliance on an order imposed either from outside, or by the planning conscious mind. But here our struggles to adapt, in infancy, to social living, provide a potent source for anxiety when we are trying to learn to paint; for the desire for the primitive rhythms, such as sucking, free bowel movement, babbling, masturbating, may all be reactivated when the adult sets himself the task of surrendering the conscious control of movement of the hand while still going on moving it.

The study of technique for achieving bodily relaxation has shown that release of any particular muscle is largely achieved by the apparently simple act of directing attention to it, letting consciousness suffuse it. But, in any one of us, if the need to relinquish the wish to return to the infantile phase of surrender to a total release, including the release of sphincter muscles, has not been adequately worked through, then the idea of the surrender of any muscular tension is bound to be associated with social anxiety, sometimes very acute. In this book, and also in others, I have tried to describe the observed effects of changes in body awareness and in muscular tension which resulted from different ways of focusing attention and different ways of drawing. But such phenomena clearly cannot be studied unless we also take into account that involuntary suffusing of the body with maximum intensity of feeling which goes with the experience of the orgasm. And the orgasm cannot be discussed, in the setting of the theme of this chapter, without also considering what are its symbols in non-logical thinking, how it is conceived of on the level of non-verbal imagery. The subject of the capacity to make one's attention suffuse the whole body, and the relation of this to the genital and pregenital orgasm, both as experienced and as thought about, would lead to a field of discussion beyond the scope of this book. Such discussion if undertaken would have to include a psychological study of the symbolic meaning of light and colour, subjects which have been only very briefly touched on in Chapter 4 [of *On Not Being Able to Paint*].

Clearly the subject of colour is, on the evidence of language alone, very closely bound up with the feelings. For instance, we talk of an emotional statement as a highly coloured one, and of its high points as 'purple patches'. We are 'green with envy', we 'see red', or we 'feel blue'. And the subject of light, which includes the inner light and the light of dreams is equally closely bound up with the theme of consciousness. The consciousness can in fact also suffuse the whole body, though it does not ordinarily do so, is perhaps expressed poetically by the psalmist's phrase 'clothed with light as it were with a garment'. There is also the fact that the sense of inner 'beingness', of 'dead' material acquiring life of its own, is the fundamental test of the goodness of a work of art; for a good picture is one in which every mark on the canvas is felt to be significant, to be suffused with subject. Similarly a good dancer gives the impression that there is maximum intensity of being in every particle of the living flesh and muscle and skin, the body itself having become the objective material suffused with subjectivity; and in good sculpture the whole mass of 'dead' metal or stone has been made to irradiate the sense of life.

Painting and symbols

I have said that the question of what kind of entity was produced by the method of the free drawings was not explicitly raised in the main part of this book. What kind of thing it was that appeared within the framed gap provided by the blank sheet of paper had become more clear to me when I thought more about the function of frames.

Frames can be thought of both in time as well as in space, and in other human activities besides painting. An acted play is usually, nowadays, framed by the stage, in space, and by the raising and lowering of the curtain in time. Rituals and processions are usually framed in space by barriers or by the policemen that keep back the onlookers. Dreams are framed in sleep and the material of a psychoanalytic session is framed both in space and time. And paintings, nowadays, are usually bounded by frames. But wall paintings are not, and when the wall is the wall of a cave the painted image must come nearer to the hallucinated images of dreams. Thus when there is a frame it surely serves to indicate that what's inside the frame has to be interpreted in a different way from what's outside it; for painters nowadays do not seem so concerned to achieve a near hallucination. Thus the frame marks off an area within which what is perceived has to be taken symbolically, while what is outside the frame is taken literally. Symbolic of what? We certainly assume that it is symbolic of the feelings and ideas of whoever determined the pattern of form within the frame. We assume that it makes sense, for instance we assume that the people on the stage are not there just by accident. In the same way, as analysts, we have learnt by experience that an apparently casual remark made within the frame of the session also makes sense if understood symbolically.

I did not make much use of the word symbol in the original edition of this book. This was because I was then still confused by the classical psychoanalytical attempt to restrict the use of the word to denoting only the defensive function of symbols, to what Ernest Jones called 'pure symbolism'. But now, having in the meantime published a technical paper, based on clinical material, on the subject of symbolization, and having come to the conclusion that I could not usefully restrict the concept in such a way, I can accept the idea that a work of art is necessarily and primarily a symbol.[3] Also in the first edition I talked about the role of images but did not recognize, and for the same reason, that a mental image is a symbol. Thus whereas before I could only talk about the artist as making new bottles for the continually distilled new wine of developing experience, now I could talk of him as making new symbols. I could look on the artist as creating symbols for the life of feeling, creating ways in which the inner life may be made knowable; which, as Freud said, can only be done in terms of the outer life. And since this inner life is the life of a body, with all its complexities of rhythms, tensions, releases, movement, balance, and taking up room in space, so surely the essential thing about the symbols is that they should show in themselves, through their formal pattern, a similar theme of structural tensions and balances and release, but transfigured into a timeless visual co-existence. Thus the artist surely amongst other things that he is doing, is making available for recall and contemplation, making able to be thought about, what he feels to be the most valuable moments in this feeling life of psycho-physical experience. And in his concern for the permanence and immortality of his work, he is not only seeking to defy his own mortality (as analysts have said), he is perhaps also trying to convey something of the sense of timelessness which can accompany those moments. He does in fact make tabernacles to house the spirit, with the result that others can share in his experiences, and he himself can have a permanent record of them after the high moment of transfiguration has passed; and it may be a high moment of rage and horror and pain as well as of joy and love. So that broadly, what the painter does conceptualize in non-verbal symbols is the astounding experience of how it feels to be alive, the experience known from inside, of being a moving, living body in space, with capacities to relate oneself to other objects in space. And included in this experience of being alive is the very experiencing of the creative process itself.[4]

In psychoanalytic terms this process of seeking to preserve experiences can certainly be described in terms of the unconscious attempt to preserve, recreate, restore the lost object; or rather, the lost relation with the object conceived of in terms of the object. And these experiences can be lost to the inner life, not only because of unconscious aggressive feelings about separation from the outer object, but also because it is of the nature of feeling experience to be fleeting. Life goes on at such a pace that unless these experiences can be incarnated in some external form, they are inevitably lost to the reflective life. Then it is perhaps possible to say that what verbal concepts are to the conscious life of the intellect, what internal objects are to the unconscious life of instinct and phantasy, so works of art are to the conscious life of feeling; without them life would be only blindly lived, blindly endured. Hence surely it can be said that a great work of art provides us with a new concept with which to give form to, to organize, find orientation in, the life of feeling. And it is just because feelings are about something, about objects, in the psychoanalytic sense, that we can easily talk of the unconscious meaning of the thing that an artist makes as a recreation of a lost object. But I think also there is much evidence to suggest that this function of art, as restoring lost objects, is in fact secondary; and that the primary role is the 'creating' of objects, in the psychoanalytic sense, not the recreating of them. The recreating of them is part of the so-called depressive position; for the theory of the depressive position attempts to describe what happens to an infant when it has reached the stage of recognizing whole external objects separate from itself, and how it deals with the guilt and sorrow about the attacks it has made in phantasy on the objects. But I think the artist is also concerned with a stage earlier than this. I think he is concerned with the achieving that very 'otherness' from oneself which alone makes any subsequent sadness at loss possible. In fact he is concerned primarily with what Adrian Stokes calls the 'out-there-ness' of his

227

work.[5] Certainly for the analyst, at certain stages in analysing an artist, the importance of his work of art may be the lost object that the work re-creates; but for the artist as artist, rather than as patient, and for whoever responds to his work, I think the essential point is the new thing that he has created, the new bit of the external world that he has made significant and 'real', through endowing it with form.

The two kinds of thinking

Perhaps the solution of the controversy over where the deepest meaning of art lies, can only be found through a fuller understanding of the differences between the kind of thinking that makes a separation of subject from object, me from not-me, seer from seen, and the kind that does not. We know a lot about the first kind of thinking, we know its basis in the primary laws of logic, which say that a thing is what it is and not what it is not, that it cannot both be and not be. We know also that these laws of reasoning work very well for managing the inanimate material environment. We divide what we see from ourselves seeing it, and in certain contexts this works very well. But it does not work so well for understanding and managing the inner world, whether our own or other people's. For, according to formal logic, all thought which does not make the total separation between what a thing is and what it is not is irrational;[6] but then the whole area of symbolic expression is irrational, since the point about a symbol is that it is both itself and something else. Thus, though separation of the seer and what is seen gives a useful picture in some fields it gives a false picture in others. I think that one of the fields in which formal logic can give a false picture is aesthetics; and that the false picture is only avoided if we think about art in terms of its capacity for fusing, or con-fusing subject and object, seer and seen and then making a new division of these. By suffusing, through giving it form, the not-me objective material with the me – subjective psychic content, it makes the not–me 'real', realizable. Clearly the great difficulty in thinking logically about this problem is due to the fact that we are trying to talk about a process which stops being that process as soon as we talk about it, trying to talk about a state in which the 'me–not–me' distinction is not important, but to do so at all we have to make the distinction. But it is only, I think, in this way of looking at it that the phrase 'art creates nature' can make sense. So what the artist, or perhaps one should say, the great innovator in art, is doing, fundamentally, is not recreating in the sense of making again what has been lost (although he is doing this), but creating what is, because he is creating the power to perceive it. By continually breaking up the established familiar patterns (familiar in his particular culture and time in history) of logical common-sense divisions of me–not–me, he really is creating 'nature', including human nature. And he does this by unmasking old symbols and making new ones, thus incidentally making it possible for us to see that the old symbol was a symbol; whereas before we thought the symbol was a 'reality' because we had nothing else to compare it with. In this sense he is continually destroying 'nature' and re-creating nature – which is perhaps why the depressive anxieties can so easily both inhibit and be relieved by successful creative work in the arts. And in this sense also it can be seen how invention, both in science and in the arts can be rooted in the same process. For instance, Ernest Jones, in his paper on 'The Theory of Symbolism', introduced the idea that in science the process of discovery and invention consists in freeing the tendency to 'note identity in difference'.[7] He thus draws attention to the non-logical aspect of the process.

I think the Mount of Olives drawing, with the dead bones blocking the way ahead, does symbolize a blocking of this kind of non-logical thought through an excessive reliance on logical processes. Thus it seems to me that the drawing has meaning, not only in terms of the not yet worked through feelings of guilt over cannibalistic phantasies of oral incorporation; but that it also refers to the artificial keeping dead of the method of thinking which does not stay detached and apart, that expresses itself pre-eminently in the arts. By its title the drawing makes a connection with the New Testament. This is a reference to a phenomenon which had been continually in my mind while writing this book; the fact that when thinking about the kind of surrender of conscious planning experienced in making the drawings, phrases from the Gospels kept cropping up in my thoughts, such as 'Consider the lilies of the field'. 'Take no thought for the morrow'. 'The meek shall inherit the earth.' In fact it almost semed that on one level the symbolism of the Gospels was a kind of poetic handbook for the way in which psychic creativity works. Certainly this non-logical type of thought does depend on a willingness to forgo the usual sense of self as clear and separate and possessing a boundary. I wondered, is it possible that the teaching of the Gospels is partly to do with a logic of non-logical thought; and also that of the *Tao Te Ching*, with its opening phrase, 'The Tao of which we speak is not the real Tao'?

Painting and imitation

I have said that I did learn to paint, in the sense that I learnt to overcome internal and external difficulties so that I could spend most of my weekends and holidays in a group painting. For, after many years of waiting, I had finally found people to teach me who did see that the essence of painting is that every mark on the paper should be one's own, growing out of the uniqueness of one's own psycho-physical structure and experience, not a mechanical copy of the model, however skilful. Incidentally, in this connection, I showed this book to a painter who, while turning over the pages to look at the drawings said, 'That one is not you, nor that, nor that, they are unconscious copies of some picture you have seen.' I had myself recognized the obvious derivation of 'Mrs Punch' from the Duchess in *Alice's Adventures in Wonderland*, just as the chair in 'Nursery' derived from van Gogh; and also that the design in the 'Blasting Witch' was a close unconscious copy of the design of a picture I had often seen in a friend's room. But the painter had never seen this friend's picture and it was a surprise to me that anyone could know, without having seen the 'copy', that the line of the drawing was not my own, not growing out of my own psycho-physical rhythms. Of the wavy line at the top left side of 'The Eagle and the Cave-man' he said, 'That is good, that is from you; though the shading is not, that is mannered, banal.' The point of view prompting these criticisms confirmed my growing conviction that a work of art, whatever its content, or subject, whether a recognizable scene or object or abstract pattern, must be an externalization, through its shapes and lines and colours, of the unique psycho-physical rhythm of the person making it. Otherwise it will have no life in it whatever, for there is no other source for its life.

I also learnt to understand something about the use of colour which made the colour in the Angry Parrot seem crude. For I remembered how I had painted the original drawing with what I would now call an intellectual attitude to colour, I had *thought* what colour I wanted to put next, rather than looking quietly at the first colour I had put and listening to it, allowing it to call for what colours it needed around it, colours that grew out of its own nature. Also I became able to see the difference between a painting and a coloured drawing and became able to paint by starting with the colour masses rather than with the outlines.

A place for absent-mindedness

The kind of thinking that does not distinguish between the seer and the seen (or perhaps we should say, the phase of thinking, for normally it seems that the two kinds alternate with each other), is certainly continually talked about by analysts under the name of phantasy. But I think it is a pity that the expressive word 'reverie' has been so largely dropped from the language of psycho-pathology, and the overworked word phantasy made to carry such a heavy burden of meaning. For the word 'reverie' does emphasize the aspect of absent-mindedness, and therefore bring in what I feel to be a very important aspect of the problem, that is, the necessity for a certain quality of protectiveness in the environment. For there are obviously many circumstances in which it is not safe to be absent-minded; it needs a setting, both physical and mental. It requires a physical setting in which we are freed, for the time being, from the need for immediate practical expedient action; and it requires a mental setting, an attitude, both in the people around and in oneself, a tolerance of something which may at moments look very like madness. The question then arises, are we going to treat all phenomena that are often talked of under that heading as symptoms, something to be got rid of, or can we, in our so objectively minded culture, come to recognize them as something to be used, in their right place? In our childhood we are allowed to act, move, behave, under the influence of illusions, to play 'pretend' games and even get lost in our play, feel for the moment that it is real. In adult life it is less easy to find settings where this is possible (we get other people to do the pretending, on the films and the stage), although we do find it within the framework of the analytic session as patients.

I have suggested that, just as sleep dreaming is necessary (said Freud) to preserve sleep, so both conscious and unconscious day-dreaming is necessary to preserve creative being awake. Clinical psychoanalytic experience suggests that many of the impediments to going forward into living are the result of a failure of the child's environment to provide the necessary setting for such absent-mindedness. For it seems likely that, in this phase of not distinguishing the 'me' and the 'not-me' we are particularly vulnerable to the happenings in the inner life of those nearest to us emotionally.[8] Two of the most disturbed patients I have had, who also had marked artistic gifts, both showed attempts to cling rigidly to the laws of formal logic (although they had never heard of the explicit statements of these laws). One of them would say furiously, in

231

response to an interpretation involving symbolism, 'But a thing either is or it isn't, it must be one thing or the other!' And the second patient would always insist that the literal meaning of any object or activity was the only possible meaning. And both of those patients had mothers who were mentally extremely ill. I suggest that such a human environment forces a child into desperate clinging to the phase of thinking that does distinguish between the 'me' and the 'not-me', because this is the only protection against an impossible confusion between their own and their parents' inner problem. But this (which is one possible meaning for the phrase 'premature ego development') leads them to great difficulties in managing their social environment, for they continually try to employ the kind of thinking (formal logical) which in fact gives a false picture of that world of human feeling (their own and other peoples') that they are trying to understand and manage. And the result is that whole areas of their experience become cut off from the integrative influence of reflective thinking. What they are essentially in need of is a setting in which it is safe to indulge in reverie, safe to permit a con-fusion of 'me' and 'not-me'.

Such a setting, in which it is safe to indulge in reverie, is provided for the patient in analysis, and painting likewise provides such a setting, both for the painter of the picture and for the person who looks at it.

References

1 Milner, M. (1957) *On Not Being Able to Paint*. (2nd edn.) London: Heinemann.
2 Milner, M. (1955) The Role of Illusion in Symbol Formation. In M. Klein, P. Heimann, S. Isaacs, and J. Riviere (eds.) *New Directions in Psycho-Analysis*. London: Tavistock.
3 There is always the difficulty, when using the word symbol in connection with art, that different writers continue to use it in different ways. I am using it here in the same sense that Susanne Langer uses it in her book *Feeling and Form*, when she says, 'Art is the creation of forms symbolic of human feeling'. Thus I am not using it in the sense that Vivante does (in his book *English Poetry*) when, in writing about Blake, he says 'Poetic expression is a moment of life and truth, but symbols are stiffened things, with the super-addition of abstract conceptions, or references to extrinsic powers and causes which are not fully realised, and lack the self-dependent, self-witnessing truth of *form*. We see sometimes in Blake's poetry *expression* overlapping in *symbols*.' I would agree with his

observation about Blake but disagree with his narrow use of the word symbol. Manangoni (in *The Art of Seeing Art* (1951) Shelley Castle: London) also talks about symbols; he says, 'This very form, this "language" or whatever one decides to call it, this is the very essence of art. Those lines, those surfaces, that play of light and shade, which the painters call into being are not, as many people still believe, symbols of what he wishes to express, but become through the miracle of art, a direct medium of expression of his whole spirit, become *his* art. "Art is direct expression".' Here, there is clearly more than a linguistic difference. Manangoni shows himself to be one of those who believe what Susanne Langer calls 'The widely popular doctrine that every work of art takes rise from an emotion which agitates the artist, and which is directly "expressed" in the work'. She adds, 'But there are usually a few philosophical critics – sometimes artists themselves – who realise that the feeling in a work of art is something the artist conceived as he created the symbolic form to present it, rather than something he was undergoing and involuntarily venting in an artistic process. There is a Wordsworth who finds that poetry is not a symptom of emotional stress, but an image of it – "emotion recollected in tranquillity".'

4 Non-psychoanalytic writers on art use various terms to describe the creative force. For instance, Vivante talks of 'the original formative principle', and Maritain talks of 'creative subjectivity'.

5 Stokes, A. (1947) *Inside Out*. London: Faber & Faber.

6 Here I am indebted to a lecture entitled The Logic of Irrationality by Harold Walsby, author of *The Domain of Ideologies*, 1947, Glasgow: Maclennan.

7 Jones, E. (1916) The Theory of Symbolism. In *Papers on Psychoanalysis*. London: Ballière Tindall (1948).

8 Maritain, in his book *Creative Intuition in Art and Poetry*, quotes Cézanne's exclamation to Ambroise Vollard, 'I damn well have to be left alone when I *meditate*'.

14

1960: The concentration
of the body

Part I: A note on a paper by Sylvia Payne

In March 1960 I wrote a small contribution to a paper by Dr Sylvia Payne given to the London 1952 Club on the subject of 'What Do We Expect from a Psycho-Analytic Treatment'.[1] I wrote that she says, as I understand it, that what we expect, hope for, from psychoanalytic treatment is an enlarging of consciousness in the particular direction of discovering, establishing, the capacity for inner observation which sees, becomes aware not only of what one is experiencing, and so producing a quantitative change, in that repression is lifted so that more of one's wishes are known, but also a qualitative change, both in the inner observer and what is observed. She quotes Einstein on the scientific attitude to show how the observer becomes unjudging, and she quotes Rappaport partly because of his description of how new conscious qualities appear in the transition from primary to secondary process. I said that as I understand it she is saying that amongst the conscious qualities that can emerge is the fact that the observer is driven to recognize the existence of unconscious ideas and processes. I said I suppose that we would all agree that a great step is taken when the observer does recognize this gap in self-knowledge, this bit of nothingness, and also discovers that it can enter into a relationship with this gap, this inner unknown. Also that this is a discovery which is perhaps as momentous as the earlier step which she talks about – that first recognition of a gap in one's own consciousness which turns out to be filled by another consciousness, another person.

I also liked very much how she links the development of the inner observer with the development of body awareness in lavatory training. I added that I think that what she says emphasizes the fact that this momentous meeting of the inner observer and the inner experience is also a meeting of mind and body. I said that from fields other than psychoanalysis there are many observations that such a meeting produces actual bodily changes as well as psychic ones, through this dialectical interplay.

I went on to suggest that this fertile meeting which goes on inside can be often symbolized by the internal parents in good intercourse. I added that there is a very interesting part where she talks about the first question mark, claiming that the breast which does live up to what is expected of it does not evoke a 'not-me' discovery, while the breast which does not, that is, which frustrates, *does* evoke a 'not-me' discovery.

I then talked about the inner rhythm in which the conscious common-sense reality ego is recurrently submerged in a changed state of consciousness, where the me–not–me distinction becomes unimportant, and added that the recognition of this rhythm can be one of the inner observer's tasks in learning how to use creative process.

I want to go on to suggest that this first not–me or gap in the quality of one's awareness of the outer world becomes also an unknown not–me gap in one's inner awareness, and that this is something that the inner observer has to reckon with. In other words, the observer is driven to recognize the existence of unconscious processes. I suppose we would all agree that the great step is taken when the observer recognizes this gap inside, this nothingness, and even discovers it can enter into a relationship with it, this inner unknown, which can then suddenly become a known, and something that has to be accepted as one's own. I added that I think we would all agree if we say that the end of the psychoanalytic situation comes when the analysand has established the capacity of continual psychic growth through the fertilizing contact of the ego function of attention with the meeting the unconscious, that is the gap. But I think it is not only the repressed that is discovered, but also some sort of active direct feeling contact with a primary body awareness.

Part II: Painting and internal body awareness

In 1960 I was also invited to give a paper at a Congress on Aesthetics in Athens.[2] I chose as my subject certain observations I had made while trying to learn to paint.

In this paper I want to try and indicate something of the direction in which, it seems to me, some most interesting things are happening in the meeting ground between psychoanalysis and painting.

The central idea that I want to talk about is something that has grown out of my own studies of what happens when one tries to paint and also out of twenty years of clinical work with patients. It is to do with first, observations of the varying moment to moment perception of one's own body, including the effects of deliberately directing one's attention to the whole internal body awareness, and second, the connection between this and both the creation of a work of art and the growth of a vital emotional involvement in the world around one. It is the direct sensory (proprioceptive) internal awareness that I am concerned with; in fact, the actual 'now-ness' of the perception of one's body, and therefore of the perception of oneself. (It was Freud who said that the ego is essentially a body-ego.)

When I first began, in 1926, trying to describe the kind of attention that this whole body awareness requires, I noticed the astonishing changes in the quality of one's perception, both of oneself and the world outside, that the deliberate use of a wide rather than a narrow focus of attention brings.[3]

In a recent (as yet unpublished) paper given to the London Imago Society, by Adrian Stokes, and called 'Some Connections and Differences between Visionary and Aesthetic Experience' he refers to the visionary experiences which Aldous Huxley induced in himself by taking the drug mescalin.[4] Stokes compares Huxley's experiences with one of Ruskin's, described in his diary: of how, as a young man travelling to Italy for the sake of his health and stopping on route at some inn, he felt so ill that he doubted his ability to continue the journey. Feeling in despair, he staggered out of the inn along a cart track and then lain down on the bank, unable to go any further. But he had found himself staring at an aspen tree by the roadside and finally he had sat up and begun to draw it. He drew the whole tree and in doing so had an intense imaginative emotional experience of understanding of all trees, as well as finding that his feeling of being close to death had disappeared. He was able to continue his journey to Italy.

Stokes also talks in this paper of certain modern artist's attempts to portray what he calls 'the naked process of being', the attempt, as they sometimes claim, to portray 'the real thing' rather than the symbol. However much it may be said that they cannot ever make good this claim, (since surely all art must inevitably be symbolic) I do believe that, in making it, they are trying to concentrate upon and realize more deeply, a highly important human capacity; that is the non-symbolic direct sensory awareness of their own state of being alive in a body.

In my own earliest studies I also (though I had never read Ruskin) had observed how, by staring at an outside object that one especially liked (or even something that one did not like, for instance, an ugly white tin mug) there gradually emerged a sense of changes in one's whole body perception – a life-enhancing effect (to borrow Berensen's phrase) as well as a becoming deeply interested in the very 'thingness' of the thing I was staring at.

If one tries to find ways of talking about what could have happened to Ruskin in this experience, there are various things to be said. Stokes himself talks of Ruskin having 'gained a potency feeling' focused by the integrated body of the aspen. He also links this with specifically psychoanalytic concepts and talks of Ruskin having 'gained the measure of a good incorporated object'. I agree but want to add something. It is that I think we are here getting near to talking about a direct sensory internal experience of the integrating processes that created and go on creating the body. I believe this to be a direct psycho-physical non-symbolic awareness, although at the same time of course an experience which is inextricably bound up with the inner images of the relation to another person ('the good incorporated object') since the force that created our bodies and goes on doing so could not have kept us alive as infants without the devoted care of another person.

Stokes also refers to Huxley's claim that such visionary experiences as those resulting from taking mescalin are to do with the experience of direct contact with the Divine Ground of Being. Whatever may be said about the transcendental implications of such a statement I feel there is a lot more to be said about one's own inner ground of being, as a real psycho-physical background to all one's conscious thoughts, something which can be directly experienced by a wide focus of attention directed inwards – in contrast with the narrow kind of attention needed for discursive logical verbal thought.

Also I suspect that the adjective 'divine' (but without a capital 'D') added to the word 'ground' can be an accurate description (quite apart from any cosmological meanings) of what happens when the consciousness does suffuse the whole body; for it does seem that such a dialectic re-union, such a meeting of opposites, after the necessary division into mind and body, thoughts and things, that we have to make in order to take practical responsibility for ourselves in the world, it does seem to be an observed fact that such a reunion has, or can have, a marked ecstatic or 'divine' emotional quality. In fact, I found the phrase 'resurrection of the body' occurring to me in connection with such experiences as those described by Ruskin. Thus it seems that, behind the states that are often rather loosely talked about by psychoanalysts as auto-erotic and narcissistic (and regarded as pathological) there can be an attempt to reach a beneficent kind of narcissism, a primary self-enjoyment which is in fact a cathexis of the whole body, as distinct from concentrating it in the specifically sexual organs; and which, if properly understood, is not a rejection of the outer world but a step towards a renewed and revitalized cathexis of it.

Part III: Aspects of technique with 'borderline' patients

I recently came across some notes I had written in 1960 and 1961 on papers by Margaret Little[5] and Masud Khan,[6] on what were increasingly coming to be called 'borderline' patients. What I said was:

I have been very interested in Margaret Little's series of papers, especially the one 'On Basic Unity', and can confirm from my own clinical experience several if not all of her statements about this kind of patient. Certainly there is discontinuity between early body memories and later experience. Also I would agree that interpretations in terms of splitting do not carry conviction or start psychic growth to begin again on the level where the deepest hold-up of development is operative. I have found too that the hold-up seems to lie partly in an inability to establish the necessary oscillation between, on the one hand, a state of coming together into an integrated whole within the body boundary and, on the other hand, a state of diffuse being in which there are no boundaries, only fluidity.

My own clinical experience does lead me to agree with the idea that the ability to find objects with whom relationship can be made does depend on the previous existence of a recurrent state of unity, one which comes originally from the mother–child fusion. Also that this feeling of unity is not a projective identification resulting from splitting a pre-existent ego, but is the result of recurrent awareness, in feeling, of an undifferentiated state of no separation, a state described by Masud Khan in his 1960 paper in terms of 'a pre-stage of infancy development where ego and id themselves emerge from an undifferentiated matrix of energic potential structure'.

I also certainty agree with what Masud Khan says in his paper that the need for the achievement of this state of undifferentiation is the source of these patients' most crucial seeking and their most adamant resistance and negativity.

Furthermore, I know only too well that Fairbairn is right when he says (and Khan quotes this passage), 'it is usual for this [final] stage to be reached only after all available methods of defending the personality have been exploited'.[7]

I think what is particularly valuable for me is what he has to say about the kind of patient who cannot make use of the transference situation in the way that an ordinary neurotic can. He describes how the primitive ego distortions in these patients prevent the establishment of the 'benign split' which is the prerequisite for the success of the clinical process in the classical psychoanalytical situation. He maintains that they cannot do this because, in their experience of it, a regressive confusion occurs, that is a blurring of boundaries of self and analyst and setting.

I value very much the idea Khan has had of making a list of the different names under which he thinks these patients are described in the literature. It is also valuable that he points out how the various different procedures advocated for dealing with their problems are in fact contradictory. I also like the description, based on his own clinical observations, of what in fact they do do, instead of behaving as a proper neurotic should. It's the fact that he has attempted to list these deviations from the 'classical' patients' behaviour that I value; I am not saying that this list is necessarily inclusive.

This is not the time to elaborate on my ideas about what I do in my struggles with such patients, but there is one aspect of the problem that I would just like to mention. In 1950, when writing about problems to do with painting, I used the term 'concentration of the body' to describe certain phenomena to do with one's way of attending to the object one is painting. During the years since then I have been finding that this kind of body attention has come to play an increasingly important part in my analytic relation to some of my patients.

What I mean by body attention or body concentration in the analyst is this: it is a state in which the direct proprioceptive body–self awareness, which I suppose is best called the body presentation, as distinct from the body representation or body image, becomes the foreground of one's consciousness rather than the pre-conscious background. As I see it, this kind of attention in the analyst differs from the free-floating kind that, when I first practised as an analyst, was the only kind I thought appropriate and which most neurotics seemed able to manage with. It differs because it is not 'in the air'; it deliberately attends to sinking itself down into a total internal body awareness, not seeking at all for correct interpretations, in fact not looking for ideas at all – although interpretations may emerge from this state spontaneously.

Other main points about this kind of attention seem to me to be

1 that it is wide focused,
2 that its object, one's own internal body perception, is inarticulate, dark, and undifferentiated,
3 that what looks like a turning away from the object and the outside world does in fact seem to result in the opposite from turning away, that is it results in an increased perception of the nature and significance of the external object, in this instance the patient,
4 that, as far as I can observe, it does seem to bring about a change in the analytic situation and freeing of the patient's material.

As for an explanation of why this should happen, I would suggest the following: it may be that what they are looking for, not all the time but sometimes, before they can make creative use of that recurrent merging with the object through blurring of the boundaries (that Masud Khan says they do, only uncreatively), a merging that I believe must precede the creation of symbols, they have to achieve an intuitive awareness of an unanxious mother figure contentedly anchored in her own body and in happy communion with it.

As I have said, I am not going to discuss the relation of these phenomena to metapsychological theory. But I do want to say that, as I see it, they must have some bearing on such statements as, for instance, that the theory of narcissism is basic to the study of object relations.

References

1 Payne, S. (1960) What Do We Expect from a Psycho-Analytic Treatment? (Unpublished paper.)
2 Milner, M. (1960) Painting and Internal Body Awareness. Published in the IV International Congress on Aesthetics, Athens.
3 Milner, M. (1934) *A Life of One's Own*. London: Chatto & Windus.
4 Stokes, A. (1959) Some Connections and Differences between Visionary and Aesthetic Experience. (Unpublished paper.)
5 Little, M. (1960) On Basic Unity. *International Journal of Psycho-Analysis* 41: 377–84.
6 Khan, M. (1960) Clinical Aspects of the Schizoid Personality. *International Journal of Psycho-Analysis* 41: 430–37.
7 Fairbairn, R. D. (1940) Schizoid Factions in the Personality. In *Psychoanalytic Studies of the Personality*. London: Tavistock (1952).

15

1967: The hidden order of art

After Anton Ehrenzweig died in 1967 I was asked to speak at a memorial meeting for him at the Institute of Contemporary Art.[1] This is what I said.

I have gained so much from my experience of Anton as a friend, so I decided that the best way I can contribute to this meeting is to tell something of the personal context in which I came to view his work. For, in my experience, he was such a personal person; he had such a gift for making vivid contacts with people, such a capacity for grasping in a flash what one was trying to say (even though one had by no means yet said it) – such a capacity for breaking through English reserve and going straight to a point, not only with a cogent intellectual comment, but also with humour, or with gentle teasing. Of course, he could easily get angry: his aggression was by no means deeply hidden and there was plenty of it, so he often got himself involved in quarrels. (Once, on the phone, he told me that some friend of his would no longer speak to him. When I asked what he, Anton, had done, he answered, a little ruefully, 'Oh, only told him to go to hell.')

My personal contact with him began when we were introduced by his old friend and schoolmate, Dr Rubenstein, at the 1953 International Psycho-Analytical Conress in London, but I only came really to know him, in 1955, at the next Congress in Geneva. It was here that I realized his sensitiveness to what someone else was trying to say, for he came to hear my 1955 Congress paper, 'The Yell of Joy' (see Chapter 10).[2]

The theme of the paper centred on the use that these patients had made of a special visual symbol, in their drawings, during analysis. It was of the type that is known in textbooks of general psychology as 'alternating perspective' and it is usually shown in the form of two complementary waved lines which can be read either as a vase or as two profiles facing each other. If one looks at the symbol with an easy enough stare, not seeking to impose either one meaning or the other, the two meanings alternate. The argument of the paper was to illustrated the hypothesis that these two patients had, unconsciously, chosen variants of this symbol to express a primary difficulty that was interfering with the whole of their creative function in daily living, that is a difficulty over how to relate themselves to the recurrent loss of that primary undivided state of unity, undifferentiation, between subject and object that Freud called 'oceanic'. In other words, they had difficulty in coming fully to accept the recurrent division into two, into separateness, that all relationship requires.

Those of you who know Anton's work can see how much common ground there was for discussion between us, after this paper. For this was just what he was primarily interested in: that is the role in art of that inherent capacity of the ego's awareness which causes it to swing between conscious, directed, deliberative attention, and an absent-minded dream-like state, in a kind of porpoise-like movement of emergence and submergence.

It was after this meeting that he lent me his first book, *The Psycho-Analysis of Artistic Vision and Hearing*, with its subtitle 'An Introduction to a Theory of Unconscious Perception'.[3] The result of this was that when, in 1956, I had to give one of the Freud Centenary Lectures, one on 'Psychoanalysis and Art' (see Chapter 12), I found that I could not do it without making extensive use of Anton's contribution.[4] As the subtitle of his book implies, it is essentially a detailed account of the part played by unconscious modes of perception of form, in all creative work (whether in science or in art), though he is primarily concerned with creation in the arts, including music.

The other half of this interchange between us, after Geneva, was that I lent him the book that I had written in 1936 (before becoming an analyst) called *An Experiment in Leisure*.[5] Reading this led Anton to write a critique of it, in a paper that he read to the London Imago Society in 1957, calling it 'The Creative Surrender'.[6] Central to the theme of his paper was an interpretation of the mythology of the Dying God in terms, not of the vicissitudes of instincts, not in terms of sadism and masochism, but in terms of the psychology of the ego. For this theme of the Dying God was something I had been obsessed with, in my book, particularly with the rituals described in Frazer's

The Golden Bough, but an obsession that I had largely lost sight of during my Freudian training (and also because the book had been blitzed out of print in 1940).[7] The argument of Anton's paper was that the fertility rites of the Dying God contain the intuitive poetic understanding of that ego-rhythm which must be deliberately made use of in all creative work: the rhythm by which the ego's ordinary common-sense consciousness voluntarily seeks its own temporary dissolution in order that it may make contact with the hidden powers of unconscious perception.

In his last book he continues the detailed study of this ego rhythm, or fertility cycle; and, as in the first book, he drew attention to the relation between religious mystical experience and artistic creativeness, so in this one he elaborates in practical detail, as well as in theory, the implications of the interplay between conscious and unconscious mental functioning in the teaching of art and the teching of art teachers.[8] In this book too he makes a, to me, useful comment about Freud and the concept of the oceanic state: the feeling of *no* boundaries, no separation. Anton points out how Freud only developed this in connection with his discussion of religious experience and did not expand it to include the experience of the artist. That the need to do this expansion was certainly in the air in the early 1950s is shown by what happened in 1953. For it was in this same year, in which Anton's book was published, that Adrian Stoke's paper 'Form in Art' appeared in the number of the *International Journal of Psycho-Analysis* that was written in honour of Melanie Klein, a paper in which the concept of the oceanic state and its relation to a state of separateness, of the 'otherness' of the 'other' was given a central place.[9] The fact that the concept of the oceanic state is now used extensively in the attempts to understand the nature of art, and yet was first formulated by Freud in his study of religious experience, seems to me extremely interesting, for it does suggest a very close connection between artistic and religious experience.

It was when thinking about all this that I kept coming back to a statement of William Blake's that had fascinated me in 1936. It was Blake's claim, when talking about the New Testament and the labour of Christ and his Apostles that these are the labours of art and science.[10] I had felt, in 1936, that this linking of the gospel of the Dying God with the labours of Art and Science, was deeply significant, but it was from Anton's last book that I came to see much more of its practical implications; for here he translates the poetic image of the dying god, not only into the conceptual language of psychology, but also into the day-to-day problems of helping students to achieve what he calls the voluntary de-differentiation of the ego, in the service of tapping the hidden sense of order. Once he said to me, 'To make someone love the unconscious, *that* is teaching art.'

Of course I by no means always found myself in agreement with his aesthetic judgement about any particular work of art, or student's achievement, but that is not the point; for what he said about it always stimulated me to some kind of fresh seeing, even in disagreeing with him. To use a pet phrase of his: it helped me to keep my eyes peeled, which I saw as meaning the stripping off of the layers of cliché-seeing, of habit-bound superficial looking. Of course, too, not all students could tolerate having their eyes peeled. But Pat Millard, then head of Goldsmiths' Art Department, who had had the vision to appoint Anton to a full-time post on the Art Teachers Course, tells me that those students who could accept his method are all doing exceptionally well in their subsequent careers. He also tells me that several students who applied to come to Goldsmiths but were not accepted said it was worth applying, just for the sake of the interview they had with Anton; who would, of course, be liable to upset the whole interview timetable by keeping an applicant he was interested in for an hour instead of fifteen minutes. They said the question he asked always made them look at their own work that they had brought to the inverview in a new way. I am told too that his success in vitalizing and inspiring whatever class he worked in was shown by the fact of how devastated the students were at the news of his so sudden death, as those of us who were his friends also were.

References

1 Milner, M. (1967) The Hidden Order of Art. Read at the Institute of Contemporary Art, London, 21 June.

2 Milner, M. (1956) The Communication of Primary Sensual Experience: The Yell of Joy. *International Journal of Psycho-Analysis* 37: 278–89. Previously read at the Nineteenth International Psycho-Analytical Congress, Geneva, 24–28 July, 1955.

3 Ehrenzweig, A. (1953) *The Psycho-Analysis of Artistic Vision and Hearing.* London: Routledge & Kegan Paul.

4 Milner, M. (1958) Psycho-Analysis and Art. In J. Sutherland (ed.) *Psycho-Analysis and Contemporary Thought*. London: Hogarth and British Institute of Psycho-Analysis.

5 Milner, M. (1938) *An Experiment in Leisure*. London: Chatto & Windus.

6 Ehrenzweig, A. (1957) The Creative Surrender. *The American Imago* 14: 3.

7 Frazer, J. G. (1890) *The Golden Bough*. Part Three: 'The Dying God'. London: Methuen (1923).

8 Ehrenzweig, A. (1967) *The Hidden Order of Art*. London: Weidenfeld & Nicolson.

9 Subsequently published as Stokes, A. (1955) Form in Art. In M. Klein (ed.) *New Directions in Psycho-Analysis*. London: Tavistock.

10 Blake, W. (1904) Jerusalem. In *The Poetical Works of William Blake*. Oxford: Oxford University Press.

----------------------------------- 16 -----------------------------------

1972: Winnicott and the
two-way journey

This paper was my contribution to the memorial meeting for D. W. Winnicott, given to the British Psycho-Analytical Society in 1972.[1]

Often, when I talked to people about D. W. Winnicott they would say, 'Oh, but of course, he was a genius.' I do not know what makes a genius. All I know is that I must take as my text for this paper something he once said to his students just before a lecture: 'What you get out of me, you will have to pick out of chaos.'

I want to describe the highlights of my contacts with him in matters of theory. I find this particularly hard to do, because I am one of those people who Freud reminded us exist, people who think in pictures. So what I want to say about Winnicott must centre around certain visual images.

One night in 1957, driving through France, I saw a crowd in the market-place of a little town, all gathered around an arc lamp where a trapeze had been set up by travelling acrobats. The star performers were there, in spotless white, doing wonderful turns and handstands on the bar. Below them was a little clown in a grey floppy coat too big for him, just fooling around while the others did their displays. Occasionally he made a fruitless attempt to jump up and reach the bar. Then, suddenly, he made a great leap and there he was, whirling around on the bar, all his clothes flying out, like a huge Catherine wheel, to roars of delight from the crowd.

This is my image of Winnicott. Often over the years when we had a gap of time and arranged to meet to discuss some theoretical problem, he would open the door, and there he would be, all over the place, whistling, forgetting something, running upstairs, making a general clatter, so that I would become impatient for him to settle down. Gradually, I came to see this as a necessary preliminary to those fiery flashes of his intuition that would always follow. He has actually written about the logic of this in one of his papers, where he talks of the necessity, when doing an analysis, of recognizing and allowing for phases of nonsense, when no thread ought to be searched for in the patient's material because what is going on is preliminary chaos, the first phase of the creative process.[2]

After the whirling clown on the bar comes another image, an actual Catherine wheel firework, nailed to a tree and lit by a small boy, in the still dark of the countryside. The wheel at first splutters and misfires, then gets going as a fizzing, fiery ring of light, sending off sparks into the darkness around. I always have an image of the dark disc at the centre whenever I read in his writings about the unknowable core of the self.

My third image, woven into my thoughts for this paper, is part of a shared joke we had. During the war I had shown him a cartoon from the *New Yorker*. It was of two hippopotamuses, their heads emerging from the water, and one saying to the other, 'I keep thinking it's Tuesday.' It was typical of him that he never forgot this joke. After all these years, I see how it fits in with a dominant preoccupation of mine – the threshhold of consciousness, the surface of the water as the place of submergence or emergence.

And from this picture of the water's surface I come to one of his images, that is, the quotation from Tagore[3] that he put at the head of his paper 'The Location of Cultural Experience',[4] 'On the sea-shore of endless worlds children play'. I too have had this line at the back of my mind, ever since I first read it in 1915. Winnicott said that, for him, the aphorism aided speculation upon the question, If play is neither inside nor outside, where is it? For me it stirred thoughts of the coming and going of the tides, the rhythmic daily submergence and smoothing out of this place where children play.

Later in this paper about the place of cultural experience he uses another image that we both had in common – only I had completely forgotten about it. He is talking about how the baby comes to be able to make use of the symbol of union and can begin to allow for and benefit from separation, a separation that is not a separation, but a form of union; and here he refers to a drawing that I made, long ago in the 1930s, showing the interplay of the edges of two jugs. He says the drawing conveyed to him the tremendous significance there can be in the interplay of edges.

I too found myself using this same drawing as a visual symbol for his concept of potential space. And it still has many overtones for me, since a patient of mine used it constantly, in the more abstract form of two overlapping circles which become two faces and then oscillate between being two and being one.

So much for the images. Now for the actuality.

I first saw Winnicott when he was giving a public lecture in the late 1930s, talking about his work with mothers and babies and the famous spatula game. He told how he would leave a spatula on the table in front of the mother and baby, well within the baby's reach. Then he simply watched what the baby did with the spatula, watched for variations in the normal pattern of reaching for it, grabbing it, giving it a good suck and then chucking it away. He told how, out of this very simple experimental situation, he could work out, according to the observed blocks in the various stages, a diagnosis of the problems betwen the mother and the baby. As he talked, I was captivated by the mixture in him of deep seriousness and his love of little jokes, that is, the play aspect of his character, if one thinks of true play as transcending the opposites of serious and non-serious.

It was after this lecture that I began to attend his clinic as an observer, and I well remember the pleasure he took in this spatula game. I feel it was the neatness that satisfied both the artist and the scientist in the man, the formal qualities so simple and clear, providing a structure within which he made his observations. And this same feeling for aesthetic form continued in his therapeutic use with children of what he called the squiggle game. In fact, as described in his book on the subject, he used these games to structure the therapeutic consultations.[5] Each account of those drawing sessions with the child exemplifies as well his beautiful concept of potential space – an essentially pictorial concept, although he defines it as 'what happens between two people when there is trust and reliability'. Thus there is also the way the account of each session organizes time. Time stretches back, not only through the child's lifetime, but also through Winnicott's own years of psychoanalytic practice, so that he has at his fingertips the tools of psychoanalytic concepts, though using them here in a different setting.

Then there is what I have gained from his concept of the holding environment. I will not say much about this, for I have already given it extensive form in my book about a patient's drawings, having even embodied the idea in my title: *The Hands of the Living God*.[6] The phrase is in fact taken from a poem by D. H. Lawrence, a poem in which Lawrence describes the ghastly feelings of terror at falling forever when contact with the inner holding environment is lost.[7]

I would in addition like to say something about Winnicott's comment, in his paper on play,[8] on my 1952 paper on the play of a boy patient (see Chapter 9).[9] Near the beginning of his paper Winnicott points out that I have related playing to concentration in adults, and that he has done the same thing. A little later he quotes my remark about 'moments when the original poet in us created the world for us perhaps forgotten . . . because they were too much like visitations of the gods'. His quoting this reminded me that one of the jumping-off places for my paper had been a growing preoccupation with certain moments in the boy's play, moments which seemed both to express and to be accompanied by a special kind of concentration, moments actually symbolized, it seemed to me, by his continual play with lighted candles and fires in the dark, as well as by explicit play concerning visitations of the gods. All this seems to me now to link up with what Winnicott came to call 'creative apperception', the colouring of external reality in a new way, a way that can give a feeling of great significance and can in fact, as he claims, make life feel worth living, even in the face of much instinct deprivation.

I realized too that this starting-point for that paper of mine had also been the starting-point for the first book I ever wrote, a book based on a diary I kept in 1926, about the sudden moments when one's whole perception of the world changes – changes that happen, sometimes apparently out of the blue, but sometimes as the result of a deliberate shift of attention, one that makes the whole world seem newly created.[10] Although when I became an analyst I tried to fit these experiences into such psychoanalytic concepts as manic defences against depression and so on, these ideas did not seem quite adequate to account for the phenomena. But then I found Winnicott making the distinction between the vicissitudes of instinct and what happens in creativity, which for him was the same as creative playing. This seemed to offer a more useful approach. Not that I found his way of putting his ideas about creativity entirely easy: sometimes he seemed to be talking about a way of looking at the world, sometimes about a way of doing something deliberately, and sometimes about simply enjoying a bodily activity, breathing, for instance, that just happens. I asked myself, in what sense are these all creative? Certainly they are different, as he says, from the making of anything, such as a house or a meal or a picture, though all these may include what he is talking about. Then I happened upon a statement that helped me clarify the problem. It was Martin Buber's remark about 'productivity versus immediacy of the lived life'.[11] He was referring to what he called the dominant delusion of our time, that creativity (meaning, I supposed, *artistic* creativity) is the criterion of human worth. Buber went on to say that 'the potentiality of form also accompanies every experience that befalls the nonartistic man and is given an issue as often as he lifts an image out of the stream of perception and inserts it into his memory as something single, definite and meaningful in itself'. This phrase – lifting an image out of the stream of perception – clearly related to Winnicott's comment, 'What you get out of me you must pick out of chaos.' Thus one gets the idea of creativeness as not simply perceiving, but as deliberately relating ourselves to our perceiving. It is a perceiving that has an 'I AM' element in it. And this brings me to Winnicott's use of the word *self*.

First, what does he say about the way self comes into being? He claims that the sense of self comes only from desultory formless activity or rudimentary play, and then only if reflected back; he adds that it is only in being creative that one discovers oneself. I have a difficulty here. I can understand him when he claims that the sense of self comes on the basis of the unintegrated state, but when he adds that this state is by definition not observable or communicable, I begin to wonder. Not communicable, yes. Not observable, I am not so sure. I think of the dark still centre of the whirling Catherine wheel and feel fairly certain that it can, in the right setting, be related to by the conscious ego discovering that it can turn in upon itself, make contact with the core of its own being, and find there a renewal, a rebirth. In fact isn't Winnicott himself referring to this when he speaks of 'quietude linked with stillness'? This reminds me of T. S. Eliot's 'still point of the turning world' or 'words after speech reach into silence'.[12]

Linked to this question of the discovery of the self is surely the discovery of one's own body. So the question arises, What is the relation of the sense of being, which Winnicott says must precede the finding of the self, to the awareness of one's own body? I think there is a hint about this when he speaks of the 'summation or reverberation of experiences of relaxation in conditions of trust based on experience'. For me this phrase stirs echoes throughout years of observation of how deliberate bodily relaxation brings with it, if one can wait for it, a reverberations from inside, something spreading in waves, something that brings an intense feeling of response from that bit of the outer world that is at the same time also oneself: one's own body. Here is what I think he means when he speaks of enjoying one's own breathing as an example of creativity.

As for his statements concerning the first toy, which he says we do not challenge as to its coming from inside or from outside, these serve as a bridge for me, particularly to the special cultural field of religion.[13] When I encounter, in a book entitled *The God I Want*, the idea that to discover God as myself is also to discover Him as other than myself, when I read that receiving implies otherness and that at the same time what we receive is our own, I am reminded of the creative paradox so dear to Winnicott.[14] And when he speaks of the transitional object as the symbol of a journey, it seems really to be a two-way journey: both to the finding of the objective reality of the object and to the finding of the objective reality of the subject – the I AM.

There was, as well as this word *creativity* and all its implications, another term that, since the late 1940s, had given me a lot of uneasiness, like a shoe beginning to feel too tight. The term was *primary process*. I had been taught that this was a form of archaic thinking that had to be outgrown. But slowly, over the years, primary process seems to have changed its meaning, so that it is now seen, certainly by some writers, as part of the integrating function of the ego: that is it serves to join up experiences and assimilate them into the ego, in order to preserve the ego's wholeness. As such it is not something to be grown out of, but, rather, is complementary to secondary process functioning and as necessary to it as male and female are to each other. It is this primary process that enables one to accept paradox and contradiction, something that secondary process does not like at all, being itself bound by logic, which rejects contradiction. Although Winnicott hardly ever uses the term, I feel that given this new meaning, the concept of primary process is implicit in all of his work and integral to his idea of what it means to be healthy.

So what the hippopotamus joke means to me now is this: One must not try to make the hippo live only on land, because it is, by nature, incurably amphibious. And whatever it means to say that someone is a genius, I do wish to make clear that I believe Winnicott was on excellent terms with his primary process; it was an inner marriage to which there was very little impediment.

References

1 This paper was published as Chapter 3 in S. Grolnick (ed.) (1978) *Between Reality and Phantasy: Transitional Objects Phenomena*. London and New York: J. Aronson.

2 Winnicott, D. W. (1971) Playing: Creative Activity and the Search for the Self. In *Playing and Reality*. London: Tavistock.
3 Tagore, R. (1986) *Collected Poems and Plays*. London: Macmillan.
4 Winnicott, D. W. (1971) The Location of Cultural Experience. In *Playing and Reality*. London: Tavistock.
5 Winnicott, D. W. (1971) *Therapeutic Consultations in Child Psychiatry*. New York: Basic Books.
6 Milner, M. (1969) *The Hands of the Living God*. London: Hogarth.
7 Lawrence, D. H. (1929) *Pansies*. London: Secker.
8 Winnicott, D. W. (1971) Playing: A Theoretical Statement. In *Playing and Reality*. London: Tavistock.
9 Milner, M. (1952) Aspects of Symbolism in Comprehension of the Not-Self. *International Journal of Psycho-Analysis* 33: 181–95.
10 Milner, M. (1952) The Role of Illusion in Symbol Formation. In M. Klein, P. Heimann, S. Isaacs, and J. Riviere (eds.) *New Directions in Psycho-Analysis*. London: Tavistock.
11 Buber, M. (1969) *The Healthy Personality*. Readings edited by Hung-min Chiang and A. Maslow. London: Van Nostrand Reinhold.
12 Eliot, T. S. (1959) Burnt Norton. In *Four Quartets*. London: Faber & Faber.
13 Winnicott, D. W. (1953) Transitional Objects and Transitional Phenomena. In *Collected Papers*. New York: Basic Books.
14 Williams, I. H. A. (1967) (ed. J. Mitchell) *The God I Want*. London: Constable.

17
1972: The two-way journey in a child analysis

In 1971, shortly before writing the 'Two-Way Journey' paper about
D. W. Winnicott (see Chapter 16), I was supervising the analysis of a
child patient. I found that the analyst concerned, Dr Lore Schacht,
did not yet know Winnicott's paper 'The Use of an Object'.[1] When
she read it she saw its relevance for the problems of the child we were
battling with. Subsequently she sent me a paper called 'Psycho-
Analytic Facilitation into the "Subject-Loses-Subject" Phase of
Maturation'.[2] In this she wrote about one week of the analysis,
quoting extensively from Winnicott's paper, but using the later
version of it published in *Playing and Reality*.[3]

I have Dr Schacht's permission to quote extracts from her paper,
because the work we did together with this child helped me to
understand far more of the implications of what Winnicott was
saying and also to see how it illustrated what I have called 'The Two-
Way Journey'. Here is part of what she wrote.

'Case history'

'The events which prompted me to write this paper occurred
during the five hours of one week of treatment of Jasper, a 4½-
year-old boy who had been in therapy about fourteen months. He
had been taken on for treatment because he had shown himself to
be extremely aggressive and physically destructive toward his
environment (his mother in particular), had shown serious self-
destructive tendencies, was unable to play with other children or
alone, and was at the point of being dismissed from his nursery

school. During the first year of analysis, Jasper had lived through so rich an emotional development that I was constantly surprised by the insights into his psyche that he revealed to me.'

At one stage Jasper asked Dr Schacht to do something he did not like so that she could be punished by being put in jail. Dr Schacht writes:

'While I was sitting in jail, Jasper came over to see what effect his actions against me had had. ("You should be dead by now; one dies in prison after some time.")

The attacks on the object (me) increased in force in the following session when the car was pushed again and again against the wall, when the Mommy doll was again buried under the falling bricks, and when the Mommy doll finally fell off the wall and was lying dead on the ground. The rescue action, which might still have been possible, turned into an attack on my room and thus on me when Jasper, in order to put out the fire of the burning ambulance, produced a smal flood. It was only during the course of the game that he decided that I was able to survive. His attack on the consulting room was launched at tremendous speed and violence and was at first not easy to meet and contain.'

This description reminded me of how, nearly forty years before, my patient Simon's violent attacks had made me let him out into my garden where he could do less damage (see Chapter 9). Dr Schacht continues:

'After his first attack on me, Jasper started to talk about the "bad Jasper" as if he were placing himself outside both himself and me by making him appear outside the window: "There he is – he is coming through the window." Later he went further than merely seeing "bad Jasper" by saying, "I don't like the bad Jasper", and by coming to the unusual conclusion, "I'll kill him – I can do that." Quite clearly the episode meant that the subject potentially destroys the subject. Here this was done in the presence of the object which earlier had resisted a similar attack by the subject.'

Here too, I remembered how, at one point, Simon had tried to shut himself into the cupboard where I kept the drawing paper etc., and taken a box of matches with him. In Jasper's case the self-destructive wish was only verbal; for Simon there was real danger if I had not intervened. And Dr Schacht is able to tell of the benign sequel for she says:

'The bad Jasper survived the threat of destruction ("I'll kill him – I can do that") and reappeared in the following hour when Jasper exclaimed, "The bad Jasper likes me — he likes me — there he is at the window."

Jasper had prefaced his statement by telling me that the people in the library liked him. This statement leads to an interesting tie-up. These people liked Jasper: the subject was saying that it felt safe in its object relations and described itself as loved. Supported by this experience, it could have an encounter with the subject in which destruction or the thought of destruction had been overcome, and Jasper thus exclaim triumphantly, "The bad Jasper likes me".'

Here there immediately came to my mind a statement of Melanie Klein's, made at the International Psycho-Analytic Congress in Paris in 1957, 'The split-off parts of the self are lonely'. Dr Schacht continues:

'The subject which the subject found to be objectively perceivable, also recognized that the subject could be destroyed by the subject. Yet the subject survived – "The bad Jasper likes me": the subject did not take revenge. There was happiness about the discovery, which Jasper expressed in the following hour by drawing a man with a bunch of flowers in his hand and with a big sun in the sky. Here, too, Jasper allowed me to participate in his work – he drew the man, the flowers, and the sun, yet the colors were added by way of the object relationship with me, since he asked me to color in the patterns he had drawn.'

Dr Schacht then says:

'Jasper's ensuing action against me showed definite signs of caution, self-control, and consideration. He happily played at being the big fish which devoured me and then spat me out safe and sound. The impulse to destroy was probably softened by the memory that once before I had been able to survive ("It is important that 'survive' in this context means 'not retaliate'") [Winnicott].

Was Jasper able to see me as more than a projective entity when he told me that I should do something he didn't like so that he could punish me? If it had been merely a question of projecting the "bad Jasper" onto me, as I assumed at first, it wouldn't have been necessary for him to ask me to do something that put me in opposition to him. I think rather that the situation was an anticipation of the development of the phase in which the object "is in process of being found instead of placed by the subject in the world" [Winnicott].'

Here I found myself again going back to Simon and to his insistence on giving me a name, in fact that of a chemical that he had himself made. In contrast to this, I found that Dr Schacht summarized what had happened with Jasper in the following terms:

'The first signs of the ability to use an object can also be seen in Jasper's changed attitude toward my name. So far there had only been one name he could or wanted to write down: his own. Now, however, he allowed me to have a name, too. While before he had called me exclusively "Doctor", now, for a time, he addressed me by my full name. I want to interpret the use of my name here as a sign of object constancy, of the continued existence of the object even outside the area of the subject's omnipotence.

To use an object in the transitional area means to give up the illusion of having created the object oneself. It means being able to endure the given reality and to use it for the enrichment of the subject. This transition from illusion to reality can constitute the leap into a new dimension of experience; it can mean that the subject is no longer supported by its subjective omnipotence.'

She adds that in this phase of his analysis Jasper was preoccupied with understanding the meaning of being born – that there was a beginning that was not of his own making. Dr Schacht summarizes her findings:

'The first part of my thesis, drawn from this part of the analysis, is the following: The potential destruction which Jasper previously had directed against the object was now being turned against the subject. ("I'll kill him – I can do that!").

The necessary precondition is that the subject has first become aware of itself *objectively*. The words "There he is – he is coming through the window" may be seen as an intensely concentrated reflection of this experience, in the sense that "he is coming through the window" constitutes what I want to call the encounter of the subject with the subject. By translating Winnicott's concept of the importance that the awareness of the object, as something that can be objectively experienced, has to this aspect of the communication of the subject with the subject, it is possible to say: The subject is in process of being found, rather than placed in the world by the subject.

The preceding rejection, "I do not like the bad Jasper", made it easier for the subject to become aware that the subject was something that had an objective existence – that it was not created by the subject himself.'

References

1 Winnicott, D. W. (1969) The Use of an Object. *International Journal of Psycho-Analysis* 50: 711–15. Previously read to the New York Psycho-Analytic Society 12 November, 1968.
2 Schacht, L. (1972) Psycho-Analytic Facilitation into the 'Subject-Loses-Subject' Phase of Maturation. *International Journal of Child Psychotherapy* 1(4): 71–82.
3 Winnicott, D. W. (1971) *Playing and Reality*. London: Tavistock.

18

1973: Some notes on psychoanalytic ideas about mysticism

This paper was originally written for a book of papers by her colleagues in honour of Paula Heimann's seventy-fifth birthday.

This paper began when I became aware of a need to look at psychoanalysts' ideas about mysticism, partly because of occasionally having patients who practised some form of meditation. This paper is therefore an account of what I found, beginning in the first part with a look at what my own ideas about it had been, both before and after becoming an analyst, and going on, in the second part, to see what has been written about it by other analysts. While writing both parts I have in fact become aware of a process going on; I can think of no better description for it than Bion's phrase (though it is a formulation that I did not in fact discover till near the end of this study) – 'an idea in search of a thinker'.[1]

With this in mind I now remembered that a first hint of such a preoccupation had occurred, in 1916, in a conversation with a schoolfriend, a very intelligent girl who won a Mathematics scholarship to Cambridge, about the nature of thinking. The discussion had ended with us both agreeing that 'it thinks you'.[2] Also, it was partly this same preoccupation which led me, in 1926, to try and record, in diary form, the results of practising different kinds of attention, especially a wide unfocused kind. This was an undertaking which eventually resulted in my first book and its sequel.[3] Amongst the great number of letters that I received about the first book were a few that made me realize that some of the experiences I had described might be called 'mystical', a fact which I had not realized; also there were some letters that forced me to ask myself the question, What is the relation between mysticism and madness?

Then, in the early 1930s, I had a phase of reading various books about mysticism, including Suzuki on Zen Buddhism,[4] the Lao Tze,[5] Patanjali,[6] and a summary of the Western mystical tradition whose title or author I do not remember, but from which I picked one statement which I never forgot because it seemed so surprising. As far as I remember, it said that a beginning of mystical experience could be learning how to attend to one's own body awareness, from inside, even beginning with one's big toe.

A little later I read Silberer's *Problems of Mysticism and its Symbolism.*[7] I do not remember what I learnt from this, but it did serve to strengthen my interest in those sudden moments of intensified perception of the outer world that I had already been studying in my first book, and that I was about to continue to study in my second.

When, in 1940, I began training as a psychoanalyst, I was so busy learning how to do it and how to pass my initiation tests into the inner circle of psychoanalysts that I forgot some of my earlier experiences – or rather, put them aside for the time being. The beginning of their return (1947) can, I think, be illustrated by a remark made to me by a boy of 6 in his analysis (see Chapter 4). He had done much painting of houses using black for the roofs and at one moment had said, 'Not horrid black, lovely black, if it's wet and shiny'. Now I found I had made a note in the margin of my notes about this, adding a quotation, 'There is in God a deep but dazzling darkness'.[8] I also remembered that the only bit that had stuck in my mind after learning something of the philosophy of Spinoza, at the university, was the phrase, as I remembered it, 'The night in which all cows are black'; also there was Edward Thomas's poem *Out in the Dark*. About this time too, my adult patient, Susan, (see Chapter 6) had told me she had just discovered the word 'mystic' and decided that she herself must be one, in the light of certain intense experiences that she had once had, before being given ECT. Soon after this I happened to find Reich's *Character Analysis* and I pondered on his insistence that all mystical experience is due to the misinterpretation of sexual feelings.[9] This seemed a possibly useful idea, as this patient had massive sexual inhibitions. However, I did not think this was at all the whole story.

It was in 1950 when this same patient did begin to draw that she produced many variants of a circle, as I have described in 'The Yell of

259

Joy' papers (see Chapter 10). Although at first I had tried thinking of the circle as standing for the breast this did not seem to get us very far, so gradually I had tried looking on it as representing, not an object, but some kind of ego state. This thought then took me back to Suzuki's book and the Chinese Cow Herding pictures that he reproduces in the appendix, for here, in the series of twelve circular pictures showing the progress in the sage's task of learning to control his attention, which is shown as a cow (in some versions a bull), the eighth one is shown as a complete blank, the sage and his hut and cow have all disappeared.

This theme of blankness, emptiness of thought, then led me on to ideas about a 'bad' blankness and 'good' blankness, just as my boy patient had distinguished between horrid black and lovely black. In fact I was gradually coming to see that there might be a kind of blankness or gap in one's perception that could be of value and even a necessary stage in a creative process, a phase of a fertility cycle comparable to the emptiness of the fields in winter. I now began to suspect too that this set of ideas had been silently active even throughout the years of my analytic training. For instance, as early as 1942, when asked to give a lecture on any subject I liked to a group of educationists, I had chosen the title 'The Child's Capacity for Doubt' (see Chapter 1) and had elaborated on the positive aspects of not-knowing. At this time too there was always in the back of my mind the memory of Keats's letters and his use of the term 'negative capability' which I had first read in the 1930s. However, apart from my patient's claim of being a mystic having directed my attention to Reich's formulation in terms of the mystification of sexuality, I had continued to put aside my queries about mysticism itself during the years from 1940 to 1950. Instead, throughout this time, apart from writing my first three psychoanalytic papers which seem to have nothing to do with mysticism, I had been preoccupied with attempts to understand my own difficulties in learning how to paint. It was in 1950 (when the first edition of the book about painting was published)[10] that something else happened which I can now see could have had something to do with what I had first read about training for mystical experience. It happened one day when sitting in a garden, at a residential art school, wanting to paint but unable to find a subject. In order to deal with the tension of the frustration I had started a deep breathing exercise and had been astonished to find that the world around me immediately became quite different and, by now, exceedingly paintable. It seemed odd, then, that turning one's attention inwards, not to awareness of one's big toe but to the inner sensations of breathing, should have such a marked effect on the appearance and significance of the world, but I had not then thought of this in terms of mysticism.

It was in 1952 that I was brought back to the subject, as the result of being present at a discussion directed by Harold Walsby (not a psychoanalyst and working almost entirely outside academic circles) whose ideas as expressed on these occasions have not, so far as I know (he died in 1973), appeared in print. He spoke about the difficulties of equating intellect with logic and how the technique of formal reasoning and its assumptions enable us to manage the inanimate world but is incapable of dealing intelligently with the territory of the self and other selves, since these require a dialectic approach; that is the capacity to embrace the very contradictions that formal logic avoids. Walsby claimed that this other kind of thinking, which can be called mystical just because of its capacity for letting go the clinging to the distinction between subject and object, became relegated to the sphere of religion and so was alienated from what should be a complementary interplay with the ways of thinking based on the rules of formal logic. He had gone on to illustrate some of his ideas from the sayings of Lao Tze in the *Tao Te Ching*.[11]

Although I had felt when first reading the *Tao Te Ching*, in the 1930s, that it meant a lot to me, I had not, as I have said, been able to relate it to psychoanalytic theory when I began to train as a psychoanalyst. The two streams of thought had therefore remained separate in my deeper preoccupations; but after hearing Walsby it had seemed it might be possible eventually to bring them together. And now, in 1973, I remembered that I had, in 1952, acquired a different, more modern translation of the *Tao Te Ching*, in fact the one used by Walsby, in which I had marked some of the aphorisms which had been especially mentioned by him as to do with what he called 'dialectical thinking.'

It was here that I remembered how, in my 1934 book, when finding much ambiguity in my ideas about the word god and having searched for an alternative term for 'ultimate reality', I had myself quoted from Lao Tze the aphorism, 'The TAO of which we speak is not the real TAO'. And now, when I looked at some of Walsby's markings about the TAO I found the following (I have added on the right side the earlier translation):

xiv	It goes back to non-existence.	This is the appearance of the Non-Apparent
	It is called the form of the formless,	The form of the Non-Existent
	And the image of non-existence.	This is the unfathomed mystery.

It is called mystery.
Meet it, you cannot see its face;
Follow it, you cannot see its back.

Going before, its face is not seen; following after, its back is not observed.

xvi   Attain to the good of absolute vacuity.

Having emptied yourself of every thing remain where you are.

xxviii He who knows the masculine and yet keeps to the feminine
Will become a channel drawing all the world towards it;
And then he can return again to the state of infancy.
He who knows the white and yet keeps to the black
Will become the standard of the world;

He who being a man remains a woman will become a universal channel.

As an universal channel the eternal virtue will never forsake him. He will re-become a child.

He who, being in the light remains in obscurity will become a universal model.

Several of these aphorisms were especially useful for me, for instance, 'It goes back to non-existence.' This seemed to be, for some patients, the crux of the matter, the paradox of being able to feel oneself in touch with non-existence while yet continuing to exist. For them non-existence was apparently thought of as forever, a total annihilation rather than a phase in the creative process of 'lifting an image out of the stream of perception'.

Similarly, 'Attain to the *good* of absolute vacuity' (my italics), did have a particular meaning for me and this, in spite of the fact that it could easily provide, if misunderstood, an excuse for a total mental self-blinding, a dangerous denial of unpleasant truths, both in ourselves and the world, denials that could in fact lead to the total disaster of a nuclear war. Also there was one memory that reminded me that I had had ideas about the value of 'absolute vacuity' on quite a practical, everyday level. It was in the 1930s, when attending a school prize-giving, the giver-away of the prizes, Lady So-and-So wearing a feather boa, had ended her speech by saying, 'and do you also know how to wipe your minds free of learning?' Perhaps arrogantly, I had wondered how she knew. I also remembered that one of the tasks I used to set myself, then, was not only to practise wiping my mind free of learning, with its visual image of a wiped clean blackboard, but also the task of stopping internal chatter of thoughts, to reach an inner silence.

As for knowing the masculine yet keeping to the feminine, this was a concept that I had eventually struggled with in my 1934 book. Also, in the saying, 'He who knows the white yet keeps to the

262

black', the key word for me was 'keeps', that is an active relating to the dark, not a passive submergence in it. For this reminded me of how the dragon-like Leviathan creature in Blake's picture (see *Figure 44*, p. 171) seems to be in danger of (or in intense desire for?) complete submergence in the sea. By contrast, in 'The Morning Stars' picture (*Figure 56*, p. 205) the moon goddess is driving a team of very active dragons, in exact complementary symmetry with the sun god's team of horses on the opposite side of the picture.

At this point I had to remind myself how, in my own 1956 lecture, I had referred to the work of Ehrenzweig, and his first book where he maintains that mystic feeling is explained by our rational surface mind's incapacity to visualize the inarticulate images of the depth mind,[12] an idea which he further develops in his second book *The Hidden Order of Art*.[13] So here, for me, the three streams were coming together with both Maritain and Walsby saying that the process which goes on in the depths essentially involves an undoing of the split into subject and object which is the very basis of our logical thinking.

Another step seems to have come from writing my Athens paper (1960: see Chapter 14) about the importance of the direct non-symbolic internal awareness of one's own body from inside; in fact, the ongoing background or matrix of one's own sense of being which can yet become foreground once one has learnt the skill of directing attention to it. Again, I had not really thought of this in terms of mysticism; however, I could now see that the idea went back once more to the 1930s, back to my amused surprise that a beginning of a mystic's training could be to become aware of one's own toe from inside. Certainly, I really had found, in my own experiments, that the deliberate effort, at times, to wipe out all conscious imaging – verbal, visual, auditory – and to descend into awareness of an imageless existing, within one's own body, this could result in a way of being that was not only highly recuperative but also a great enrichment of one's appreciation of the outer world. And this reminded me how, in the Cow Herding pictures, after the blank circle the last one shows the sage returned to the market-place. No doubt it was this feeling about what happens to one's body awareness that had made me borrow from somewhere for the Athens paper the phrase 'divine ground of one's being' – because this was as accurate a description as I could then find for what seems to happen to one's sense of self when consciousness does suffuse the whole of the body from inside and all focused images are got rid of, an inner action that seemed to be a kind of dialectical reunion of body and mind. As I have said, it was not till later that I realized what had been left out in the Athens description was the awareness of one's own breathing.

This thought of a felt imageless state now reminded me that also in the mid-1930s I had developed a technique for dealing with 'bad' moods of my own, moods of restless unease, by saying silently to myself, 'I have nothing, I know nothing, I want nothing.' I did not then know where the phrase came from, I might even have invented it – but it certainly worked. Then I had given it up when I started training to be a psychoanalyst for I thought it surely contained a most massive denial and so could not be looked on as healthy at all. Now however I was beginning to guess that there might be more sense in this inner gesture than I had recently allowed. Also I found out that I had certainly not invented it for I was now told that it came from the thirteenth-century German mystic, Meister Eckhart, whose books I had not read but who had most likely been quoted in the 'forgotten' one that I had read.

Another landmark had been when, during the middle 1960s, after writing the account of the analysis of my patient, Susan, who had at one time thought she was a mystic, I had chosen the title *The Hands of the Living God* (from D. H. Lawrence's poem).[14] This was because she had claimed that, before they gave her the ECT, she had felt she had known what St Paul meant by 'the length and breadth and depth and height of the love of God',[15] but after, she did not know any more. Certainly I thought that this god, being so spatially containing, holding, sounded very much more like a mother god than a father god.

I was now ready to begin the second half of my undertaking; that is to see what other analysts had felt about mysticism.[16] I decided to do it by seeing if they thought the subject of sufficient importance to be mentioned in the indexes of their books. This meant that I would not include paperbacks, which usually have no index, and, to keep the study of manageable size, I would include only qualified Freudian psychoanalysts.

My psychoanalytic books (the hardbacks) were arranged alphabetically on the shelf; I began at the end with Winnicott, and found only two references in all the indexes of his many books. In one he talks of mysticism in terms of a secret communication with a subjective satisfying object.[17] In another place he compares the mystic and the behaviourist in terms of where they find infinity, either at the centre of the self or 'beyond the moon to the stars and to . . . time that has neither an end nor a beginning'.[18]

Next came Silberer. He makes only three page references to

mysticism, one being to what he calls the diabolic, as contrasted with the divine kind and which he describes as phantasmic appearances that partly flatter the wish for power and other wishes. Also he says that the true mysticism is characterized by an extension of personality, the false by a shrinking.

There were no references in Ella Sharpe.

Then came Reich. I found he elaborates at length, in many books, his view of mysticism as distorted sexuality, insisting that the mystical response does not allow the perception of sexual excitation and precludes orgastic release.[19] Also in his book *The Mass Psychology of Fascism* he gives many examples of what I think Silberer would have classified as the diabolic kind of mysticism.[20]

Next was Rycroft, with no references in his hardback books but in his study of Reich (a paperback with no index so not really belonging here) he gives extensive summaries of Reich's views; for instance, the view that orgasm, since it unites the bodily and the spiritual, thereby breaks down the dichotomy between the natural scientific and religious–poetic vision of reality.[21] However, says Rycroft, Reich's view was that anyone who achieves such a unification becomes a threat to the established order and is liable to be martyred, as Jesus was, and Giordano Bruno (1548–1600). Rycroft also tells of Reich's claim that, owing to the defensive character-armouring the majority never achieve orgasm in this sense.

I could only find one reference in Rickman, that is to the use of magical words in most mystical cults.[22]

I found no references, amongst the volumes that were on my bookshelf, in the works of Hanna Segal, Herbert Rosenfeld, Money-Kyrle, Meltzer, Bertram Lewis, R. D. Laing (hardback only), nor in the works of Melanie Klein; but in the *New Directions in Psycho-Analysis*, which contains papers by sixteen different people (including one by me), there is one reference and that is by Joan Riviere.[23] Although she refers to the unconscious *sources* of our being and the *reality* of sensations, emotions, and so on, and claims that these realities are the origin of mystical tendencies, she maintains that their *explanation* is to be found in *phantasies*, such as of bodily incorporation, union, fusion and inner possession.

In all my Ernest Jones books I could find only two references, both in the third volume of the life of Freud.[24] These are to do with Freud's admitting that his study of religious belief was limited to that of the common man, and that he regretted having ignored 'the rarer and more profound type of religious emotion as experienced by mystics and saints'.

In Freud's own work I found three references. In *Civilization and its Discontents*,[25] after discussing whether the oceanic feeling of oneness with the universe can be considered the source of religious needs he goes on to tell of the friend who claimed that the practice of yoga, in fixing attention on a bodily function, especially breathing, brings new sensations and coanaesthesia. Freud sees in this a physiological basis for much of the wisdom of mysticism.[26] In *Moses and Monotheism* he talks of how Jewish monotheism, borrowed from Egypt, included the rejection of magic and mysticism.[27] In his posthumously published *Findings, Problems, Ideas* he says, 'Mysticism is the obscure self-perception of the realm outside the ego, of the id'.[28]

In the works of Anna Freud I found no references.

In Fenichel's introduction to *The Psycho-Analytic Study of the Neuroses* I found one reference.[29] He maintains that the science of psychoanalysis does include the rudiments of mystical tradition but compares these to the activities of the police dog in police investigations, which Reik saw (1925) as the survival of the animal oracle.

Now came Brierley, *Trends in Psycho-Analysis*,[30] and Bion's *Attention and Interpretation*.[31] I had bought the Bion but not yet read it. Now I found that both had much to say about mystics and mysticism.

Brierley is concerned with the Christian mystics and quotes extensively from Evelyn Underhill.[32] For instance:

'The mystics are fond of this metaphor – "I live in the ocean of God as a fish in the sea". That is the life of union, of conscious abiding in God: . . . It brings with it great creative power. Once more we come back for our best definition to St Paul's "I live, yet not I".'

Brierley herself says that blissful experience is not the element most emphasized by Christian mystics, rather it is their overwhelming conviction of the reality of God: and she speaks of the mystics' conviction that religion is the only true realism.

In addition to talking about mysticism, Brierley also discusses the pros and cons of what she calls the 'integration of sanctity' and speculates about what psychotic elements may be included in it. In general her conclusion is that the true spiritual vocation is very rare. She says that the findings of psychoanalysis suggest:

'that the high road for the majority does not lead to super-ego autocracy and selective idealisation, but to a more inclusive and democratic harmonization of id, ego, and super-ego systems, to the development of a more comprehensive reality-sense and to the more enlightened ego-direction of personal life.'

In short, Brierley tries translating the Christian mystics' accounts of their experiences into psychoanalytic terms although she does not think that this is all there is to be said about it.[33]

Bion on the other hand does the opposite (twenty-one years later) in that he tries using religious terminology to denote what happens in psychoanalysis. He is able to do this because of an initial decision to use the terms mystic and genius interchangeably, even including the term 'messiah'. I was not unsympathetic to this usage, having thought so much about how creativity evolves out of darkness, especially when Bion follows Meister Eckhart's use of the word 'godhead' as 'that which contains all distinctions as yet undeveloped and which is therefore Darkness and Formlessness'.[34]

Bion goes on to ask whether it is possible, through psychoanalytic interpretation, to pass from knowing the phenomena of the real self to being the real self. His answer is that the further steps to bridge the gap must come from the analysand, 'or from a particular part of the analysand, namely his "godhead", which must consent to incarnation in the person of the analysand'. But he adds that this is not the same as for the analysand consenting to become god (or the 'godhead' of which 'god' is the phenomenological counterpart) as this latter would seem to be nearer to insanity. He maintains that the difference here is a matter of direction.

Bion also discusses the relation of the mystic or genius to the group, or 'Establishment' as being one in which they both need each other, and he illustrates this by reference to psychoanalytic societies. He sees the dynamics of this relation in terms of an explosive force within a restraining framework, as for instance 'the art form outmoded by new forces requiring representation'. He adds:

'The most powerful emotional explosion known so far, spreading to many cultures and over many centuries, has been that produced by the formulations of Jesus.[35] The effects are still felt and present grave problems of containment even now, though some measure of control has been established.'

Besides his use of religious terminology, Bion uses another representation to denote the ultimate reality, or God. He calls it '0' and defines the mystic as a thinker who claims the capacity for direct contact with it. He adds that '0' is unknowable, except for the mystic.

'For the same reason that makes it impossible to sing potatoes;

they may be grown or pulled or eaten, but not sung. Reality has to be "been"; there should be a transitive verb "to be" expressly for use with the term "reality".'[36]

However, although '0' is Darkness and Formlessness, it can, says Bion, be conjectured phenomenologically, through knowledge gained by experience and formulated in terms derived from sensuous experience.

So also, Bion points out, psychoanalytic events cannot be stated directly, any more than those of other scientific research and he demonstrates the use of this sign '0' to denote what happens in psychoanalytic sessions. Thus he says that 'what takes place in the consulting room is an emotional situation which is itself the intersection of an evolving "0" with another evolving "0" '; and he adds that the messianic idea is a term representing '0' at the point at which its evolution and the evolution of a thinker intersect. Then, following up his use of this term he says that there are also messianic ideas, which may be confused with the person, he may believe he is the messiah. Bion adds that there is a profound difference between 'being "0" ' and rivalry with '0', the latter being characterized by envy, hate, love, megalomania.

Bion also makes the statement that the suspension of memory and desire promotes exercise of aspects of the psyche that have no background of sensuous experience. Also his last sentence in the book, after having talked of the 'mathematics of growth', is:

> 'What is to be sought is an activity that is both the restoration of god (the Mother) and the evolution of god (the formless, infinite, ineffable, non-existent), which can be found only in the state in which there is no memory, desire, understanding.'

Yes, I thought, no memory, desire, or understanding, that's all right, but what about sensory awareness of breathing, which plays such a crucial role in Eastern mystical training systems? Still my own guess was that part of the task of the restoration of the Mother consists in consciousness becoming able to relate itself to, suffuse, every part of one's own body, Mother Nature, through attending to one's own breathing. But surely also there is needed the restoration of the father as well as the mother; for here I remembered Silberer's quoting the seventeenth-century mystical fable in which the hero becomes responsible for two lovers within a crystal globe, who are drowned, and it is the hero's task to restore them to life. In fact, it even seemed possible that the task of consciousness becoming able to relate itself to one's own body, from inside, could be symbolized, in phantasy, by the idea of the internal father and mother in creative union.

Finally, on my bookshelf, Balint and Abraham, with no index reference to mystics in either of them. But Balint's concepts of the 'philobat', always seeking the outer empty spaces, and the 'ocknophil', always wanting to cling so that there is no space between self and object, both seemed to be possible defences against making a dialectic relation to one's inner space, the space that is discovered when there is no clinging to knowledge, memory or desire – in fact, making a reliable contact with what Bion calls '0', the empty circle which is also the inner silence.[37] But to get this does seem to involve a long journey for many of us.

I received this letter from Marjorie Brierley after I had sent her a copy of this paper.

'24 January, 1975

Dear Mrs Milner,

Thank you for your letter and paper and the return envelope, which was most considerate. Unfortunately they arrived at a rather unfavourable time because I have to be out most of tomorrow and have someone coming to lunch on Saturday so, though I would have liked a bit longer to think about it, I must do what I can quickly today if you are to get paper back in good time for your dead-line. One tends to remember people as one last saw them. It was quite a surprise to hear that Paula Heimann was having her 75th birthday. I am glad she is having a Zeitschrift. If opportunity offers will you give her my congratulations?

First, *Webster's Biographical Dictionary* gives the dates for Eckhart as 1260?–1327?, i.e. not exactly known but presumably approximate.

Next, the paper itself. I found the account of your mental Odyssey most interesting. You certainly seem to have been sped on by learning from your patients, which is as it should be. I think you are probably right about the common factor between mysticism and creativity and the creative nature of perception. Every fresh perception assimilated into the pre-existing pattern must modify this, i.e. create a more or less new pattern. Your increase in perception following the breathing exercise, suddenly finding everything paintable, must have been striking. Without wishing to be too mundane, I suspect the breathing had to do with

269

it because it would have resulted apart from anything else in much better oxygenation of your brain.

It doesn't seem to have occurred to you that the '0' symbolises not only the emptied mind and the infant's open mouth but also the womb. It could be that a kind of temporary psychic regression to the womb is a prerequisite for both creativity and mystical experience. Christian literature abounds in references to the need to be re-born. It is a theme by no means limited to Xty. Primitive initiation ceremonies include such symbolizations, including giving a new name to the initiate. Antaeus renewed his strength every time he retouched Mother Earth, etc., etc.

It also struck me that your emphasis was on darkness, rather than light. Darkness can connote many things but most commonly the unknown, the Unconscious and also, the safe darkness of the womb (your little boy's good blackness when he and his mother were one, as he now wishes you and he were? His horrid blackness could refer to his night fears when alone with mother?) The mystic's dark night of the soul, in which all sense of the love and presence of God is lost, often said to precede illumination and the unio mystica, would be a most horrid blackness too. It would seem that both creativity and mystical experience emerge from or are mediated through, the Unconscious. I believe in the existence of telepathy in its literal sense of empathetic communication, so that I think games of telecard-reading etc. are a bit off the beam. When your idea finds its thinker I fancy the unconscious is sensitised to a kind of mental climate which comes through and is translated into conceptions.

Emptying of the mind, frequently aided by breathing methods, seems to be a common feature of "spiritual" life of most major religions. I am not sure how common your becoming aware from the big toe up is. Certainly no "still small voice" can be heard above what you aptly call the chatter of the mind. A feature of experiences of the "peace that passeth all understanding" is timelessness; they have a quality of eternity, though themselves transient.

Re your summary of my efforts, I do not think you have misrepresented me. Naturally you couldn't give more than a brief sketch but I am glad you said I didn't think that was all there was to it. Because I don't think we have any right to make assertions on ultimate issues like the existence or non-existence of God, etc. Re Bion I would agree that mystics and geniuses have features in common but am not at all sure the terms are interchangeable. His "godhead" in Christian terms would be God Immanent, the counterpart to God transcendent. But I have't read this book of his (I don't blame you for not always reading books you buy!) and your summary needs much more thought than there is time now to give it, as indeed the whole paper does. I don't think these hasty ruminations and first impressions will be much use to you but they are the best I can do in present circumstances.

Hoping the birthday, your paper and Zeitschrift itself will be a great success.

Yours sincerely,
Marjorie Brierley

P.S. Had never heard of Walsby before but have long been convinced that our intelligence is intended to cope with the external environment and thus not a good instrument for dealing with subjective experience. Intuition is more serviceable here but not necessarily reliable because more difficult to evaluate and far more open to selective influence of personal bias etc.?

Here are a few extracts from a letter I received from Bion after I had sent him my mysticism paper.

'A few immediate reactions to your paper. I found it both interesting and stimulating. . . .

Have you read Gerard Manley Hopkins "Habit of Perfection", "Candle indoors" and the "terrible" poem all very illuminating in this context. Also Chaucer's "Book of the Duchess" which I am sure you know better than I do but it may be worth reading again if you haven't read it recently. I also find very sympathetic St John of the Cross though unfortunately I depend on translation which is very bad, even the best like a little of Roy Campbell . . . likewise Lorca . . . Meister Eckhart unfortunately I cannot get in any reasonably compact form altho' it is obvious from the effect that he had on the "Establishment" that he was right on the nail. Dante, in spite of his somewhat off-putting letters, must, I think, at the end of the Paradiso, be after the same thing. The *Bhagavadgita* I think is marvellous in spite of the translation. I cannot now undo my mispent youth by learning French, Spanish, Sanskrit. Why is one almost fit to start one's education when it is nearer one's second childhood than one's first? I don't know. Perhaps I had better write a paper on it! . . . Like a fool I cannot find your letter so I shall have to send this off without being able to answer it.'

271

I cannot remember what I said in my letter, but suspect it may have been asking his views about some mystical training insisting on becoming aware of one's body, even one's big toe, from the inside.

References

1 Bion, W. R. (1970) *Attention and Interpretation*. London: Tavistock, p. 88.
2 H. Guntrip, having read this paper, wrote to me: 'Re: "it thinks you" and "Ideas in search of a thinker", I have come to feel there is an insistent pressure of a hidden, undiscovered True Self in search of an owner, with roots in the unmothered infant in search of a parent.'
3 Milner, M. (1934) *A Life of One's Own*; (1937) *An Experiment in Leisure*. London: Chatto & Windus.
4 Suzuki, D. T. (1927) *Essays in Zen Buddhism*. First series. Kyoto, Japan: Luzac & Co. for the Eastern Buddhist Society.
5 Lao Tze (*c.* 600 BC) *Tao Te Ching*. Trans. W. Gosser Wild (1927) London: Rider & Co. A book of aphorisms, the title sometimes being translated as 'The Simple Way'.
6 Patanjali (1974) *Apohorisms of Yoga*. London: Faber & Faber.
7 Silberer, H. (1917) *Problems of Mysticism and its Symbolism*. New York: Moffat.
8 Henry Vaughan (1621–95) in his poem *The Night*. Here is the relevant verse:

> 'There is in God – some say –
> A deep, but dazzling darkness; as men here
> Say it is late and dusky, because they
>   See not all clear.
> O for that Night! where I in Him
> Might live invisible and dim.'

9 Reich, W. (1950) *Character Analysis*. London: Vision Press.
10 Milner, M. (1950) *On Not Being Able to Paint*. London: Heinemann.
11 Lao Tze (*c.* 600 BC) *Tao Te Ching*. Trans. Ch'u Ta Kao (1937) London: Buddhist Society.
12 Ehrenzweig, A. (1953) *The Psycho-Analysis of Aesthetic Hearing and Perception*. London: Routledge.
13 Ehrenzweig, A. (1967) *The Hidden Order of Art*. London: Weidenfeld & Nicolson.
14 Milner, M. (1969) *The Hands of the Living God*. London: Hogarth.

'It is a fearful thing to fall into the hands of the living God
But it is a much more fearful thing to fall out of them.'

15 In his letter to the Hebrews, 10: 31.
16 While working on this paper I often found myself not entirely satisfied
    with the use of the word 'mysticism' for psychoanalytic thinking; it
    semed too liable to get associated with 'mystification'. But when I tried
    to find another word to denote a particular kind of enlargement of
    consciousness different from the everyday 'common-sense' kind, I
    failed to find one.
17 Winnicott, D. W. (1965) *The Maturational Process in the Facilitating
    Environment.* Ch. 17. London: Tavistock.
18 Winnicott, D. W. (1971) *Playing and Reality.* Ch 8. London: Tavistock.
19 For example, Reich, W. (1927) *The Function of the Orgasm.* (1942 edn.)
    New York: Orgone Institute. Here Reich does not seem to have known
    about the Indian cult of ecstasy, Tantra.
20 Reich, W. (1934) *The Mass Psychology of Fascism.* London: Souvenir
    Press.
21 Rycroft, C. (1971) *Reich.* London: Fontana.
22 Rickman, J. (1957) *Selected Contributions to Psycho-Analysis.* London:
    Hogarth.
23 Riviere, J. (1955) The Unconscious Phantasy of an Inner World
    Reflected in Literature. In M. Klein, P. Heimann, S. Isaacs, and J.
    Riviere (eds.) *New Directions in Psycho-Analysis.* London: Tavistock.
24 Jones, E. J. (1957) *The Life and Work of Sigmund Freud.* Vol. 3. London:
    Hogarth.
25 Freud, S. (1930) *Civilization and its Discontents.* Standard Edition 21.
26 Later I found another reference to mysticism in Freud's writing, though
    not mentioned in the index. In Freud, S. (1920) *The Psychogenesis of a
    Case of Female Homosexuality.* Standard Edition 18, on p. 165 this
    sentence occurs: 'I know, indeed, that the craving of mankind for
    mysticism is ineradicable.' This follows his referring to 'the unconscious,
    the real centre of our mental life, the part of us that is so much nearer the
    divine than our poor consciousness'.
27 Freud, S. (1939) *Moses and Monotheism.* Standard Edition 23. Compare
    Bakan, D. (1955) *Sigmund Freud and the Jewish Mystical Tradition.*
    Princeton, NJ: Van Nostrand.
28 Freud, S. (1940) *Findings, Problems, Ideas.* Standard Edition 23.
      Paula Heimann, on seeing the manuscript of this paper, writes that
    this is one of the translations she does not agree with. Hers would be
    'Mysticism is the dark self perception of the realm of the id, the realm
    outside the ego'. She adds that Freud's word is 'dunkel' and that 'dark'
    has far more poetry than 'obscure'. . . . Having more poetry it is more

true. Moreover, the word 'dark' is associated with natural phenomena, whereas 'obscure' suggests something made by men.

She also says that Freud uses 'Mystik' in an article 'Psycho-Analysis and Telepathy' (1921), Standard Edition 18. He says there: 'Psycho-Analysis . . . stands in opposition to everything that is conventionally restricted, well-established and generally accepted. Not for the first time would it be offering its help to the obscure but indestructible surmises of the common people against the obscurantism of educated opinion.'

Again Paula Heimann prefers a different translation: 'Not for the first time would it be offering its help to the dark but indestructible, inarticulate hunches of the people against the arrogant know-all of the educated.'

29 Fenichel, O. (1946) *The Psycho-Analytic Study of the Neuroses*. London: Kegan Paul.

30 Brierley, M. (1951) *Trends in Psycho-Analysis*. London: Hogarth.

31 Bion, W. R. (1970) *Attention and Interpretation*. London: Tavistock.

32 Underhill, E. (1913) *The Mystic Way*. London: Dent. (1927) *Man and the Supernatural*. London: Methuen. (1946) *Collected Papers* (ed. L. Menzies). London: Longman Green.

33 A paper on the 'Psycho-analytical Aspects of Mystical States', including the practice of yoga, was given to the British Psycho-Analytical Society in 1970 by F. W. Graham but as it is not yet published it does not come within the scope of this study.

34 If I had been allowed more space I could have gone on to see what Jungian analysts have said about mysticism. However, after finishing this paper I did happen to be looking at Jung's *Psychological Types* and came upon extensive quotations from Eckhart, which helped me to amplify the passage quoted from Bion. (C. J. Jung (1933) *Psychological Types*. London: Kegan Paul.)

35 This reminded me of the exploding lines of light radiating out from the figure of Jesus in Blake's *Job* pictures.

36 Reading this book sent me back to an earlier one which I also had not read: Bion, W. R. (1965) *Transformations*. London: Heinemann. Here the word mystic does not appear in the index, but does in the text, as if Bion had not yet quite realized how important the word was going to become in his thinking and in his next book. But in it I found much elaboration of his use of the symbol '0' and some of what I have tried to describe here of his use of this is taken from that book.

37 Balint, M. (1959) *Thrills and Regressions*. London: Hogarth.

19

1975: A discussion of Masud Khan's paper 'In Search of the Dreaming Experience'

Masud Khan's paper was given to the International Psycho-Analytical Congress in London in 1975 and I was one of the discussants.[1]

When Dr Pontalis wrote asking me to contribute to this discussion he said it was because I seemed to use dreams in a very personal way, as described in my last book about a patient who did doodle drawings.[2] I answered that I did not think I used them in any special way, as I only looked for associations, and if there were none I tried to see if I could find understandable symbols. I therefore asked him for examples of what he meant. He wrote back quoting what I had said in the book, about two of the patient's dreams; he then said that I had considered the dream neither as a message or text to be deciphered nor as a compromise between repressed desires and ego defence mechanisms, but as a witness of a state of being; in fact as an attempt at symbolization, rather than as a symbolic language to be decoded, and how this makes it possible to work on the manifest content without necessarily considering it as a distortion of the latent content. He said he wants this approach, although it may be 'usual' for me, made explicit. I will try, very tentatively, at least to make some comments on this problem.

First, I think that what I do is perhaps not so way out: I think it does follow from Ernest Jones's list of what gets symbolized, since he includes the word 'self' in his list. So this is perhaps the central problem, just because what it is that this word self denotes is so very elusive.

In listening to the discussions here this week on change in patients

275

I have heard much argument about analytic concepts, the abstract tools we use. But the best tools tend to get blunted after much use and need periodical resharpening and one of the ways of doing this is for me, at least, to sharpen them on the hone of more intuitive formulations, sometimes from other disciplines.

So in trying to understand what Masud Khan means by his term 'dreaming experience' I was taken back to something I was trying to formulate in 1956 for my Freud Centenary lecture on 'Psycho-Analysis and Art (see Chapter 12). There I found I had to go outside psychoanalytic theory to find a conceptual tool which seemed to me to be at all adequate for talking about art. I needed a cross-fertilization from another discipline, and in fact found that Jacques Maritain provided just such a tool, that is in what he calls the unnameable something or the incommunicable world of 'creative subjectivity'.[3]

So I noted now that what Maritain says about this is very close to what Khan says about dreaming experience. In fact, at one moment Maritain actually calls it 'a margin of dreaming experience' and says that many have murdered it in themselves.

Actually I think that perhaps it was this aspect of the psyche that may have been hinted at near the end of the discussion on changes in the patient when it was said that something seemed to be being left out. In fact much of the discussion had been in terms of the fate of internalized objects and very much less about the subject, the 'I' and what models we have for talking about this thing we know as the 'I' of experience and call the self. I think Masud Khan is trying to explore ways of making good this omission by making his own model. Incidentally when he talks about 'dreaming experience' as something which never becomes available for ordinary mental articulation he is obviously not talking about what Freud called the latent content of the dream because this, when uncovered, can be expressed in discursive language. Nor is he talking about something which happens only in sleep.

In trying to find my own model for what he is talking about I do in fact find I have to go back to another cross-fertilization that I made use of from another non-analyst – Ehrenzweig – who, after a long study of art and Freud, came to the conclusion that the inarticulate structure of what he calls the 'depth' mind is totally ungraspable by the 'surface' mind, not because of repression of offensive content but because of its structure; and that, because of its peculiar structure it can achieve tasks of integration that are quite beyond the capacity of the conscious surface mind.[4] *And*, this is the point – its activities are experienced by the surface mind as a gap in consciousness. So here

276

what seemed to be emerging was the possibility of there being something positive about emptiness, nothingness, whether empty unstructured space or the empty unstructured time that is silence (hence the enormous importance of Freud's invention of the psycho-analytic silence).

But here I come to a point of disagreement with Masud Khan, when he says there 'is no clue to the dreaming experience' in the manifest content of the dream. I think that, in some dreams, where an empty undifferentiated space is an important item in the dream's manifest content then it has to be considered whether one should not look behind the obvious theme of loss, loss of the needed object, to the dreamer's wish for direct contact with his own sense of being.

So when in 1950 I found my patient, Susan, continually drawing circles, sometimes empty, sometimes with a dot in the middle, I did not feel that my interpretation of them as symbols for breasts was the whole story. I came to see that although the empty circle could stand for the empty mouth with no nipple in it, and even for the destroyed nipple, it could also be necessary to look for the dreamer's wish to relate himself to what feels like non-being as part of the process of coming to be. By the way, Bion has used the symbol '0' (or zero) for this ultimate reality both of analyst and patient.

Maybe others will prefer other names than 'dreaming experience' for this basic activity of the psyche. For instance, how does it relate to what Shakespeare in *Hamlet* meant by his 'divinity that shapes our ends, rough-hew them how we will', which of course emphasizes the shaping aspect of it, the potentiality of form? Or to Blake's 'each man's poetic genius'?

In this connection I find it interesting to see how my patient described what she felt she had lost when, as she said, she 'got rid of herself' by deciding to have ECT.[5] She said she had lost her background as well as her feelings but also her appreciation of music, which before had been the centre of her life but now was nothing but a jangle of sound. Perhaps music is the nearest of all the arts to communicating what can't be communicated, or what Khan in one place calls 'the viccissitudes of the self'. So perhaps it is significant that the jumping-off place for his paper was the experience of a musician in a moment of creating.

Dr Pontalis talks of my way of seeing dreams as an attempt at symbolization. I agree, but not with his words 'rather than' a com-promise between repressed desires and the ego defence mechanisms. I see it as both. I do see the drive to get in touch with the self, know the self as well as not to, as crucial, not just bits of the self but the wholeness of the self. So what Masud Khan calls the dreaming experience can be related to the sleep dream in the sense that he says that dreaming experience is to do with knowing who, what, one is. What one is. What any self is. Do we know the answer to that?

References

1 Khan, M. (1975) In Search of the Dreaming Experience, taken from Khan (1975) The Changing Use of Dreams in Psychoanalytic Practice. *International Journal of Psycho-Analysis* 57: 325–30.
2 Milner, M. (1969) *The Hands of the Living God.* London: Hogarth.
3 Maritain, J. (1953) *Creative (?) in Art and Poetry.* New York: McClelland.
4 Ehrenzweig, A. (1967) *The Hidden Order of Art.* London: Weidenfeld & Nicolson.
5 She also said to the therapist, who asked how she felt, that she had lost her soul and, according to Susan, the therapist had replied, 'You look very cheerful about it'.

20

1977: Winnicott and overlapping circles

This paper was written in 1977 when I was asked to contribute to an issue of the French journal *L'Arc* which was to be devoted entirely to papers about Winnicott.[1]

In this paper I have decided to limit myself to certain ideas of D. W. Winnicott's that seem to have been most fertilizing for my own thinking. To do this I will take as my starting-point a reference of his to the drawing of the two jugs that I made in the 1930s. I have also chosen this drawing because it foreshadowed, for me, the image of overlapping circles made many years later by my patient, Susan, an image which had, still later, become a kind of flag or model for my own thinking about my work with patients and with myself.

Winnicott's reference to my drawing was in his paper about the place for cultural experience.[2] It occurs when he is talking about how the baby comes to be able to make use of the symbol of union and becomes more able to allow for and benefit from separation and a separation that is not a separation, but a form of union. As I have said, my drawing had been made from nature years before I ever knew of Winnicott or his work. The two jugs were placed side by side, one slightly in front of the other so that they could, in fact, be seen as two circles overlapping.[3] As I have said my concern in making the drawing had been with observing how shadows cut across or bring about a merging of boundaries; his response to it was to say that I had drawn his attention to the tremendous significance that there can be in the interplay of edges. My concern now in using the image is with the area of overlap in the circles just because it is

279

impossible to say which circle the area belongs to since it belongs to both. Because of this is seemed to me an apt symbol for Winnicott's concept of the transitional area that he says is the place where all culture belongs.

The second place of overlap occurs in his paper on play,[4] where he refers to the paper I wrote about the play of the boy, Simon, moments particularly concerned with lighted candles and fires in the dark (see Chapter 9).[5] Now I realized that this starting-point of moments in the boy's play had also been the starting-point for the first book I ever wrote, those sudden moments when one's whole perception of the world changed, or as Winnicott has put it, became coloured in a new way.

There is the further overlap in his paper on playing when he says that I related playing to concentration in adults and that he has done the same thing, but he then goes on to talk of a difference between us. He says that, while I was talking about the prelogical fusion of subject and object, he was trying to distinguish between this fusion and the fusion or defusion between the subjective object and the object objectively perceived. But he adds that he thinks this theme is inherent in the material I presented.

I therefore tried to see more clearly what this difference between us might imply. For instance, as I have said, my paper had also been an attempt to work through some misgivings I had felt about what seemed to me to be the too-narrow aspects of the classical Freudian concept of symbol formation. It was as a result of this attempt that I had tried out wording Freud's 'two principles of mental functioning' in terms of this fusion or defusion between subject and object; that is in terms of two ways of being which differ according to whether one feels joined up, merged with what one looks at, or separate from it. It had only slowly become apparent to me that we know a lot about the separated state of mind, since our very speech depends on it (subject, verb, object), but that the unseparated phase, that of merged boundaries, is quite a different matter and is defended against, partly out of fear, fear that it means some kind of loss of definition, loss of identity, even loss of sanity.

What had followed had been this idea that the illusion of no-separateness between either the subject and the object, or between what Winnicott came to talk about as the subjective object and the objective object, could possibly be a necessary phase in all creativity, even in the process of coming to perceive the reality of the external world at all. In fact it had seemed that perception itself is a creative process. So it was here that I had had to think of Santayana's way of putting it:

'Perception is no primary phase of consciousness; it is an ulterior function acquired by a dream which has become symbolic of its own external conditions, and therefore relevant to its own destiny.'[6]

In fact this is the statement which had become so important to me when writing *On Not Being Able to Paint*, from 1940 onwards.

'Symbolic of its own external conditions', surely this was another way, though a more academic one, of describing what Winnicott talks about of how the mother's breast becomes felt by the baby to be what he needs; or as Winnicott puts it, the baby comes imaginatively to 'create' the breast? In short, by now I was nearly coming to believe that this recurrent phase of feeling one with what one sees is part of the rhythm of oneness – twoness, unity – separation that the creator in all of us has used, from earliest infancy, to make the world significant to us, a capacity which is perhaps what William Blake meant by his phrase 'each man's poetic genius'.

Having struggled to reach this point it was no surprise to me to read Winnicott's statement that creativity belongs to being alive, that it belongs to the whole approach of a person (if not ill) to external reality.[7] Yet when I settled down to consider the various other ways in which he uses this word creativity I had to draw on further experiences on my own. In the first place, I thought about how he says that anything that happens to one is creative, unless stultified by the environment. I asked myself just exactly what does he mean by this? Sometimes he seems to be talking about a way of looking at the world, sometimes about a way of doing something deliberately and sometimes about simply enjoying a bodily activity that just happens, such as, he says, enjoying breathing.

Certainly I did have to ask myself, in what sense are all these creative? I could agree when he says they are different from the making of any thing, such as a house or a meal or a picture, though, as he says, all of these may include what he means by creative. And when he talks of just enjoying breathing, I found it linked up with the whole collection of observations about different kinds of concentration that I have already written about in the Athens and the mysticism papers (see Chapters 14 and 18).

While trying to link up these statements of Winnicott's with my own enquiries I even remembered an example of how I had, long before becoming an analyst, observed the effects of simple non-purposive looking. For example, I had noticed how, through staring at an outside object that one especially liked (or even an object that one did not like, for instance, an ugly white tin mug), staring at it in a contemplative way, without any ideas about making use of it, there had gradually emerged a feeling of change in one's whole body perception as well as a move towards a feeling of intense interest in the sheer 'thusness', the separate and unique identity, of the thing I was staring at.[8]

This effect of the changing awareness of one's own body on one's perception of the object and also the opposite set of phenomena, the effect of certain kinds of concentrating on the object on one's own body awareness naturally took me back to my Athens paper and Ruskin's experience with the tree. It also took me to my own attempts to describe what happened in terms of change to proprioceptive sensations, a change from a body image, or images, to body perceptions, that is from body re-presentation to body presentation. In fact, to a perception that is concerned with the actual coenaesthetic awareness of one's existence in space and time, including the sense of one's own weight and natural speed of moving and awareness of one's breathing. In addition, there was the fact that this deliberately directing one's attention to the body presentation requires a wide focus of attention; it cannot be done with the narrow focus which is a characteristic aspect of discursive argumentative thought. Also, when it did happen there was, as I have said, not the narcissistic impoverishment of one's relation to the external world that one might have expected, but an actual enrichment of it. Not only this but also I had found that it resulted in a sense of well-being that is a different kind from that which results from lack of tension between the ego and the super-ego, as when feeling one has lived up to one's standards.

Something else that I had to consider in all this was the fact that the direct body presentation has no clear boundary. This now reminded me of the child's first 'not-me' possession, what Winnicott called the transitional object, the bit of blanket or its equivalent, and later the teddy bear or woolly animal and how they are nearly always fluffy, perhaps partly suggesting, I thought, the fuzziness of the sense of the body boundary in direct sensation.[9] Further, it seemed that this kind of direct body awareness must be, developmentally, a capacity intimately bound up with the mother's, or her substitute's, loving care of the infant's body and so can be an important aspect of what Winnicott calls 'the facilitating environment' that is necessary for the infant if fullest maturation is to occur. I suspected too that Winnicott himself knew a lot about this kind of relation to the body and that it could have entered into his so astonishing awareness of what was going on in all those child-therapeutic consultations where he used what he called the squiggle game, that is when he and the child in turn drew a squiggle and the other made it into whatever caught his or her fancy.[10]

As for what Winnicott calls the 'holding' aspect of the facilitating environment I have already given extensive form to my debt to this concept in the book about my patient, Susan, and even embodied it in the title of the book, *The Hands Of The Living God*, with its association to falling in D. H. Lawrence's poem.[11] Significantly Winnicott himself talks about the feeling of falling for ever, as an aspect of what he calls 'unthinkable anxiety'.

There was another and related area of overlap which was connected with what Winnicott says about relaxation. He talks of

'the summation or reverberation of experiences of relaxation in conditions of trust based on experience.'[12]

This sentence had echoes for me throughout years of observations of how deliberate bodily relaxation brings with it, if one can wait for it, deep reverberation from within, something spreading in waves, something that brings an intense feeling of response from that bit of the outer world that is yet also one's self, one's own body.

This theme now brought me once more to consider something of what he has to say about the sense of self in relation to creativity. As I have said, up to now I had found that I could go a long way with him in his ideas about creativity, that is with the idea of it as not just perceiving, but as deliberately relating outselves to our own perceiving, which has an 'I am' element in it. I therefore continued to consider what he has to say about the sense of 'I am' – or lack of it – in relation to creativity and the difficulty I had had here. Thus, although he says that it is only in being creative that one discovers one's self, he also says that the actual work of art, the finished creation, never heals an underlying lack of sense of self. I thought I could agree here with what he says about the finished creation but I felt a need to consider further just what his use of the phrase 'sense of self' implies. For instance, I still thought I could agree when he says that the sense of self comes into being on the basis of a rudimentary kind of play that reflects back. But I still could not agree wholeheartedly that it is also unobservable. However, it could be that observable is the wrong word and that one should say 'contactable'. Certainly I had found that there is a contact that can result in a renewal, a rebirth; provided, that is, that one is prepared to stop the inner chatter of introspective arguments and face the inner silence, the basic formlessness from which all form comes, and which at first can feel like total emptiness, annihilation even, and be defended against at almost any cost. And especially so when this inner silence is liable to get mixed up with the phantasy of the destruction of the inner needed object. In fact, for some patients this is a crucial issue, especially those who are afraid of, intolerant of, being alone. Often it seems they cannot find renewal by relating themselves to the formless core of their own being, and it may be that they cannot do this partly because of fears of the results of their own destructive phantasies against their good inner objects. Thus inner silence can mean that everybody is dead.

It was after I had just read for the first time Winnicott's paper on the destruction of the good object that I rang him up and said, 'Yes, but just why does the good object have to be destroyed?'[13] He thought for a little and then said, 'Because it is necessary.' This idea led to a welding process in me, it joined up his idea of the need to destroy the satisfying object with all that I had thought about primary omnipotence and the intensity of the shock of disillusionment, the sheer incredulity and abysmal depth of dread that can come at the discovery that one is not omnipotent, if it comes, through environmental failure, at a moment when the ego is not strong enough to bear it, when it has even been feeling, not only that it was king of the castle but also that it was both king and castle itself.

Such ideas naturally led me on to the theme of nothingness, or zero, and the thought that one of the advantages of the overlapping circles model was that it can be adapted by bringing the two circles closer and closer together till they coincide as a single circle; in fact, a unity which can be seen as either everything or nothing, as a total eclipse of the sun, a dark night of the soul, or a blissful consummation.

Since Winnicott died in 1971 it is unlikely that he knew about a saying of Freud's which was not published till 1975. In a short paper Bruno Goetz tells of how he, as a young poet fascinated by the *Bhagavadgita*, had had talks with Freud (during 1905 and 1906) in which Freud said:[14]

> 'Do you know what it means to be confronted by nothingness? . . . the Hindu Nirvana is not nothingness, it is that which transcends all contradictions. It is . . . the ultimate in superhuman understanding, an ice-cold, all-comprehending yet scarcely comprehensible insight. Or, if misunderstood it is madness.'

Could Winnicott's concept of 'unthinkable anxiety' fit in somewhere here?

Re-reading this paper at the end of 1986 and nearly ten years after it was written, I felt the need to add to my flag another visual model; I remembered once hearing Wilfred Bion say that one should not have too many theories but could have as many models as one liked. The added model that I now found myself enjoying was a diagram said to have been used by Wittgenstein with his students. He asked them to say what they thought the diagram represented.

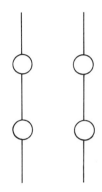

His answer was 'A koala bear climbing a tree'. In practice I have found that this answer usually brings a gasp of surprised laughter, following the imaginative leap of filling the emptiness, the nothingness between the two lines and the four circles, filling this no-thing with a some-thing and that something very much alive.

For myself, I found the experience of the four small circles suddenly coming together to form the unseen image of a living wholeness useful in clinical work. It provided me with a symbol for thinking about those patients with a precarious sense of self who can suddenly come together, even though maybe only momentarily, instead of existing in isolated fragments. It also provided me with a condensed symbol for the infant's achievement of coming to recognize that all the different contacts with the mother, both 'bad' and 'good' do come together and add up to a whole living person.

In fact, here was the imaginative leap which can be looked upon as ushering in what Melanie Klein called the 'depressive position'[15] and what Winnicott, on the whole, prefers to call 'the phase of concern'.[16]

I also found myself using the diagram with its empty space between the two lines as a way of reminding myself how emptiness, formlessness, must be the basis of new forms, almost perhaps that one has to be willing to feel oneself becoming nothing in order to become something.

As for the area of overlap in the two circles model, I found myself using it, amongst many other ways, as standing for the overlap between, on the one hand, whatever it is that we call mind, psyche, consciousness, and on the other hand, what we call body, a model for what can happen when consciousness does deliberately suffuse the whole body, when 'soul' and 'body' do meet again.

It is also, for me, a convenient way of thinking about what could perhaps be seen as the aim of all therapy, the bringing together of both the accepted and the rejected part of the personality; in fact, to allow the interpenetration of opposites to form a new whole.

References

1 Milner, M. (1977) Winnicott and Overlapping Circles. *L'Arc* 69. The issue of this French journal was devoted to articles on D. W. Winnicott.

2 Winnicott, D. W. (1967) The Location of Cultural Experience. *International Journal of Psycho-Analysis* 7: 48 pt 3. Also in (1971) *Playing and Reality*. London: Tavistock.

3 Milner, M. (1950) *On Not Being Able to Paint*. London: Heinemann. Figure 8.

4 Winnicott, D. W. (1971) Playing: A Theoretical Statement. In *Playing and Reality*. London: Tavistock.

5 Milner, M. (1952) Aspects of Symbolism in Comprehension of the Not-Self. *International Journal of Psycho-Analysis* 33(2): 181–95.

6 Santayana, G. (1920) The Suppressed Madness of Sane Men. In *Little Essays*. London: Constable.

7 Winnicott, D. W. (1971) Creativity and its Origins. In *Playing and Reality*. London: Tavistock.

8 Milner, M. (1934) *A Life of One's Own*. London: Chatto & Windus.

9 Winnicott, D. W. (1951) Transitional Objects and Transitional Phenomena. In (1958) *Collected Papers*. London: Tavistock.

10 Winnicott, D. W. (1971) *Therapeutic Consultations in Child Psychiatry*. London: Hogarth and Institute of Psycho-Analysis.

11 'It is a fearful thing to fall into the hands of the living God. But it is a much more fearful thing to fall out of them.' Milner, M. (1969) *The Hands of the Living God*. London: Hogarth.

12 Winnicott, D. W. (1971) Playing: Creative Activity and the Search for the Self. In *Playing and Reality*. London: Tavistock.

13 Winnicott, D. W. (1971) The Use of an Object and Relating through Identification. *International Journal of Psycho-Analysis* 50: 711–16.

14 Goetz, B. (1975) That Is All I Have to Say about Freud. *International Review of Psycho-Analysis* 2(2): 139–43.

15 Klein, M. (1935) A Contribution to the Psychogenesis of Manic-depressive States. In (1948) *Contributions to Psycho-Analysis*. London: Hogarth & Institute of Psycho-Analysis.

16 Winnicott, D. W. (1954–5) The Depressive Position in Normal Emotional Development. In (1958) *Collected Papers*. London: Tavistock.

21

1986: Afterthoughts

Of the many strands of a main thread from all these papers that called out for further attention, I am selecting only those that seem to me to be crucial for my current clinical work with my last few patients. There were two of the patients who particularly reminded me of those described in my comments on Masud Khan's paper (see Chapter 19). They forced me to think more about the question of 'the suppressed madness of sane men' for both were 'sane' in their professional work but not in the emotional satisfactions of their private lives and both in different degrees showed, under analysis, that they were, to use Winnicott's phrase, suffering from 'a flight into sanity'.[1]

Some of the problems of these two patients now took me back to Susan's claim that, when on the farm, at the age of 19, before the ECT, she had 'broken down into reality', but that after it the world was no longer outside her. Thus with both these patients, I had had the feeling, for a long time, that I was in some way, not outside them, not 'real' for them. For instance, one of them, for the first two or three years, never used the pronoun 'you' when talking to me. The other patient (Mr X) constantly said he had told me things that I knew he had not, he must have said them only to an inner me, but it was no good telling him this, he would just say he had told me and I had forgotten. However, one day, after having long given up lying on the couch and having insisted on sitting up, facing me, seemingly looking at me, he had suddenly said, 'Something quite new has happened.' Slowly he added that he was seeing me for the first time. Shortly after this, during agonies of crisis over having to find a new

287

place to live in, he volunteered that he really felt that he was being born. The analysis from now on had a quite different quality.

All this took me back to the viewers' comments on Susan's drawings, how many of them said she was living inside her objects (see Chapter 10). I also thought of her play with the toys, (which the viewers had not heard about) and how, through the toys, she seemed to have been able to express an awareness of feeling stuck inside something (breast, womb?), but also through the swan supported on the clay, able to foresee a time when she might be able to get back to the state she had achieved on the farm, when what she was inside was her own body and the world that was outside was in fact, supporting her, since she had become aware of her own weight.

The sense of one's own weight

In this connection it was during the months before Susan did get back into the world (January 1959) that she drew many pictures of ducks swimming on water, even a swan with its head down under the water, as if seeking sustenance there. Thus it did seem to me that here she had invented an apt symbol to denote what she had discovered at the farm; that is the capacity for consciousness deliberately going down within one's body, not drawn there because of instinctual excitement or frustration, but in a quiet frame of mind. Also that through this making contact with her sense of her own weight she had been helped to discover her own sense of existing as a unit.

The fact that she used water as the symbol for what supported her (although she did do a drawing right at the end, of a tree with its roots deep in the earth) did seem to me to denote an important recognition of the fact that the sense of one's own weight, whether on one's feet or buttocks or whole body, is actually without a clear boundary, in pure sensation; one knows with one's mind that there is a boundary, one's skin, but it is not there in direct experience, only a sense of warmth, coldness, hardness, pressure, etc. In fact it was Mr X, whose sense of being a unit self was very precarious, who told me he was quite incapable of lying flat on his back while letting the sense of his own weight spread in a vague boundary-less puddle and holding it there, holding it long enough for a flow of feeling to spread through all his body, leading to getting up again feeling totally refreshed. However, to get to the boundary-less puddle state it does seem necessary to have established a realistic idea of where one's skin is, to have something to come back to. Here I remembered the little boy in the Montessori Nursery School more than sixty years ago, who had seemed to me to be trying to get some idea of where his own boundary was.

Dual union or differentiation?

When the editors of this book mentioned the need for an index I realized for the first time how very few technical psychoanalytic terms there were in it. This reminded me how my professor of psychology, in the early 1920s, used to say, 'If you want to be a good psychologist only use an ordinary English Dictionary.' Apparently I had taken this to heart more than I knew, which in some ways seems to be a pity, since the abstract terms used by psychoanalysts are certainly essential tools for thought and communicating with one's colleagues, as long as not cut off from their perceptual roots. However, it may be that this disinclination to use technical terms has helped me to get a better hold on what seems to have been my deepest preoccupation over the years: that is it do with one's sense of being alive and inhabiting one's own body, what I have called one's body presentation, as against body representation or body images, this sense of the inner dark matrix from which emerges drives to action or thoughts or emotional expression or new perceivings.

I noticed too that I had often used the work 'undifferentiated' to describe this matrix, out of which actions or images or words begin to take shape. This reminded me that a whole paper had been published about my psychoanalytic writings by Michael Eigen, a New York psychotherapist I had been in correspondence with over many years.[2] We had first really met at a conference in 1955 and in our letters we had seemed to be in pretty close agreement. However the whole tone of this paper was critical, especially on the subject of my use of this term 'undifferentiated', he saying that he preferred the term 'dual union'. I was puzzled by the paper and sent it to several friends and colleagues to help me sort it out. Here is part of a letter from one of them, Heather Glen, a don in the English Faculty at Cambridge University whose book about Blake's Songs and Wordsworth's Lyrical Ballads is called *Vision and Disenchantment*; her letter (December 1983) also refers to my paper about Winnicott and overlapping circles (see Chapter 20).[3]

She wrote:

'Perhaps the most radical thing you do in this paper is the one you don't comment on at all because it is so natural to you: the use of a visual image to express a concept which is actually paradoxical, not expressible in verbal form – "a separation which is not a separation". I think it might be worth emphasising (for such as Eigen) that this is what you are doing. (You note on p. 5 that "our very speech is dependent on the separated state of mind; there is something in the grammatical shape of language – subject, verb, object – which makes it difficult or impossible to express such a concept in it). It does not seem to me that you're not talking about a merger between self and other, as Eigen claims, but about a state in which both are there, and the same and not the same at once. "There is an 'I am' element in it": This makes me wonder about the use of the word "undifferentiation". I'm not sure that I understand the second-last paragraph. Is there an "I am" within the undifferentiation if one can get through the threat of "unthinkable anxiety"? What is that state where the overlapping circles coincide?'

Another of my friends, not an analyst but an anthropologist now turned writer and sculptor, Jean Kadmon (who had also had an analysis) read the Eigen paper and wrote to me the following:

'It seems to me your "undifferentiated union" is the same as the sort of dissolving into whatever one is contemplating during a meditation and of the becoming one with one's lover, if only for those few moments. On the other hand, the self is always there or one is mad. But then, people do go mad and also sexual union and ecstatic rites are a way of being mad[4] with a shelter around one and a rope back to the usual way of being. Their function is something else but the dissolving does seem to be helpful to existence and perhaps is necessary. My thinking suggests that unless one is insane dissolving can happen only when one is in a general state of wholeness. And yes, I have found that my dreaming will indicate when something in me is cockeyed – when I am not in that state. So Michael Eigen does have something to say.'

My own thought was that Eigen's use of the term 'dual union' clearly had also to be considered in relation to and in contrast with what Margaret Little writes about delusions of what she calls 'basic unity'.[5] Also there was certainly much more to be worked out here in connection with Bion's ideas about mysticism.

Having written to Eigen about my difficulties with his paper and some of my friends' comments, he wrote back giving me permission to quote the following extract from the letter:

'1 January, 1984

I'm now sorry (to say the least) that I didn't send you the paper when I wrote it to get your comments, and rewrite it in the light of them. I would, I hope, bring out more thoroughly how the "I-yet-not-I" pervades your work – and how speaking about it in terms of "undifferentiation" blurs (for me, at least – and perhaps you and Heather Glen as well) the essential vision/feeling. I think I could now much more clearly bring out the advance in "mystical"-psychological thinking that the "I-yet-not-I" expression offers over the "undifferentiation" language and mystique, and how even in your work they tend to get lumped together, thus somewhat blunting/distracting from the moment at stake. Speaking about the confusion (rather than the polarization) of these two "languages" and possibly "dimensions" might have made the paper more palatable.

Too late for this paper unless it generates discussion in print.

Yet in passages I still think (for me) you got off and the "I-yet-not-I" gets split into isolation vs merger or fusion. These are real enough as extremes of the "I-yet-not-I" foundation. I think I've tried to say this more explicitly (or as Heather Glen might say, more obviously). I suspect *part* of the "polarizing" comes from milieu. In the USA I have to "combat" the tendency to use the notion of "undifferentation" promiscously.'

Two years later when I asked for his permission to quote from his letter, I received the following reply.

'6 July, 1986

Dear Marion

The enclosed is the quote you want – very slightly edited (I omitted something at the end of the first para). It comes from my letter of Jan. 1 1984. You may use it, of course, only with the proviso that the whole of it be used without deletions. If there are minor editing changes which will help the passage, please let me know.

Now, a few years later, I still feel your work does superimpose an "undifferentiation" language over the "I-yet-not-I" language. I think this is important. The "I-yet-not-I" experience is better, more wholesome and more fruitful. It maintains the ambiguity and tension of our basic position. Winnicott's paradox. I still feel that the term "undifferentiation" too often leads to mystification, rather than the properly mystical. As my letter suggests, if I were to write my paper on you over today, I would try to better bring out how both kinds of discourse tend to fuse in your work, and to try to free the "I-yet-not-I" moment from unnecessary trapping.

I am grateful that my work has stimulated further work of your own, and that you find it useful in working out some part of your *Collected Papers*, which I very much look forward to.

As ever

Michael Eigen

(PS If there is anything in this note you may want to use, please do so also.)'

This theme of lack of differentiation, fusion, illusion of unity, or whatever term one wants to use also took me back to my 1952 paper and the boy Simon (see Chapter 9). Soon after I was considered qualified as a child analyst I told Melanie Klein that, although very grateful for her supervision, I now wanted to work on my own with Simon. Thus the work I did with him when I had to be his 'lovely stuff' that he had made and also the solemn ritual kind of play were all unsupervised.

Also it was somewhere about 1954 that I stopped going to Melanie Klein's seminars for analysts because I could not accept her idea of inborn envy. The high degree of envy that I undoubtedly came across in some of my patients seemed to me to be related to far too little allowance having been made in their infancy for their primary omnipotence; in fact, related to the idea of premature ego formation that I had first been driven to consider because of Simon's difficulties.

As for my preoccupation with the overlapping circles, this symbol, which has become a kind of flag for me (originally based on the drawing of the two jugs) appeared again in Peter Fuller's book *Art and Psycho-Analysis*.[6] However, I noticed that the printer had confirmed my idea about people's fear of lack of boundaries for he had put a frame round the drawing, even making the frame cut off bits of the jugs (see *Figure 62*).

Autism in adults

In the early 1970s a student I was supervising for Child Psychotherapy gave me as a parting present Frances Tustin's book, *Autism in Childhood Psycho-Analysis*.[7] In this book she claims that autism arises when the infant is required to recognize its separateness too soon and at a time when there is not enough ego, to face bodily separation or recognize the 'me'–'not-me' distinction without what is felt to be unbearable grief. Although I had not worked with any child

Figure 62

diagnosed as autisitic I began to see that something of what she said could be applied to certain of my adult patients. For instance, it was Mr X who for years would talk to me endlessly about his dealings on the Stock Exchange, taking no notice of my various attempts at interpreting. Eventually he was able to tell me that he never did anything with the money when he did make it, he just had to have it there. This seemed to fit in with Frances Tustin's account of how autistic children were liable to hold on tight to some particular hard toy which then came between them and relationship to other people and to the therapist. When I became able to talk to Mr X about this the analysis grew far more productive. Frances Tustin also says these children do not admit to any need for help which was certainly true of this patient; he came to analysis only to fill in time between work and going home.

Frances Tustin's view also is that these children who have been unable to face what they felt to be intolerable grief at recognizing their bodily separateness have often had mothers who were in a state of depression at the time of their infancy. This certainly fitted in with Mr X's problems. Also with Mr X, who in fact had a fairly successful professional life, but a very impoverished private one, interpretations in terms of projection had seemed to come up against a blank wall. But when I began to think about him in terms of a split-off autistic part, the whole feeling of the transference and counter-transference changed. Puzzling over this I actually rang up Frances

Tustin to ask about the difference between autism and schizophrenia in childhood and she wrote back:

'9 April, 1986

I have come to see that autism is different from any other psychopathology in that the core feature is that the patient has not established a primal attachment to the breast and thus has no sense of self and other.'

I now thought that if there is no sense of the separate self to be split and projected and no self-contained 'other' into which to project them this certainly fitted in with one of my apparently very 'sane' patients who rejected any interpretation which involved the idea of projection of parts of himself.

Frances Tustin also introduced me to a paper by a Kleinian psychoanalyst, Sidney Klein (no relation to Melanie Klein), about autism in adults.[8] I found he had written about how these patients who have successful professional lives

'sooner or later reveal phenomena which are strikingly similar to those observed in so-called autistic children. These autistic phenomena are characterised by an almost inpenetrable encapsulation of part of the personality, mute and implacable resistance to change and a lack of real emotional contact either with themselves or with the analyst.'

In addition, he maintains:

'we have to recognize that although the patient appears to be communicating at one level, there is also a non-communication corresponding to the mute phase of the autistic child, and that what is not communicated are not only the aggressive but also the loving feelings which accompany the growth of the sense of separateness and the associated sense of responsibility for the self and objects.'

He also notes that these patients were extremely verbally fluent and adds that this may be partly a defence against underlying feelings of emptiness and non-existence, and partly to overcome the infant's anxiety that his primitive feelings are not understood and contained. He ends his paper with the following statement:

'There is one other important feature which repays observation in these patients, and indeed all patients, namely the process of oscillation, which repeatedly occurs for example, between states of omnipotence and helplessness, activity and passivity, adulthood

294

and infantility, psychosis and neurosis, primitiveness and sophisti-
cation of thought, and paranoid-schoizoid depressive. Analysis of
the oscillation leads hopefully to a more balanced state of mind
and personality, in which the knife-edge of opposites is broadened
to become a more solid basis of reflective thought.'

Clearly there was here an overlap with Susan's oscillating drawings
as well as the overlapping circles. Thus what I wanted to add to the
'knife-edge of opposites broadening to a more solid basis for
reflective thought' was that surely this is the same as Winnicott's idea
of the 'transitional area', the place where opposites can interpenetrate
and allow the acceptance of paradox as an essential element in certain
areas of experience, particularly the 'I-yet-not-I' area.

Meanings for the word 'mad'

If I were going to write another paper, which I will not as I am too
old, it would have to be about possible meanings of the empty space
at the centre of Susan's 'Catherine wheel' drawing (see *Figure 20*, p.
128) and would have to be about inner emptiness both in its benign
and malign aspects. It would also have to take into account Andre
Green's paper 'Potential Space in Psycho-Analysis: The Object in the
Setting'.[9]
   In addition it would have to include an attempt to study the
different ways in which the word 'mad' is used, both colloquially, in
literature and in psychoanalysis. I did in fact actually try to see what
Santayana seems to mean by it in the essay the title of which I have
stolen for this book.[10] He seems to be concerned, in the rest of his
essay, with people or states of mind in which one is cut off from what
he calls 'instincts' – which must surely mean, cut off from the body.
And this seemed to me to relate to what Winnicott is describing
when he talks about 'psychotic anxieties'. Thus, in his posthumous
paper 'Fear of Breakdown' he lists some of the anxieties (he calls
them agonies, saying anxieties is not a strong enough word here) that
can occur at the times of absolute dependence 'when the mother
supplies the auxiliary ego-function, the time when the infant has not
separated out the "not-me" from the "me".'[11] Here he uses the
phrase 'lack of indwelling' to describe one aspect of what he calls
'madness' and also 'lack of psychosomatic collusion'. In other words,
head and heart not working together?
   Another way of describing madness came from one of my
colleagues, James Home, because, after the publication of my book

about Susan's drawings, some of my colleagues asked for a seminar about it, so I suggested each of them might like to write to me beforehand, raising any special questions.[12] Here is what James Home said (in 1971) about madness.

> 'I see Susan's conflict as arising from the experience of living with a "mad" mother. In such cases simply to be sane (reality adjusted) involves loss of feeling relation with mother. Madness involves a rigid restriction of the personality and therefore of the ability to share "meanings" with other people. All cliché partakes of this sort of madness. I feel therefore that effective therapy in this sort of case requires that the analyst struggles to be free of his own clichés of thought. I think that your willingness to do this was the main therapeutic factor rather than the formulation of any specific interpretations.'

I now realized that for myself the definition of madness that I had in the back of my mind all this time was from J. Bronowski's splendid little book about William Blake, which he called *The Man Without A Mask*.[13] Bronowski writes:

> 'Certainly the men who thought Blake mad were wrong; but they were not silly. *Each kind of madness is a distortion of privacy, at its boundary with the social world* [my italics]. The privacy of the mad may collapse inward, like Cowper's, or explode outward, like Burke's; but it does so under the strain of the world. The men of Blake's day felt the strain in him, because they feared it in themselves. William Wordsworth held it anxiously in his language, until thought withered in him. But Dorothy Wordsworth went mad. Blake knew what discontent made him and others pit their language against the world's and drove them to madness "as a refuge from unbelief" . . . the men of Blake's day who called him mad were less glib than others who have since called him sane. For they did not miss the larger content of his discontent.'

But Bronowski's definition of madness in terms of distortion of boundary does I think leave out the overlapping of boundaries, that is, the area of the 'I-yet-not-I' which is also the area of what Blake calls 'each man's poetic genius' by means of which each of us creates the world that we perceive.

References

1 Winnicott, D. W. (1964) Review of Jung's *Memories, Dreams, Reflections 1963*. *International Journal of Psycho-Analysis* 45: 450–63.

2 Eigen, M. (1983) Dual Union or Undifferentiation? A Critique of Marion Milner's View of the Essence of Psycho-Creativeness. *International Review of Psycho-Analysis* 10: 415–28.
3 Glen, H. (1983) *Vision and Disenchantment*. Cambridge: Cambridge University Press.
4 I thought that this might provide an answer to Heather Glen's last question about what is the state when the overlapping circles coincide.
5 Little, M. (1981) *Transference Neurosis and Transference Psychosis*. New York: Jason Aronson.
6 Fuller, P. (1981) *Art and Psycho-Analysis*. London: Writers & Readers.
7 Tustin, F. (1973) *Autism in Childhood Psycho-Analysis*. London: Hogarth.
8 Klein, S. (1980) Autistic Phenomena in Neurotic Patients. *International Journal of Psycho-Analysis* 61: 400.
9 Green, A. (1978) Potential Space in Psycho-Analysis: The Object in the Setting. In S. Grolnick (ed.) *Between Reality and Phantasy: Transitional Objects Phenomena*. London and New York: J. Aronson.
10 Santayana, G. (1920) The Suppressed Madness of Sane Men. In *Little Essays*. London: Constable.
11 Winnicott, D. W. (1974) Fear of Breakdown. *International Review of Psycho-Analysis* 1: 103–07. See also his (1951) Transitional Objects and Transitional Phenomena. In (1958) *Collected Papers*. London: Tavistock.
12 Milner, M. (1969) *The Hands of the Living God*. London: Hogarth.
13 Bronowski, J. (1947) *The Man Without a Mask*. London: Secker & Warburg, p. 14.

Note: 1987

In spite of the fact that my own copies both of Freud's *The Future of Illusion* (1949, Hogarth) and Anna Freud's *The Ego and its Mechanisms of Defence* (1948, Hogarth) are full of my own pencil annotations, I now find that both are left out of my bibliographical references. I can only see these omissions as symptomatic of the constant struggle both to use the 'parents'' insights and at the same time to be sensitive to my own experience, to see with my own eyes.

Name Index

Note: pseudonyms of patients are included in the subject index.

Abraham, K. 269
Augustine, St 82

Balint, M. 192, 269
Bartlett, F. C. 39
Berenson, B. 97, 192, 237
Bion, W. R. 258, 266–69, 270–71, 274, 284–85; letter from 271
Blake, W. 10, 232–33, 263, 277, 281, 289; on art and science 243; *Auguries of Innocence* 63; on imagination 82; madness of 296; *Illustrations to Book of Job* 9, 168–87, 189, 190, 199–214 *passim*; Job's error, nature of 172–74; descent to depths 174–76; recovery 176–87
Bowlby, J. 60
Brierley, M. 266–67; letter from 269–71
Bronowski, J. 296
Bruno, G. 265
Buber, M. 249–50
Butler, S. 9, 15

Caudwell, C. 99, 104, 107, 111
Chardin T. de 206
Chaucer, G. 271
Clarke, K. 192

Dante, 209, 271
Darwin, C. 136

Eckhart, Meister 264, 267, 269, 271
Ehrenzweig, A. 192, 241–44; on depth and surface minds 194–97, 211, 213, 263, 276; on articulating tendency 194–95; on mysticism 195–96, 263; on primary disintegration 209–10
Eigen, M. 289–90; letters from 290–92
Einstein, A. 234
Eissler, K. 108
Eliot, T. S. 250
Empson, W. 192

Fairbairn, A. 59, 192, 239
Fenichel, O. 86, 100, 104, 266
Flugel, J. C. 2
Follett, M. P. 64–5
Forster, E. M. 206
Frazer, J. G. 15, 242–43
Freud, A. 6, 109, 138, 188, 192, 216, 266
Freud, S./Freudianism 3, 206, 276; on analysis 6, 195; on articulating tendency 194; on battle 169, 187, 210; on cosmic bliss 179; on dreams 213, 231; and education 187–90; on ego 45–6, 133, 236; on infancy 173; on internal reality 45–6; on introjection 50, 54; on libido 59; on love, growth of power to 186; on mental functioning 250; on mysticism 266, 273–74; on myth 57; on negation 44,

Freud, S./Freudianism (*cont.*):
58; on nothingness 284; on oceanic
feeling 195–97, 208, 243, 266; on
phantasy 45, 48, 57, 207; on pleasure
and pain 45–6, 63; on poets 199; on
primary object 83; on questionings of
childhood 178–79; on reality-ego 58;
on religion 265; on silence,
psychoanalytic 277; Sprott on 40, 48,
50, 55, 57–8; on super-ego 55; on
unconscious 2, 215, 273; on work,
hard 188
Fuller, P. 292

Glen, H. 289, 291
Goetz, B. 284
Gombrich, E. H. 192, 211
Gordon, J. 8
Green, A. 295
Guntrip, H. 59, 272

Heimann, P. 95, 258, 269, 273–74
Home, J. A. 4, 295–96
Hopkins, G. M. 271
Hourd, M. 79
Huxley, A. 236–37

Isaacs, S. 3, 47

James, W. 194, 195
Janet, P. 3
Jesus 181–82, 204, 265, 267
Jones, E. 64, 83–5, 102, 192, 226, 229,
265
Jung, C./Jungians 6, 57, 113, 274; and
paintings by patients, 140, 143, 144,
147, 150, 151, 155, 162, 164

Kadmon, J. 290
Kant, I. 64
Keats, J. 10, 260
Khan, M. 216, 238–40, 287; on
dreaming, 275–77
Klein, M./Kleinians 6, 42, 79, 83, 192,
243, 265, 292; and analysis of Rachel
21–2, 60–1; and analysis of two-and-
half-year-old boy 16–20; on artistic
creation 209; on depressive position
285; on femininity phase 91; Guntrip
on 59; letter from 109–11; on
loneliness 255; on original object 87;

on paintings by patients 140, 141, 143,
144, 147, 150, 152, 153, 158, 162,
164–65; on paper on Blake 168; on
phantasies 59; Sprott on 40; on
symbolism 84, 102, 105
Klein, S. 294
Kohnt, H. 64
Kris, E. 192–93, 211

Langer, S. 113, 192, 213, 232, 233
Lao Tze 259, 261
Lawrence, D. H. 248, 264, 283
Lichtenberg, J. D. 61
Little, M. 238, 290

MacDougall, W. 40
MacMurray, J. 81
Malraux, A. 192
Maninsky, B. 82
Manangoni, M. 233
Maritain, J. 192, 233; on creative
subjectivity, 193–94, 196–97, 204,
206, 208, 263, 276; on Freud and
psychoanalysis, 210–11, 213
Mayo, E. 3
Michelangelo 210
Millard, P. 244
Milner, M. *see* preliminary note of
subject index
Montessori, M. 2
Myers, C. S. 3, 9, 39

Nietzsche, F. 209

Patanjali 272
Paul, St 82, 204
Payne, S. 6, 234
Piaget, J. 3, 47
Pontalis, J. B. 275, 277

Raine, K. 191
Rank, D. 85, 98, 195
Rappoport, D. 234
Read, H. 85–6, 192–93, 208, 210, 214
Reich, W. 136, 259, 260, 265
Reik, T. 266
Richman, J. 213
Richmond, K. 5–6
Riviere, J. 45, 265
Rosenfeld, H. 265
Rubenstein, H. L. 241

Subject Index

visionary experiences 236–37; *see also* mysticism *and* Blake *in name index*
visual images, author's tendency to use 289–90; *see also* art

war, effect of 89, 93, 102, 165
water as symbol 288
weight, sense of one's own 288
will, role of 81
'Winnicott and Overlapping Circles' (1977); 279–86
wishes and feelings 14, 42–3, 47, 52, 55 *see also* emotion
woe 63

words/verbal expression 14, 280; fluency as defence 294; and internal perception 46; problems with 67–8, 99, 105, 119, 121, 123; and symbolism 86, 113
work, hard 188–90

X, Mr 287, 288, 293

yell of joy *see* primary sensual experience

Zen Buddhism 259